YOUR STEP-BY-STEP TECHNOLOGY GUIDEBOOK

for SENIORS®

**Stay Protected, Save Money, and
Navigate Your Phone, Tablet, Apps,
and the Internet with Confidence!**

Publisher's Note

This book is intended for general information only. It does not constitute medical, legal, or financial advice or practice. The editors of FC&A have taken careful measures to ensure the accuracy and usefulness of the information in this book. While every attempt has been made to ensure accuracy, errors may occur. Some websites, addresses, and telephone numbers may have changed since printing. We cannot guarantee the safety or effectiveness of any advice or treatments mentioned. Readers are urged to consult with their professional financial advisers, lawyers, and health care professionals before making any changes.

Any health information in this book is for information only and is not intended to be a medical guide for self-treatment. It does not constitute medical advice and should not be construed as such or used in place of your doctor's medical advice. Readers are urged to consult with their health care professionals before undertaking therapies suggested by the information in this book, keeping in mind that errors in the text may occur as in all publications and that new findings may supersede older information.

The publisher and editors disclaim all liability (including any injuries, damages, or losses) resulting from the use of the information in this book.

The heart of the discerning acquires knowledge,
for the ears of the wise seek it out.

— Proverbs 18:15 (NIV)

Your Step-By-Step Technology Guidebook for Seniors: Stay Protected, Save Money, and Navigate Your Phone, Tablet, Apps, and the Internet with Confidence! and all material contained therein copyright © 2025 by FC&A Publishing. All rights reserved. Printed in the United States of America.

This book or any portion thereof may not be reproduced or distributed in any form or by any means without written permission of the publisher. For information, or to order copies, contact:

FC&A Publishing®
103 Clover Green
Peachtree City, GA 30269

Produced by the staff of FC&A

ISBN 978-1935574996

Table of Contents

Easy ways to get started on your tablet 61

Harness your tablet's full potential. 67

Make the most of your tablet's bells and whistles 85

Assistive tech redefines aging in place 289

Elevate your lifestyle with smart home devices 295

Be prepared, stay safe with emergency planning 301

Navigate the world of streaming services with confidence 309

Take charge in the tech world

The essential toolkit: Understanding your electronic devices

The tech world can be overwhelming. In order to make the most out of all the gadgets, devices, and software out there, you need to have a good understanding of what is available and how it can be used. With this information at your fingertips, you'll be ready to take charge and master the world of tech.

Desktop computers. Despite being one of the oldest types of computing devices around, desktop computers still have a role to play in the tech world. While you can't easily move them around or take them on the road, they're often reasonably priced, simple to use, and easy to upgrade. You have two main options when choosing a desktop.

- Windows computers. These are typically known as PCs (personal computers). Although this term can apply to any computer, it has typically been associated with anything that uses the Windows operating system. The latest version is Windows 11, 2024 Update (also known as 24H2). If you have a Windows computer and want to check which version of the operating system you have, go to *Settings* and click *System*. Many different companies manufacture and sell Windows computers.

- Macs. These computers run on Apple's operating system, which is called macOS. Apple makes both the hardware and software for their desktop computers. There are no other companies that produce Macs. The latest version of macOS is Sequoia.

To check which version your computer has, go to the Apple menu, click *About This Mac*, and select *More info*.

Laptop computers. These are more mobile versions of desktop computers. They are smaller, lighter, and generally have more than enough power for most day-to-day computing tasks. However, this convenience comes at a cost. These laptops are often more expensive, and are harder to upgrade or repair.

In addition to Windows and Apple laptops, you can also buy Chromebooks. These devices run a version of the Android operating system that is also used on tablets and smartphones.

Tablets. You may think tablets are slimmed down laptops, but that's not the case. Tablets are designed with portability and ease of use in mind. They're smaller than laptops, and generally not as powerful, but they're sleek and have touch screens. If you just need a device for simple tasks, like video chatting, web surfing, and streaming, chances are a tablet is more than up to the job. You have two different types of tablets to choose from.

- iPads. Apple's line of tablets comes in many different sizes and styles. The Pro line features bigger screens and powerful hardware, while the iPad Air is small and portable. They both use the iPadOS operating system.

- Android tablets. Android is an operating system owned by Google that was originally created for mobile devices. It is an open-source operating system, which means manufactures can customize it to offer unique features. You can buy Android tablets from a number of companies, including Samsung and Lenovo.

Smartphones. Almost everyone owns a smartphone these days. The latest estimates say that 9 out of 10 Americans have one of these devices, and it's easy to see why. You can use a smartphone to play games, take photos, surf the web, make calls, and so much more. When choosing a smartphone, you have two main options.

- iPhones. Apple's offering is the most popular smartphone in America. They run an operating system called iOS, which is updated annually.

- Android smartphones. Much like Android tablets, these smartphones are available from a number of manufacturers. Because different companies offer slightly different features and designs, Android users have a wide range of options to choose from.

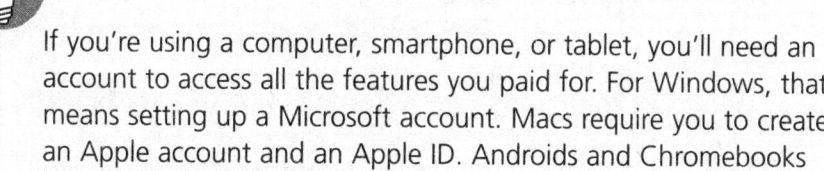

If you're using a computer, smartphone, or tablet, you'll need an account to access all the features you paid for. For Windows, that means setting up a Microsoft account. Macs require you to create an Apple account and an Apple ID. Androids and Chromebooks may require a Google account.

Don't already have one of these accounts? Don't worry. You can create one for free when you first set up a new device. All you'll need to do is follow along with the on-screen instructions to enter your email address and create a password.

A beginner's guide to important software security and updates

Computer software can be a tough thing to wrap your head around. That's because it's not something you can physically get your hands on. It's the invisible code that brings your devices to life.

Keeping your computer's hardware in tiptop shape requires cleaning and protection from spills and other damage. Maintaining your software, on the other hand, can be a bit more involved. Here are two things you should always do.

Keep everything up to date. Always upgrade to the latest version of your device's operating system when it's available. These updates usually come out at least once a year.

Look out for security updates. Companies release smaller, more frequent updates throughout the year to fix bugs, patch security issues, and improve performance. It's important to never skip these.

While many devices will automatically perform any necessary updates, that's not always the case. Here's where to go to check if there's anything to install on your computer, tablet, or smartphone.

- On Windows computers, go to Settings > Windows Update.

- On Macs, go to System Settings > Software Update.

- On Android tablets and smartphones, go to Settings > System > System Update.

- On iPads and iPhones, go to Settings > General > Software Update.

Learn to navigate this fundamental app to master your devices

The term app, which is short for application, originated with smartphones. But now it's used as shorthand for anything that used to be called a computer program. You'll find apps for tablets, computers, and smartphones alike.

And there's one app that appears on pretty much any tech device you can imagine, regardless of its make or operating system. It's the Settings app, and you need to know its ins and outs. To access this app, tap the icon that looks like this.

Here are some of the most important features in the Settings app and what you can do with them.

- Wi-Fi and Network Settings let you connect to the internet.

- Personalization settings let you change certain aspects of your device's appearance, such as color themes or the screen background.

- Notifications let you know when you have new emails, updates available for apps, and more. You can also use this setting to specify the alerts that you want and when you want to receive them.

- Privacy and security settings help you protect your personal information when you're using your computer, smartphone, or tablet.

Whenever you get a new device, spend some time exploring the menus and options within the Settings app.

3 tips to pick the perfect device

Deciding on a new device can feel like an impossible task if you don't know much about electronics. Stores are flooded with dozens of phones, laptops, TVs, cameras, printers, and more. That can make it overwhelming to choose the best one for your needs, especially if you don't feel confident about deciphering all the tech terms used in the marketing language.

- Research your options online. Tomsguide is a fantastic, unbiased website that you can use to cut through the jargon and find information on new tech. Search for product reviews in categories such as "Best Picks" or "Phones and Computers," or visit the forums where users discuss issues or share their experience with certain products. Go online to *tomsguide.com* to start your search for new electronics.

- Write down all your needs. For example, do you plan to use your new device to surf the web? Or do you want something that you can use to edit photos of your grandkids? Do you want a light and portable device, or something with a long-lasting battery? Once you've listed everything, you'll have a better sense of the features you want in a new device.

- Consider compatibility. You need to make sure your new device pairs well with the ones you already own. For example, if you have an Apple iPad and you're in the market for a new smartphone, an Apple iPhone could be a great choice. It will make it easier to share files and use all the features of both devices.

Tech devices consist of two main components — hardware and software. Hardware is any physical part of a device, be it a computer keyboard, a tablet screen, or a smartphone camera. Think of it as something that you can physically touch or interact with.

When you're choosing a tech device that you're going to be using or carrying around, test out the hardware to make sure you find it comfortable and easy to use. For example, you want the device to feel sturdy, and you need to make sure that you can easily access the screen.

Score major savings on technology with these simple tricks

You can count on tech companies to release brand-new versions of their devices every year to drum up sales. But you don't need to pay full price if you're in the market for new electronics. Here are two ways you can save a bundle.

Use this secret word to save on computers, phones, appliances and more. When you're shopping, you don't need to get the latest, most expensive version of a device. Instead use the keyword "refurbished" to score big savings on your next device.

This term refers to used electronics or appliances that have been restored and tested to make sure they're almost as good as new. You'll find they are often significantly cheaper, and are just as long lasting as brand-new gadgets.

Many major brands sell refurbished tech on their own websites. You can also find more options online at these two websites.

- Back Market, at *backmarket.com*.

- Newegg, at *newegg.com*.

When you're purchasing refurbished electronics, check to make sure that you're buying from a reputable retailer. Carefully read over whether or not there is a warranty to cover any potential problems with the equipment, and know what the return policy is in case you need to exchange the device or get your money back.

Time your shopping right to score the best deals. Savvy shoppers know that they don't have to pay full price for phones, laptops, and other gadgets if they buy them at the right time of year.

- Keep your eyes peeled for Black Friday sales. You don't need to head to the store in person to take advantage of the best deals. Most companies let you shop for sales online.

- Cyber Monday. Retailers created this sales event to encourage people to shop online after their Black Friday spending sprees. You can often find great deals on electronics and other goods from online stores.

- Amazon's Prime Day. If you're an Amazon Prime member, you can take advantage of this biannual sale. It's usually held sometime in July and October, and is often a great chance to score deals on Amazon products like Echo speakers or Fire tablets.

- Back-to-school sales. Retailers know that more and more students are using laptops and tablets in the classroom, so they often have great deals on electronics at the end of the summer. You don't need to be a student or teacher to take advantage of the savings, either. Check out online and traditional retailers to see what sales they offer.

Offload your used electronics and put money in your pocket

After years and years of buying electronics and upgrading devices, you may have accumulated a nice little collection of tech. Instead of letting these old devices sit in a box or a desk drawer, why not sell them or trade them in to make extra cash? Here are a three ways to earn a few dollars from your old devices.

- Sell your old devices direct to buyers. Websites like eBay and Facebook Marketplace are a great way to offload your old electronics. You'll need to do a bit of research beforehand so that you can make sure you're setting a good price, though. Search these sites to see what similar items are listed for.

- Use a buyback company for quick, easy cash. Websites like *decluttr.com* and *gazelle.com* buy old electronics directly from consumers to refurbish and resell. All you have to do is go to the website and enter information about your old laptop or tablet to get a quote. If you accept an offer, they will provide a shipping label so that you can send the device to them for inspection. If the gadget meets their standards, they'll send you payment.

- Trade in your old electronics for store credit. Some stores, including Costco, Walmart, and Best Buy, have trade-in programs in exchange for gift cards.

Before you sell any of your old tech, make sure it doesn't have any sensitive personal information stored on it. To do that, go to the Settings app on your device and restore it to factory settings.

Try these easy — and free — ways to learn how to use your devices

Not everyone has family members who can help them use technology, but that shouldn't stop you from using it. With a little know-how, you can practically become a computer pro. And the best part? You won't have to spend a single penny.

- Find free classes in your area. Go to social media, read local newspapers, or visit senior centers to see if you can find any information about courses that can help you become more tech savvy. You may want to check out a local computer store to see if they have a notice board or flyers with information about available courses.

- Check out your local library. You may be able to find books and other reference material that can help you brush up on computers, tablets, smartphones, and more. But that's not all. Many libraries offer free classes or have someone on staff who can give you advice. Ask for information at the main desk.

- Talk to people in your neighborhood. You may find tech-savvy members of your community who are more than willing to help you out. Talk to your neighbors, fellow church members, or any other friends you have in the community. Even if they're not able to help, you may find more resources once word gets out.

Slow computer? Follow this expert advice

Is your computer running like molasses? Chances are, you don't need to buy a new one to make it work like the newest model on the market. These two tricks can help it run faster and smoother than ever before.

Speed up your sluggish computer with this one-time upgrade. The trick is to upgrade your hard drive, which stores all the data on your computer, from a Hard Drive Disk (HDD) to a Solid State Drive (SSD). The latter is more efficient at storing large amounts of data, and works faster than an HDD. You can buy them from online electronics retailers and install them yourself, but that takes a bit of know-how. You also need to be sure that whatever you purchase is compatible with your current computer.

If you're not comfortable making that change yourself, head to an electronics or computer store to see if they can do the job. They can also ensure that you get the right parts for your machine.

Do this easy task once a month to keep your machine lightning fast. Apps and files that you're not using take up valuable space on your computer. And they may run in the background from time to time, which can make your computer run slower.

To keep your machine from getting bogged down, delete unused files and apps once a month. To do that, go to File Explorer on a Windows Computer or Finder on a Mac. Click the trash icon to send them to the Recycle Bin or Trash. In order to delete them completely, right-click on the Trash or Recycle Bin and select the *Empty* option.

File Explorer

Easy fixes for common computer problems

When your computer starts to act up, don't rush to call tech support. These tips can solve almost any problem.

Get out of frozen programs with this simple solution. From time to time, apps will simply stop working and freeze. If that happens, you won't be able to do anything within the app. Fortunately, though, there's a quick and easy way to try to close out of the app.

If you're using a Windows computer, press Alt+F4. Or press Ctrl+Alt+Delete and select *Task Manager*. Then go to the app that isn't responding, click on it, and select *End Task*. If you're on a Mac, press Option+Command+Esc or right-click on the app's icon and select *Force Quit*.

Once the app is closed, open it again and continue using it normally. Just know that you may have lost any unsaved work if your app crashed.

Try this quick fix to solve any hardware problems. Something will eventually go wrong with your computer. But chances are, numerous people have had the exact same problem and have probably figured out a way to solve it. If you run into any kind of technical problem, don't waste your money and time calling an IT professional. The first thing you should do is search online for a solution.

Simply go online to a search engine and describe the problem you're having. Make sure to include as many details as you can, such as the model of computer you have, which operating system you're using, and any error codes that you've seen.

Made a mistake on your computer? Maybe you accidentally closed out of the web page you were using. Or perhaps you deleted an important file. Don't panic. There's an undo key that can help you correct all sorts of "oops" moments. For example, you can bring something out of the trash or reopen a browser tab.

If you're using a Windows computer, simply press Ctrl+Z to undo the last action performed on your machine. If you're on a Mac, press Command+Z.

Unlock the hidden power of your keyboard with these shortcuts

It's a fact — your computer's keyboard is loaded with hidden features. Instead of using your mouse to click on icons and scroll through menus, you can navigate around your device with a few basic short-cuts. Here are some of the most useful ones everybody should use.

If you're on a Windows computer, use the WinKey to try these.

- WinKey+E, to open File Explorer.

- WinKey+I, to open the Settings app.

- WinKey+L, to lock the computer and activate the Lock screen.

- WinKey+S and WinKey+Q, to search local files on your computer or find information online.

- WinKey on its own, to access the Start menu.

Mac users can use these 5 basic keystrokes with the Command key.

- Command+H, to hide the current window.

- Command+N, to open a new Finder window.

- Command+O, to open a selected item in the Finder in a new app.

- Command+Shift+A, to open the Applications folder in the Finder.

- Command+Shift+H, to open the Home folder in the Finder.

Get more out of your computer with some can't-miss accessories

Recently bought a new computer or laptop? If so, you may want to invest in a few accessories to make the most of your purchase. Here are a few that may be worth your while.

- Flash drives and external hard drives. These small devices let you load data onto them for safekeeping. They also help you easily transfer data from one computer to another. They're a great option for backing up important files in case something ever happens to your computer.

- External CD readers. Many modern computers don't have a place for you to load CDs, so you may think that all the home videos or old movies you have stored on a disc are worthless. Fortunately, you can buy a device that connects to your computer and lets you use CDs again.

- Webcams. If your computer doesn't have a built-in webcam, you'll want to buy one so that you can broadcast video and chat online with friends and family.

- Laptop stands. Consider using an ergonomic stand with your laptop. This way you won't have to crane your neck to see the screen.

When you hit the delete button, you may think that files and apps are gone from your computer for good. But that's not so. Anything you delete is initially sent to the Recycling Bin on a Windows machine or the Trash on a Mac.

Believe it or not, it may still be possible to access deleted data even after you delete it from these locations. So if you want to make sure that you've permanently wiped private information from your computer's hard drive, you'll need to take an extra step. A great option is to use an app called Parted Magic. This software has a subscription fee, but it will allow you to erase any information on your hard drive. For details on how to use the app to securely erase information, go to *partedmagic.com*, click *Secure Erase*, and follow the instructions.

Use these top tools to keep your computer working for years to come

Computers aren't cheap, so you'll want to make sure you get your money's worth out of your investment. One of the best ways to do that is to keep them in good working order. If you follow the 10 habits practiced by people with the fastest, healthiest computers, you'll be able to keep your machine purring along like new.

1. Regularly keep your operating system up to date. This will help make sure it's performing at its best and keep its built-in security up to date.

2. Clean out junk files and unwanted apps on a regular basis. This helps to keep digital clutter from bogging down your computer's performance.

3. Use anti-virus software to protect your device from malware and hackers. And make sure to check for regular security updates.

4. Clear out the Recyling Bin or Trash to avoid unwanted files slowing down your machine.

5. Keep it clean and dust-free. Grime in your computer can drastically shorten its life span.

6. Make sure your device stays in a well-ventilated area. Without enough airflow, computers can overheat and break down.

7. Shut your computer down properly when you're done using it. Don't just use the power button or close the lid.

8. Reboot your computer regularly to clear out temporary files and free up your computer's memory.

9. If you're using a laptop, don't keep it plugged in all the time. That may overcharge the battery and cause it to wear out faster.

10. Be cautious when browsing the internet, and avoid downloading files from strange websites. You may accidentally infect your computer with a virus or other malware.

When you're trying to navigate the tech world, you may stumble across a bewildering range of terms. If you don't know what they mean, you might find yourself confused while you try to diagnose problems or learn new skills. These basic terms will help you talk tech like a pro.

Operating System (OS). This is essentially the program that brings your computer to life. It provides all of the functionality and enables you to interact with the computer. Without it, you would be staring at a blank screen. The main operating systems are Windows and macOS.

Processor. Also known as the CPU (Central Processing Unit), this is the part of a computing device that processes all of the instructions and commands from the operating system and apps. The speed of processors is usually measured in gigahertz (GHz) and the higher the number, the faster the processor. Look for a minimum of 2GHz.

Random Access Memory (RAM). This stores apps and data the computer is using, and is one of the most important indicators of how quickly it can operate. It is usually measured in gigabytes (GB). Look for a minimum of 8GB.

The fundamentals of PCs and laptops

Your desktop: Key features to know

The first thing you'll see when you turn on your computer is the desktop. So it's important to be able to identify and customize its most important elements. Here's what you need to know.

Background. This is the image that appears on the desktop. You can customize it to fit your personal style. Here's how to change the image in Windows.

1. Click on the Start button and go to Settings.

2. Select *Personalization* and click *Background*.

3. Choose *Picture* to use a still image, *Solid Color* for a plain background, *Slideshow* to use a series of images that change every few minutes, or *Windows Spotlight* to see a new image from around the world every day.

To change the background on a Mac, go to the System Settings app and click on *Wallpaper* in the sidebar. You can use a wallpaper from one of these categories.

- *Dynamic Wallpapers* are images that get brighter or darker based on the time of day in your current location.

- *Landscape*, *Cityscape*, *Underwater*, and *Earth aerials* are still images with dramatic views.

- *Shuffle aerials* show still images that change at custom intervals.

- *Pictures* are a collection of still images.

- *Colors* lets you apply a solid background color to your desktop.

Bottom bar. This feature houses a collection of apps, which makes it a great way to quickly access your favorite programs. The bottom bar is known as the Taskbar on a Windows device.

The bottom bar is called the Dock on a Mac.

To customize your Taskbar in Windows, right-click on an empty space in the Taskbar and select *Taskbar settings*. You can change the icons in it by selecting *On* or *Off* under *Taskbar corner icons*.

To add an icon to a Mac's Dock, open an app. The app's icon will appear on the right side of your Dock. Right-click on it and select *Keep in Dock*. To remove an app from your Dock, click, hold, and drag the icon into an empty space on your desktop until you see the word *Remove*.

Desktop icons. These are shortcuts that give you quick and easy access to apps and other files. You can add and remove these icons by going to the Start menu in Windows or by using the Launchpad app on a Mac. Find the app you want to add, click it, and hold. Then drag it onto your desktop.

Transform your computer with custom colors

Want your computer to feel truly unique? If you're on a Windows computer, you can add a splash of color to all the menus, Taskbar, and Start menu. Here's how to do it in Windows 11.

1. Open the Settings app and click the *Personalization* tab in the left-hand sidebar.

2. Click the *Colors* option.

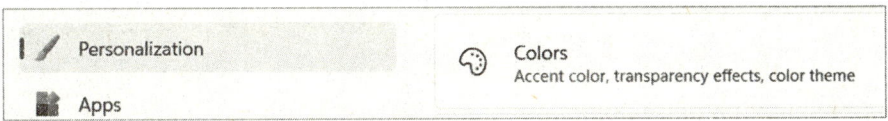

3. Go to *Choose your mode* and click the drop-down menu to select *Light*, *Dark*, or *Custom*. *Light* uses colors that work well for brightly lit environments, and lets you add a custom accent to app windows' title bars and borders. *Dark* uses colors that work well in low light, and lets you add color to the Start menu and Taskbar. *Custom* lets you choose features from both Light and Dark mode.

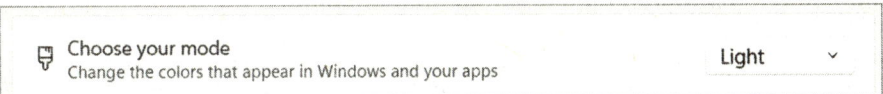

4. After choosing which mode you prefer, expand the Accent color section.

5. Manually select a color under *Recent colors* or *Windows colors*. Or have your computer pick one by selecting *Automatic*.

6. If you chose *Custom* or *Dark* mode, scroll down and select the toggle for *Show accent color on Start and taskbar* and

Show accent colors on tile bars and windows borders to turn them *On* or *Off*.

If you're on a Mac running macOS Sequoia, follow these steps to add a splash of color to your computer.

1. Open the System Settings app and select *Appearance* from the sidebar.

2. Select a color from the *Accent color* menu. This will change the color of buttons, pop-up menus, and other controls.

Use these shortcuts to navigate your computer like a pro

Switching between all the open windows on your computer can feel like a daunting task. You have to either shuffle through all the pages you have on your screen or keep opening and minimizing windows to find the right app or file. But there are a few simple tricks that will help.

Windows. Use these tips on a PC.

- Click in the bottom, right-hand corner of the screen to go back to your desktop from another app.

- Press the Alt+Tab keys to view thumbnails of all of the open windows on your computer. While holding down the Tab key, press Alt to cycle through the thumbnails. Your currently selected thumbnail will have a border around it. Release both keys to go to the selected item.

Macs. Try these hacks on your Mac.

- Press F3 to minimize all the windows you have open.

- Press F4 to open the Launchpad, which will display all your open apps.

Don't miss these keyboard tips

Ever wondered what those F keys along the top of your keyboard do? They have several useful functions. Here's an example of what they can do on a Windows computer.

- F1 — Access the Help menu for your current app.

- F2 — Rename your selected file or folder.

- F3 — Search for a file or folder in File Explorer.

- Alt+F4 — Close the window you're working on. If you're not in an app, a shutdown box will appear.

- F5 — Refresh the window or app you're using.

- F6 — Cycle through screen elements in a window or on the desktop.

- F10 — Go to the menu bar in your selected document or app.

- F11 — Enter full-screen mode.

Certain functions may vary depending on the app you're using. If pressing the F keys alone doesn't work, check to see if your keyboard has an Fn key. You may need to hold it down while pressing an F key.

On Macs, the F keys can be used for tasks like changing your screen's brightness or adjusting your computer's volume.

Keep your desktop clutter-free

When you open an app on your computer, it's displayed in a new window. Use these tips to manage them and keep your screen from becoming cluttered.

- To move a window to a new spot on your screen, click and hold on the top bar. Drag the window around and release the mouse button to place the window in a new spot.

- If you're using a Windows computer, use the buttons on the top, right-hand corner of the window to minimize it and send it to the Taskbar. You can also maximize it so it fills the entire screen or close out of it entirely.

- Mac users can access the buttons in the top, left-hand corner of a window to close it. You can also minimize it and send it to the Dock or maximize it to fill up the entire screen.

- Change the size of a window by hovering your mouse over its border until your cursor changes to an arrow symbol. Click and drag the border to make the window bigger or smaller.

Unlock your computer's potential with the Settings app

The Settings app in Windows 11 is vital to making sure your computer works exactly how you need it to. To open it, click on this icon in the Taskbar.

The app will open to the Home section, which displays several recommended settings and general information about your computer. You can also view additional categories in the left-hand sidebar. Click on one to view more details.

Windows also offers a series of Quick Settings that you can change directly from the Taskbar. These let you alter the computer's volume, check your Wi-Fi settings, or view your device's battery status without having to go through the main Settings app. You can customize the Quick Settings options by following these steps.

1. Click below one of the Wi-Fi, sound, or battery icons, located at the right-hand side of the Taskbar.

2. A Quick Settings panel will be displayed above these icons.

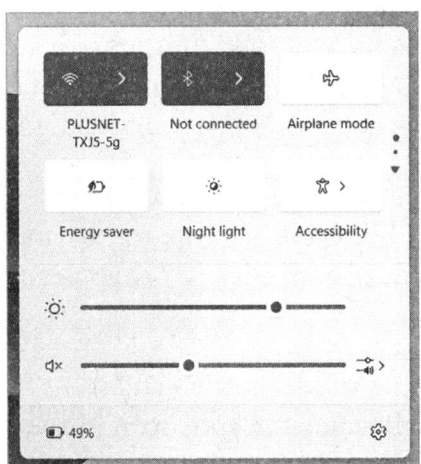

3. Select individual buttons to add or remove options. Click the buttons on the right-hand side of the panel to view more settings.

4. If a button has a right-facing arrowhead on it, click it to access additional options.

5. To go from the Quick Settings panel to the Settings app, click on the gear at the bottom-right side of the window.

To access settings on a Mac, click the System Settings icon in the Dock.

Use this helpful guide to master your favorite apps

You'll use computer apps to do everything from surfing the web to sending emails. Follow these steps to help you open, close, and find your favorite apps.

Opening and closing Windows 11 apps. To access an app on a Windows computer, click on its icon in the Start menu or the Taskbar. Any open apps will appear in the Taskbar.

If you want to close the app you're using, you can move your cursor over the X button in the top, right-hand corner of the window. Once it turns red, click it. Or you can press Alt+F4 on your keyboard.

If you have multiple windows open and want to make sure you close them all, right-click the app's icon in the Taskbar. Select *Close all windows*.

Pinning apps in Windows 11. Instead of digging through menus to find your favorite apps, you can pin them to the Taskbar or Start menu so they're just one click away. Here's how.

1. Click the *Start* button to open the Start menu.

2. Find the app you're looking for and right-click on it.

3. Select *Pin to Start* to add it to the Start menu. Any apps you add to the Start menu will appear under the *Pinned* heading.

4. Select *More*, then click *Pin* to add the app to the Taskbar. The app's icon will remain in the Taskbar whether the app is open or closed.

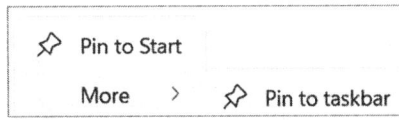

Apps in macOS Sequoia. To open an app on a Mac, double-click the app's icon in the Dock or in the Launchpad. To view all the apps on your Mac, click the Launchpad icon in the Dock.

Once opened, the app will appear in the Dock with a dot below its icon. If you want that app to stay in your Dock for easy access, click the dot and select *Options*, then *Keep in Dock*.

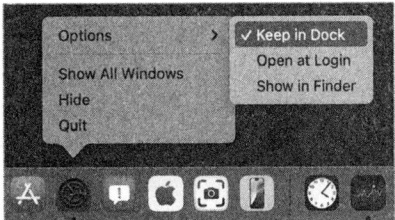

Widgets made simple — stay up to date with these powerful tools

Widgets are mini apps that display a small amount of information on your computer's desktop at all times. You can use them to, say, add things to a shopping list, check today's weather forecast, and read the latest headlines, without having to open an app. Here's how to access widgets in Windows 11.

1. Click on the Widget icon in the left-hand corner of the Taskbar. If you don't see it, go to *Settings*, select *Personalization*, and toggle *Widgets* to *On* under the *Taskbar items* heading.

2. The Widgets panel will open. Scroll down the page to view all of your widgets. Click on one to view more information about it.

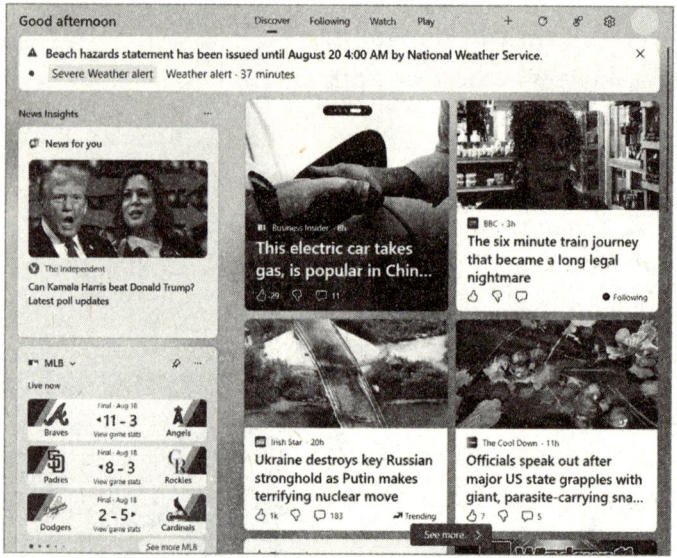

3. If you want to add more widgets to the panel, click the + button in the top toolbar.

If you're using a Mac with macOS Sequoia, you can add widgets to your computer's desktop by following these steps.

1. Open your Mac and make sure you are on the desktop. Press and hold Control on your keyboard and right-click in an empty space on the screen.

2. Select *Edit Widgets*.

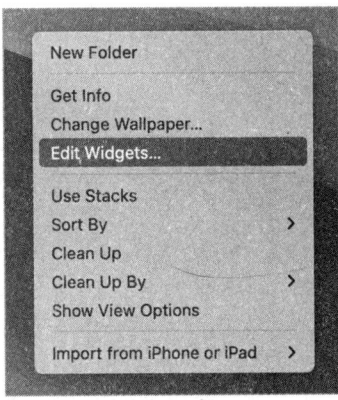

3. The Widgets panel will open. Click on the options in the left-hand sidebar to view all the available categories. You can scroll up and down in the main window to view widgets in that category.

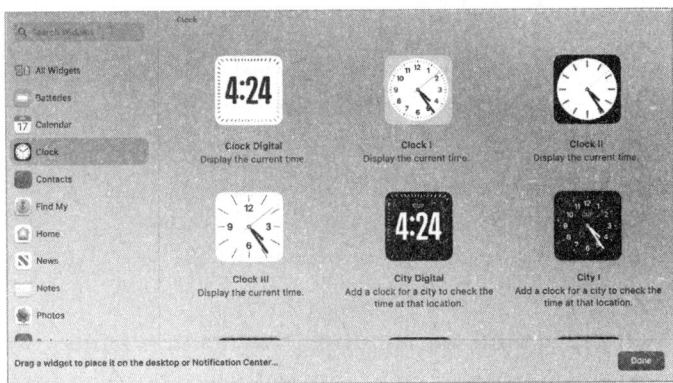

4. Move your cursor over a widget and select the + button to add it to your desktop. Or you can click it and drag it your

desktop. You can change where widgets are on your desktop by clicking and dragging them to a new spot.

5. To delete a widget, repeat steps 1 and 2. Click on the – button in the top, left-hand corner of the widget.

Don't miss a beat: Understanding alerts in Windows and macOS

Windows 11 helps you stay on top of updates and notifications from your apps so that you'll never miss an email or an event on your calendar. These alerts appear in your Taskbar at the bottom of the screen. If the bell icon is colored in, it means you have new messages available to view.

- Click the bell icon to open the Notification panel, which will display your current alerts. You can click on each individual notification to view more information.

  If you want to delete all the items in the Notification panel, click the *Clear all* button.

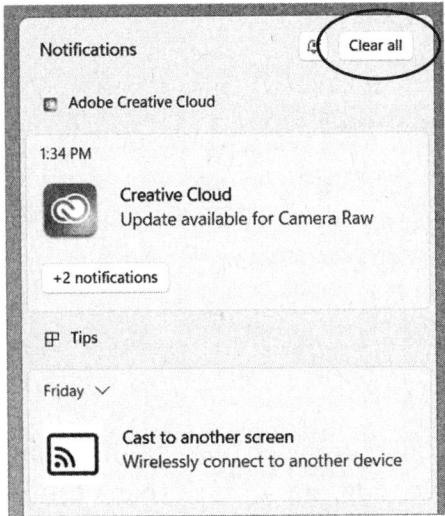

You can manage which apps send notifications. This well help you stay current with information that you need while keeping unnecessary alerts from slowing down your computer. Follow these steps to change these settings.

1. Go to *Settings* and click *System*. Select *Notifications*.

2. Make sure the button next to *Notifications* is set to *On*. Otherwise, you won't receive any alerts.

3. To change which apps are allowed to send notifications, scroll down to *Notification apps and other senders*. If you want notifications from an app to appear in your Taskbar, toggle the button next to it to *On*.

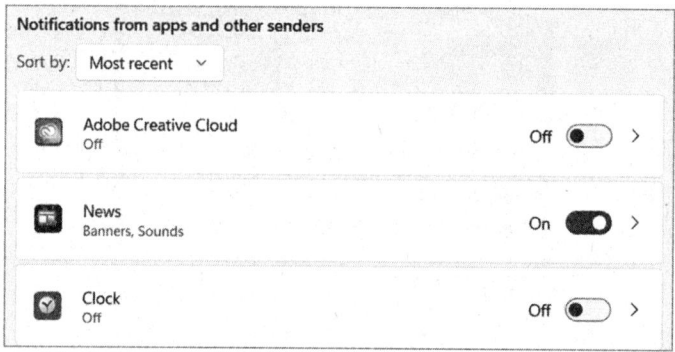

4. To further adjust how each app's notifications look, click on the app's name. You can set it so that alerts appear in a banner on your screen, or play a sound so you don't miss them.

In macOS Sequoia, you can view notifications by clicking the date and time in the top, right-hand corner of the screen. To adjust how they appear on your computer, go to *Systems Settings* and click *Notifications*.

Control digital clutter with 3 smart approaches

File Explorer is vital for viewing and organizing all the files and folders on a Windows computer. You can access it by going to the Taskbar and clicking on the *File Explorer* icon, pressing WinKey+E, or right-clicking on the Start button and selecting *File Explorer*. Use these tips to manage your files and folders with ease.

Use tabs to keep your screen from getting cluttered. File Explorer has introduced a feature that lets you use tabs to view different areas within a single File Explorer window. This can help you quickly move between folders, allowing you to view or move files without having multiple File Explorer windows open. To add a new tab, click on the + button at the top of the window. To close a tab, click on the small X on the right-hand side of the tab.

Find all your files with the Navigation pane. When you open a File Explorer window, you'll see the Navigation pane on the left-hand side. You can use it to access different folders, drives, libraries, pinned files or folders, and network locations.

To view more information about files, you can use the Preview pane or the Details pane. To access them, go to the *View* button in the top menu bar and select which one you want to use.

Manage all your menu options with a single click. The menu bar at the top of a File Explorer page displays a list of buttons that you can use to manage files. For example, you can select a file and go to the top menu bar and click *Rename* to change the file's name. You can also right-click on a file to open a menu displaying all the actions you can take.

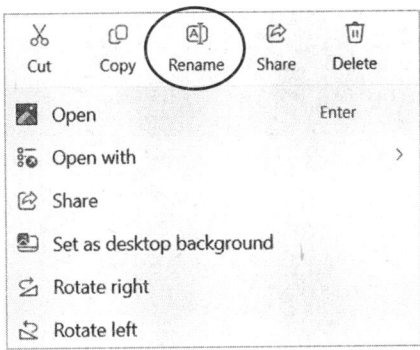

To manage options for folders instead of files, click on this button in the File Explorer menu bar and select the *Options* button. This will open the Folder Options panel. Use this menu to change how files and folders are displayed in File Explorer.

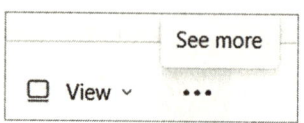

Make multitasking on your computer a breeze

Switching back and forth between apps while you're working can be frustrating and slow. But Windows offers a feature that lets you view multiple apps at the same time. That can make it easy, for example, to review your online accounts while you put new entries into a budgeting spreadsheet. Or you could work on a Word document without having to switch windows to review your notes. Here's how.

1. Open all the apps you want to use.

2. Hover your cursor over the square button in the top right-hand corner of one of the app's windows to open the Snap Layouts panel.

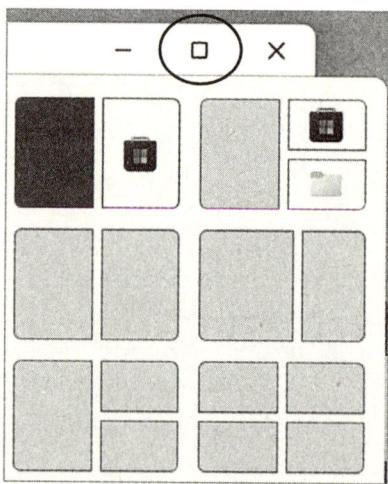

3. Click on one of the options to select a location for your current window. The panel will also show you where other open apps can be displayed.

4. The apps will open on your desktop in your selected layout. You can use them all without having to switch between windows.

On Macs, you can view up to four windows at a time. To do this, press and hold the green button at the top left-hand side of a window. Select where you want the window to appear on your screen. Do this for each app you want to use. You can also move windows by dragging them into the left or right side of the screen while holding the Option key.

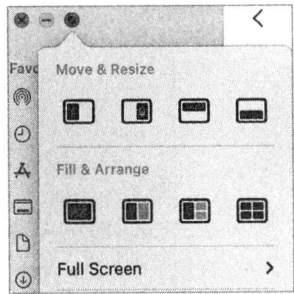

Streamline your searches and locate your files fast

Finding files on your computer or quickly searching the web is an easy task in Windows 11. Instead of scrolling through dozens of menus or pages of search results, try these quick and simple methods instead.

> If you're on a Mac, you can view all your files and folders in the Finder app.

Use the search box to find anything from your home page.
Windows has a built-in search feature right in the Taskbar. It's located next to the Start button. Here's how to use it.

1. Enter text in the box to start a search. You can search for apps, files, or even information you want to find on the web.

2. The search box will expand to accommodate the results. Click on one of them to view more details.

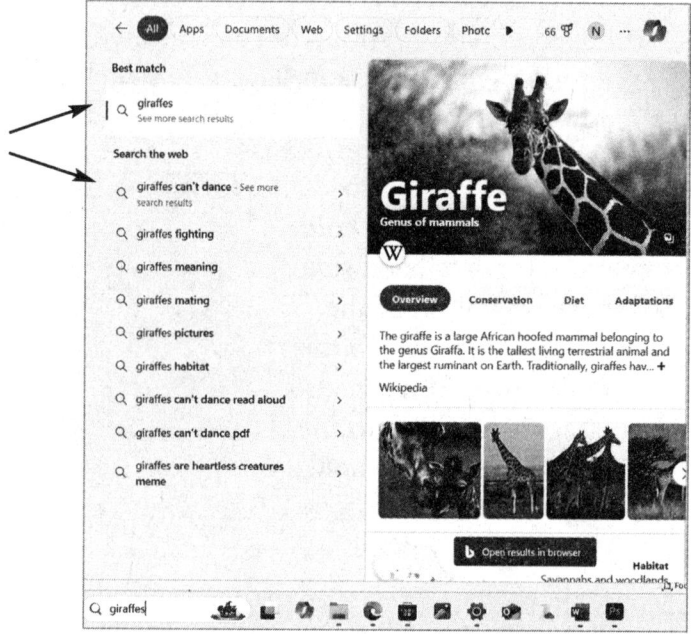

3. You can further refine your search results by clicking on the categories displayed in the top toolbar.

The search box features a small image on the right-hand side that changes daily. You can click it to view details about the icon in a new window.

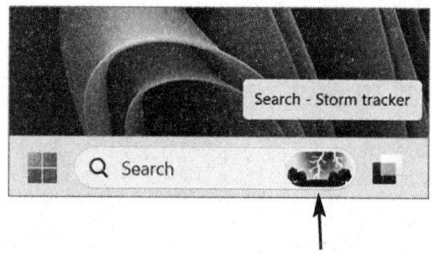

If you want to turn off this image, go to the Settings app and click *Privacy & security*. Go to *Search permissions* and scroll down to the *Search Highlights* button. Toggle it to *Off*.

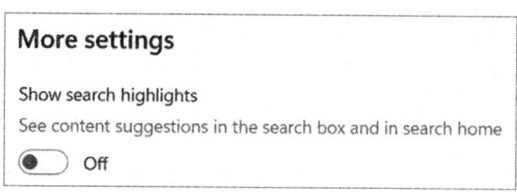

Find answers in a snap with Copilot. Microsoft's AI tool, Copilot, is designed to help users find answers to questions and use their computers more productively. You can find it in the Taskbar by clicking this icon.

1. After opening Copilot, a dialog window will be displayed.

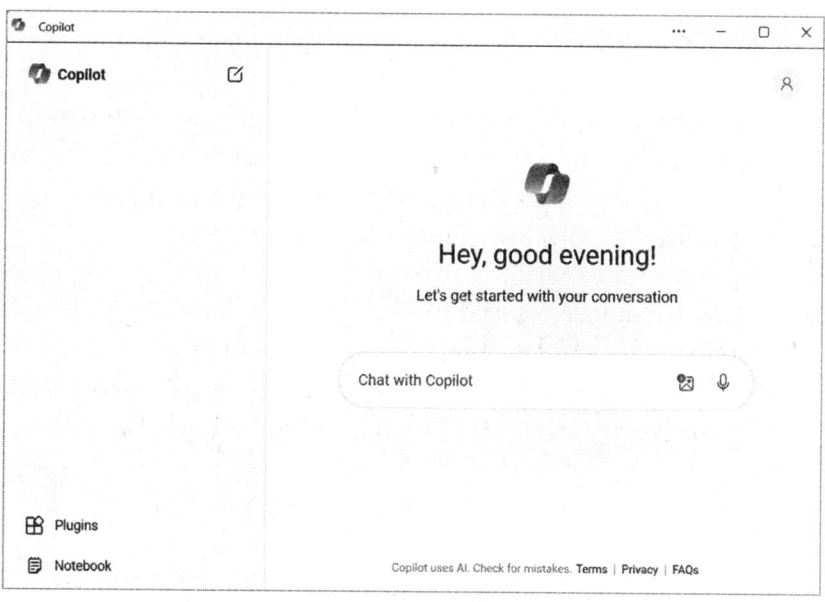

2. Click the box at the center of the Copilot panel and type in a question.

3. Click the up arrow button to display an answer. You may need to scroll down to read the full text.

4. You can continue typing in the box to ask follow-up questions.

5. If you want to start a new search, click this icon in the left-hand sidebar.

Mac users can find files by using the digital assistant, Siri, which has new features thanks to Apple's new AI. To set up Siri on your Mac, go to *System Settings* and click *Siri*.

Set up automatic backups to keep your digital memories safe

People use their computers to store treasured photos, important tax records, emails, and business documents. Of course you don't want to ever lose these important files, so it's best to make sure everything is backed up. Fortunately, it's easy to do.

Windows. In the latest version of Windows 11, File Explorer is closely integrated with the Windows cloud storage and backup service OneDrive. You can enable automatic backups so that your favorite apps save your data to a secure cloud server. Here's how.

1. Go to the Settings app and click *Accounts*.

2. Go to *Windows backup* and select *Manage sync settings*.

3. Make sure the button next to any folders you want backed up is toggled to *On*.

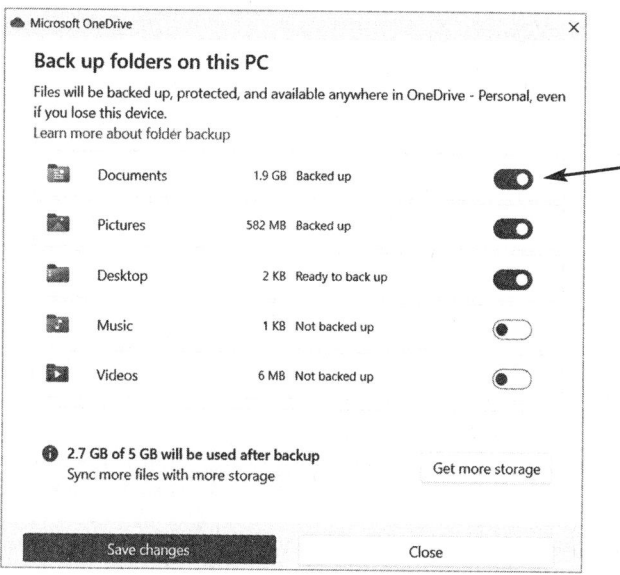

Macs. Apple's iCloud service allows users to store data from their favorite apps in the cloud. Here's what you need to do to make sure your files are automatically backed up.

1. Click the Apple icon in the top menu bar and select iCloud.

2. Sign in using your Apple ID and password. If you don't have an Apple ID, go online to *account.apple.com*.

3. Select which apps you want backed up under the *Saved to iCloud* section. If you don't see an app, click *See All* for the full list.

3 ways to make your computer secure

If hackers or scammers get access to your computer, they can wreak havoc on your life. Fortunately, the right settings in Windows can help keep you safe.

Security settings. Protecting your computer from viruses and other malicious software is a vital part of computer security. Fortunately, Windows 11 has a number of built-in settings that will help you create a solid defense.

1. Go the Settings app and select *Privacy & security*.

2. Click *Windows Security*.

3. The Protection areas panel will open. You can use it to scan for viruses, modify your computer's firewall, set up protections against potentially dangerous apps and files, and review other security options. If an icon has a yellow caution sign, click on it to view more information.

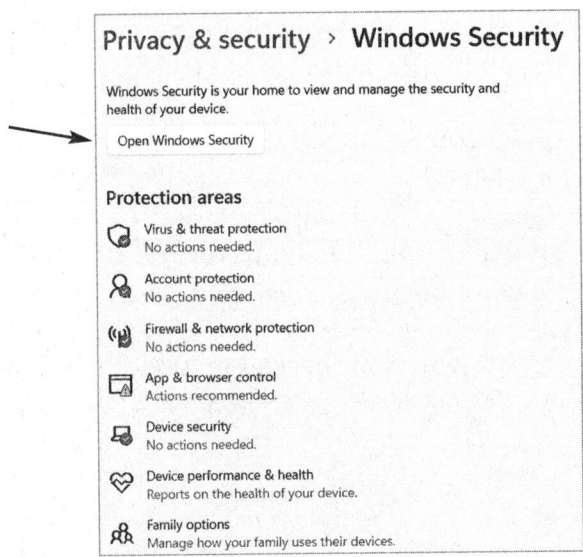

Lock screen. Computer thieves shouldn't have easy access to your data. One way to make sure that they can't sign into your device? Set up a Lock screen. Doing so means your computer will require an ID verification or password before it can be used.

Here's how to set one up.

1. Go to Settings and click *Accounts.*

2. Select *Sign-in options.*

3. Choose a sign-in option.

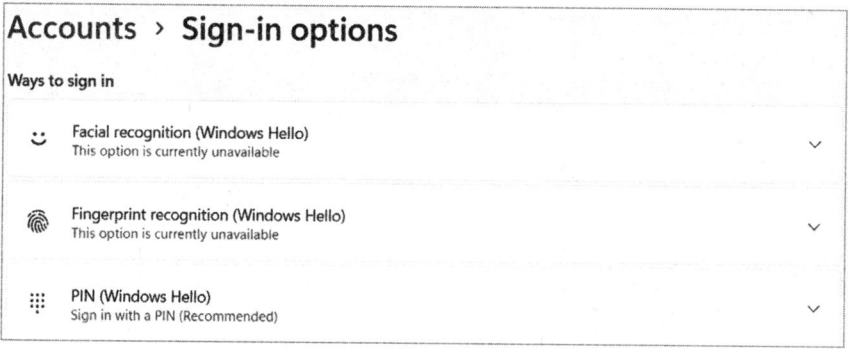

Privacy. Microsoft collects data from your computer. Some of this info is used to troubleshoot problems and identify security flaws, while other data may be used for advertising. If you want to limit the information your computer is allowed to share, follow these steps.

1. Go to the Settings app and click *Privacy & security.*

2. Click on *General* under the *Windows permissions* heading.

3. Review the privacy options and decide whether you want to toggle them *On* or *Off*.

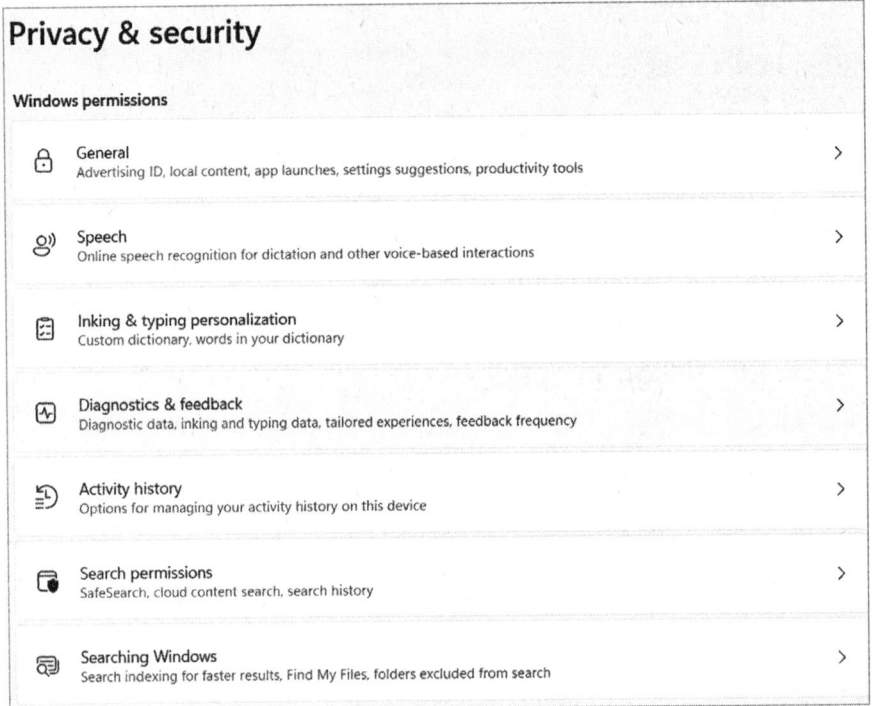

Delve deeper into the world of computers

The ABCs of computer sharing

Do several people in your family work on the same computer? If so, they should each have their own user account. This way, everyone will be able to edit and save their own files and personalize the computer's settings. Here's how to create a new user profile in Windows 11.

1. Log in to your account and go to the Settings app.

2. Select *Accounts*, and go to *Family*.

3. Scroll down the page and click the *Add someone* button under the *Your family* heading.

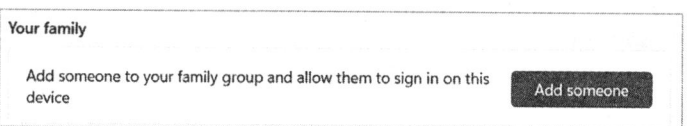

> **Your family**
>
> Add someone to your family group and allow them to sign in on this device   [Add someone]

4. If the person you wish to create a profile for already has a Microsoft account, enter their email, password, and other account details. If they don't have one, type in the email address they use and click on the *Sign up for a new email address* button. You can also

> Microsoft account
>
> **Add someone**
>
> Enter their email address
>
> No Microsoft account? Create one for a child
>
> Cancel   Next

select *Create one for a child* to make an account without using an email.

5. After the account has been created, the user can sign in to the computer by selecting their profile from the Lock screen.

Follow these steps to create a new user on a Mac.

1. Log in to your account and go to System Settings > Users & Groups.

2. Click *Add User*. You may need to enter your password.

3. Enter information into the Add user panel. You'll need to fill out the new user's full name and account name and select a password hint for them.

4. Click the *Create User* button to finish setting up the account.

5. The user can log in to the account with the password from the Lock screen.

When setting up a new account, pay attention to the account permissions. If you create an Administrator account for someone, that person will be able to access files saved to other accounts or change settings for all other users.

A step-by-step guide to managing your recycle bin

When you want to delete files, you send them to the Recycle Bin on a Windows computer or the Trash on a Mac. But your work doesn't end there. You'll still need to do some housekeeping.

Take out the trash regularly to keep your computer running smoothly. When you send a file to the Recycle Bin or the Trash, it doesn't automatically get deleted. That can be problematic because these old files can eventually cause your computer to slow down. So you should regularly empty the trash. Here's how.

1. Right-click on the Recycle Bin or the Trash.

2. Click the *Empty* button.

3. A confirmation button will appear, asking you if you're sure you want to continue with the action. Files that you delete may not be recoverable, so double-check to make sure there's nothing you want to save.

4. If you're ready to delete, click the *Yes* or *Empty Trash* button.

Follow these steps to rescue files you accidentally deleted. If you've accidentally sent an old file to the bin, don't panic. You can still recover it as long as you haven't emptied the bin. Here's how.

1. Double-click the Recycle Bin or Trash to open a list of your deleted files.

2. Scroll through the list of files to find the one you accidentally deleted.

3. On a Windows computer, click on an item you want to save. Select the *Restore the selected items* button. You can also use the *Restore all items* button to save everything in the Recycling Bin from being permanently deleted.

4. On a Mac, right-click the file you want to save and choose the *Put Back* option.

Don't miss this housekeeping hack for your hard drive

Old files and apps can accumulate on your computer over the years. If you leave them there, your device can get bogged down and run slowly. The good news? Using the Windows Cleanup tool can help keep your machine in tiptop shape. Here's how to use it.

1. Open the Settings app, go to *Systems*, and select *Storage*.

2. Toggle the button next to *Storage Sense* to *On* and select the *Cleanup recommendations* option.

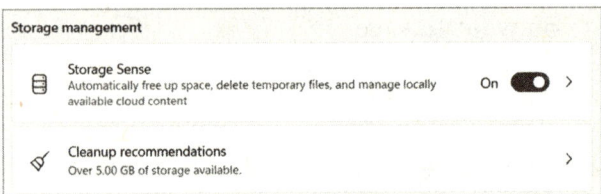

3. A list of items recommended for deletion will be listed. Review them, turning options *On* or *Off* as required. Any items you select will be deleted, so make sure you go over this list carefully.

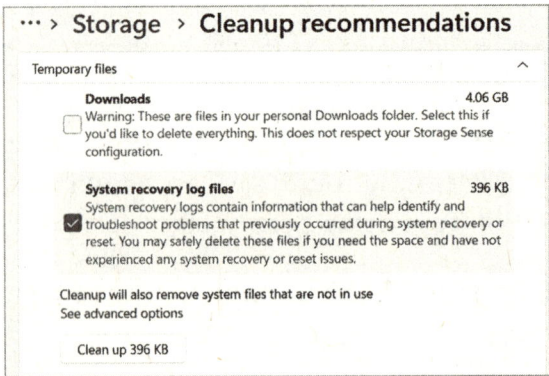

4. Click the *Clean up* button.

5 ways to speed up a slow computer

Like many things, computers get sluggish with age. But if your device is running very slowly, you may want to try the following tips to get it up to speed.

- Close apps when you aren't using them. If they're open and running, they may use power that your computer could devote to other tasks.

- Tweak your computer's appearance to make it perform better. On a Windows computer, enter "performance" into the search box on the Taskbar. Select the *Adjust the appearance and performance of Windows* option. Click on the *Visual Effects* tab, and check the *On* button for *Adjust for best performance.*

- Update your drivers. These are small programs that help the hardware on your machine run more efficiently. On Windows, search for "device manager" in the search box on the Taskbar, and open the Device Manager app. Right-click on one of the pieces of hardware listed, and select *Search automatically for updated driver software.* If there is a new driver available, click *Update Driver.* On Macs, drivers will install as part of the operating system updates.

- Adjust your search settings on Windows. Your computer will sort through and index all the files, emails, and apps on your computer. This process makes it quicker to get search results but can make your computer run slowly. If you want your computer to run faster during day-to-day tasks, go the Settings app. Select *Privacy & security*, and go to *Searching Windows.* Click the box next to *Classic option* below the *Find my Files* heading.

- Keep your operating system up to date. To check for updates on Windows, go to the Settings app and click *Windows Update*. On a Mac, go to System Settings, select *General* and click *Software Update*.

Quick pointers for building your contact list

You don't need an address book or a Rolodex to keep track of the contact info for your friends and family. Instead, you can use the built-in apps on your computer.

Use the Outlook app to stay in touch. Windows now has combined your email and contacts list into the Outlook app. Here's how to manage your contacts in Windows 11.

1. Open the Outlook app. By default it will open to the Mail section.

2. Click the *People* icon in the left-hand sidebar to access the address book.

3. Click the *New contact* button at the top of the window.

4. Fill out the contact details and click the *Save* button.

5. You can view your saved contacts under the *All contacts* heading.

6. Click on an existing contact to select it.

7. Click the *Edit* button in the top toolbar to change the contact's details or the *Delete* button to remove the contact.

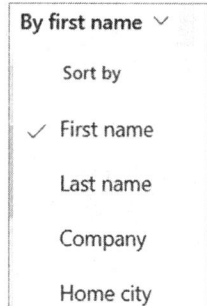

8. Click the *Sort by* button at the top of the *All contacts* heading to change how your contacts are sorted. You can sort them by *First name, Last name, Company, or Home city.*

Keep track of your address book with Contacts. Mac users with macOS Sequoia can use the Contacts app to sync all their contacts from their iCloud, Yahoo, or AOL accounts to their computer. Here's how.

1. Open the Contacts app.

2. Choose Contacts > Add Account.

3. Select the account that you want to download your contacts from. If you don't see the right one, select *Other Contacts Account.*

4. Click *Continue.* Then enter your account details and make sure the *Contacts* box is selected.

Manage your schedule with Outlook

You need to be able to stay on top of all your upcoming appointments and events. If you use a Windows computer, the Calendar section of the Outlook app is a great way to keep track of your schedule.

Add an event to your calendar. Instead of jotting down important dates on scraps of paper, you can save them in Outlook by following these steps.

1. Open Outlook and click the *Calendar* icon in the left-hand sidebar. The calendar will open on the current date.

2. You can change the display format by clicking these buttons on the top toolbar. Your calendar can be displayed using the *Day, Work week, Week,* or *Month* view.

3. To add a new event, click the *New event* button in the toolbar at the top of the window.

4. Enter all the details for the event, such as the name, time, and location. If you set the time to *All day*, you won't be able to set a specific start and end time.

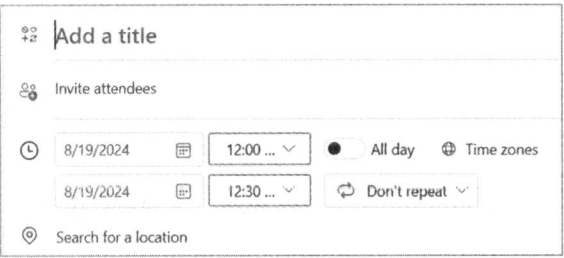

5. Click the *Save* button.

6. To modify events that have already been added to your calendar, click on an event and select *Edit*. The event window will reopen so that you can change the details. You can also remove the event by selecting the *Delete* button.

Keep track of your calendar when you're on the go. If you need to look at your schedule but don't have your computer handy, don't worry. All you need is internet access and the login details for your Microsoft account.

1. Go online to *microsoft.com/en-us/microsoft-365/outlook/log-in.*

2. Enter your Microsoft account username and password.

3. Outlook's online app will open. To find your events, click on the Calendar icon in the left-hand sidebar.

Set up your home network for a seamless internet connection

One of the first things that you'll want to do after getting a new computer is hop online and start browsing the web. You'll need a modem to get on the internet, and if you want to connect wirelessly, a Wi-Fi router. Once you have your equipment in place, follow these steps to get your Windows 11 computer online.

1. Go to the Settings app and select the *Network & internet* option in the left-hand sidebar.

2. Set the *Wi-Fi* button to *On*.

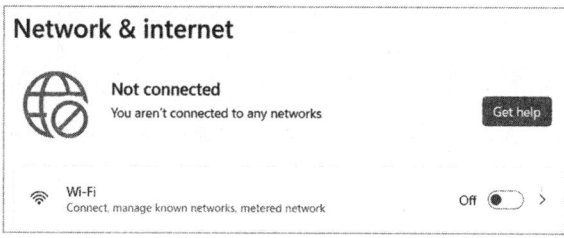

3. Click *Show available networks.*

4. Select the network you want to use. If you're not sure which one to choose, your router should have the network name and password on it.

5. Click the *Connect* button.

6. Enter the password for your Wi-Fi network.

7. Click the *Next* button.

8. Once you're online, the network status will say *Connected*.

You can view your internet connection information at the top of the Network & internet settings window or by clicking this icon in the Taskbar.

To connect to the internet on a Mac, either connect your computer to your modem with an ethernet cable or click on the Wi-Fi icon in the top menu bar. Select your home network and enter the password.

If you don't see the Wi-Fi icon, click on the Apple button on the top left-hand corner of your screen. Go to *System Settings and select Control Center*. Click on the pop-up menu next to *Wi-Fi*, then select *Show the Wi-Fi status menu*.

Choose an app to navigate the web your way

If you want to surf the web, you'll need to use a web browser. This type of app translates all the code on a website so that you can read and interact with it. Windows 11 uses the Microsoft Edge browser. Macs use Apple's Safari.

However, you don't need to use the pre-installed browser that comes with your computer. Many people choose to use a third-party app, such as Mozilla Firefox, DuckDuckGo, or Google Chrome in order to access special features or more robust privacy settings. You can find alternative options by going to the Microsoft Store on a Windows computer or the App Store on a Mac and typing "web browsers" into the search bar.

If you've downloaded a new browser, you'll need to change your computer's settings so that this app becomes the default option. That means any link you click will automatically open in your new browser. Here's how to do so on a Windows computer.

1. Go to the Settings app.

2. Select *Apps* and go to *Default Apps*.

3. Scroll down and click the *Web Browser* option.

4. Choose the app that you want to use as your default browser.

Follow these steps to change your default browser on a Mac.

1. Click the Apple button in the top menu and select *System Settings*.

2. Click *Desktop & Dock* in the left-hand sidebar.

3. Scroll down to the *Default web browser* option. Click on the drop-down menu and select your chosen web browser.

Surf safely with customized browser settings

Adjusting your web browser settings is a great way to make sure that you're protecting your privacy while surfing the web. You can also tweak your settings to make websites easier to read, or change how certain pages or tabs open when you click on a link. Here's how to access the settings in Microsoft Edge.

1. Open the Edge app and click on the *Settings and more* icon in the top, right-hand corner of the window.

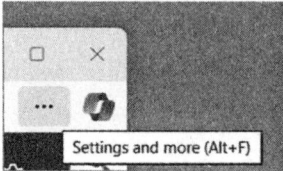

2. Click on the *Settings* option.

3. The sidebar will show the available categories. If you can't see them all, click this button in the top, left-hand corner of the window.

4. Click on a category in the left-hand sidebar to view more information in the main panel.

The steps for accessing the settings menu in other browsers may differ slightly. Look for a settings button at the top of the browser window or in the menu bar.

Simple steps make it easy to pick your home page

When you open a web browser, it will take you to a default home page. This is the first website you'll see whenever you access your browser or open a new tab. But you don't have to stick with this option. Here's how to change the home page in Microsoft Edge.

1. Go to the website you'd like to use as your home page. You can choose from any of your favorite sites.

2. Click on the website's address at the top of the page, hold down your cursor, and drag to highlight the text.

3. Right-click on the highlighted text and select *Copy.*

4. Open the Edge browser settings menu and select *Start, home, and new tabs* in the left-hand sidebar.

5. Go to *When Edge starts* and select *Open these pages.*

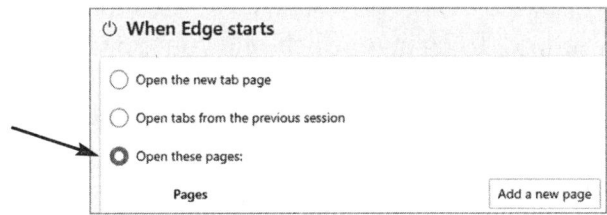

6. Click the *Add a new page* button.

7. Right-click the box under *Enter a URL* and select *Paste.*

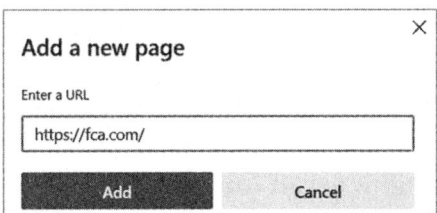

8. Click the *Add* button to complete the process. Whenever you open Edge, the web page you chose in Step 7 will be the first thing you see.

A beginner's guide to getting around the web with tabs

You don't need to have multiple windows open if you want to browse more than one website at a time. Instead, you can use tabs to quickly switch from page to page. Here's how to use tabs.

1. Click on the + button at the top of your browser window.

2. A web page will open in the new tab. This is usually the same as your home page, but it may vary depending on which browser you use.

3. All of your open tabs will be displayed at the top of your browser window. To change which one you are viewing, click it.

4. To change the order of your tabs, click and hold on the tab and drag it into a new position.

5. To close a tab, hover your cursor over it until you see an X button. Click the button.

Find your favorite online pages in a flash

Tired of typing in the full web address every time you want to visit a website? If so, you can use your browser to save your favorite pages so that you can find them in a snap. Here's how to do this in Microsoft Edge.

1. Type one of your favorite websites into the URL bar at the top of the page and press Enter on your keyboard.

2. When the website is loaded, click on the star at the top of the page.

3. Enter a name for the web page so you can easily remember what it is.

4. Optionally, click the drop-down menu next to *Folder* to select a different folder where you want to save this page.

5. Click the *Done* button.

6. The star will turn a solid color, which indicates that the web page has been saved as one of your favorites.

To navigate to your favorite pages in Edge, follow these steps.

1. Click on the *Favorites* icon at the top of your toolbar. You can also press Ctrl+Shift+O on your keyboard.

2. Select the folder where you saved the page.

3. Click on a saved page to go directly to that website.

These steps will be similar for most other web browsers. However, some menu names and icons may appear slightly different.

Save any site to your Dock with this feature

Apple has introduced a feature that lets you use the Safari browser to save any web page to your Dock as a web app. Once you've saved it, you'll be able to click on the page's icon in your Dock to open the website. There are a couple things that make these web apps special.

First, they function completely independently of your web browser. That means these apps won't share browsing history, cookies, or other data with Safari. They'll also send notifications right to your desktop, so you won't miss out on any important alerts. You may want to take advantage of this feature, say, if you use AOL to read your emails instead of the default Mail app. This way you'll get notified when you have a new message and be able to access your inbox without having to open Safari.

Follow these steps to create a web app.

1. Open a website that you wish to save as an app in Safari.

2. Select *File* in the menu bar and click *Add to Dock*.

3. Type the name you want to use with the app. The name will be visible when you hover the cursor over the app's icon.

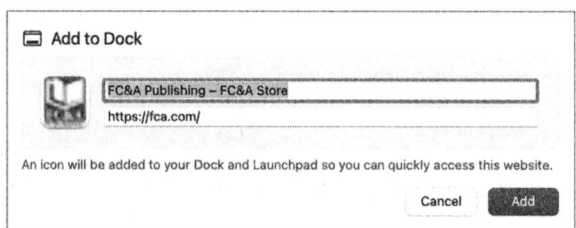

4. Click the *Add* button.

5. The icon will be added to the Dock. Click on it to open the web page.

To edit the notification settings for these web apps, go the Apple menu and click *System Settings*. Go to *Notifications*, find the web app in your list of applications, and select it to make changes. Any of your web apps will be listed under the name you gave them, not the web address of the original site.

If you want to delete a web app, follow these steps.

1. Open the Finder app.

2. Click on *Go* in the menu bar and select *Home*.

3. Open the *Applications folder* and find the web app.

4. Drag the web app to the Trash.

This feature is only available on Macs running macOS Sonoma or more recent versions.

These tools take your browser to the next level

Many browsers have a sidebar feature on the left or right side of the window. It has several useful options and apps. In Microsoft Edge, you can find the sidebar on the right-hand side.

Here's how to customize the sidebar and access all of its features.

- Click on the + button to add apps, tools, or websites to the sidebar.

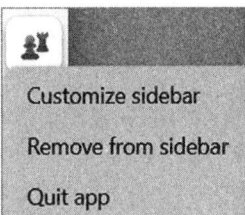

- Right-click on an item in the sidebar to access more options.

- Click the gear icon at the bottom of the sidebar to access the settings menu. Make sure *Always show sidebar* is selected so that the sidebar is enabled no matter what web page you're on.

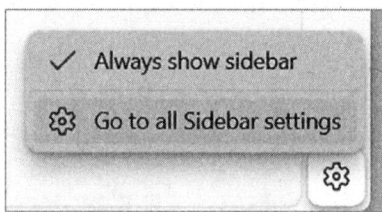

You may have to follow different steps to customize or use the sidebar if you're using a different browser.

You can also add small apps, known as plug-ins or extensions, to your browser. They can do things like change a website's appearance or find coupons when you're shopping online. Here's how to add them to Microsoft Edge.

1. Click on *Settings and more* at the top, right-hand corner of your browser window.

2. Select *Extensions* and click on *Get extensions for Microsoft Edge*.

3. This will take you to an online app store where you can browse extensions. To add one to your browser, hover your cursor over the extension. Then click the *Get* button to install it.

Different browsers will vary on how they download plug-ins or extensions. But never add one to your web browser if it doesn't come from a trusted source or app store. It may contain viruses or other malware.

Focus mode: Your secret weapon against annoying disruptions

Pop-ups and notifications on your computer screen can make it nearly impossible to focus. For example, you may be in the middle of balancing your budget when an alert tells you that an email has arrived. Next thing you know, you've forgotten which financial transaction you were working on.

Fortunately, though, you can temporarily stop these messages with your computer's Focus mode. Here's how to turn it on in Windows 11.

1. Go to Settings > System > Focus.

2. Click on the down-facing arrow to view more settings.

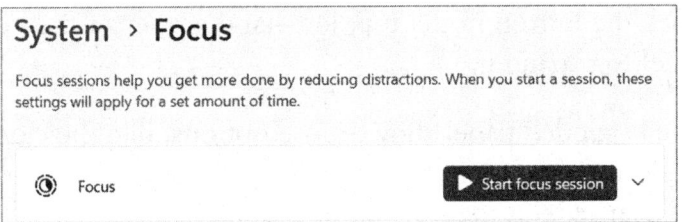

3. Review the settings that you want to use. For example, the menu option *Show the timer in the Clock app* will display a countdown on your screen that tells you how long the Focus session will last. *Hide badges on taskbar apps* will prevent app icons from showing alerts, such as when you have a new email. *Hide flashing on taskbar apps* will prevent apps from blinking when you get a notification. *Do not disturb* will silence all other notifications.

4. Use the checkbox next to these settings to toggle them *On* or *Off*. When you're done, click the *Start focus session* button.

5. The Focus session will begin and display the Focus panel.

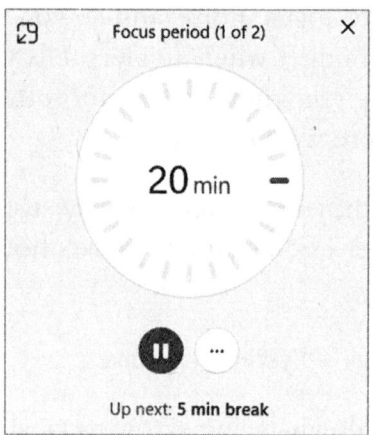

Focus period (1 of 2)   ✕

20 min   ━

Up next: **5 min break**

6. Click the button in the top, left-hand corner of the Focus panel to expand it.

7. The expanded panel shows more options, like the clock and timer in the left-hand sidebar. For all available options, click the gear icon at the bottom of the sidebar.

Here's how to use Focus mode on a computer with macOS Sequoia.

1. Click on the Control Center icon in the top menu bar.

2. Select the *Focus* button and click *Do Not Disturb*. You can also change how long the session will last or turn it off.

3. Click anywhere on your desktop to close the Control Center panel and begin the Focus session.

Easy ways to get started on your tablet

Choosing the best: How to pick the perfect device

Shopping for a tablet? If so, you're in good company. These handy, portable, easy-to-use gadgets could be the perfect replacement for a computer for most folks over 50. But there are dozens of options to choose from. Here's how to cut down on the confusion and make sure you get the best device without paying for more than you need.

First, decide whether you want to get an iPad, Android tablet, or a Chromebook. Apple iPads tend to be more expensive. But, you might want to buy one if you already have Apple products like an iPhone or a Mac. That's because these devices share some of the same apps and have similar features. An Android tablet, on the other hand, could be a good choice if you already use an Android smartphone. Chromebooks, which are made by Google, are a mix between a laptop and a tablet. They run a unique operating system, called ChromeOS, and have a physical keyboard as well as a touch screen. They're smaller and lighter than most conventional laptops.

Here are some other factors you should consider when shopping for a tablet.

- Screen size. Tablet screens are measured diagonally, from the top of one corner to the bottom of the opposite corner. If you want a device for watching videos, viewing photos, and browsing the web, you might consider getting one with a screen that measures at least 10 inches diagonally. But if you plan to use your tablet mostly for reading, and want it to easily fit in a bag or purse, you can choose one that's smaller.

- Weight. Tablets can be used when you're out and about, so make sure yours isn't too heavy to tote around. Look for one that weighs less than 2 pounds. You may want to go to a computer store and pick one up to see how heavy it is.

- Battery life. You don't want a tablet that needs to be recharged every few hours. Look for one that has a minimum of 10 hours of battery life for everyday tasks like surfing the web and watching videos.

Upgrade your tech experience with these accessories

If you've got a tablet, you might consider investing in a few accessories. The right ones can prevent your device from getting damaged, make it more comfortable to use, and ensure that a dying battery doesn't prevent you from using your tablet.

- Cases. These help protect your tablet from dings and dents. If you're worried about the screen getting scratched, consider a case that covers the entire tablet. Or you could get a separate screen protector.

- Tablet stands. These gadgets are designed to hold your device in a fixed position. This way you won't need to hold your tablet to use it. They also promote better posture by elevating the tablet to eye level. A stand could be a good investment if you frequently use your tablet to make video calls with your family or friends, or if you think you'll use it to watch movies.

- External keyboards and mice. Plan to write a lot on your tablet? Or perhaps you'll use it to track your household spending. Either way, you may want to buy a Bluetooth keyboard and mouse so that you can use your tablet more like a traditional computer.

- Portable battery chargers. You don't want to worry about your tablet dying in the middle of the day if you plan on using it when you're not at home. That's where portable power banks come in. You can use them to top off your battery no matter where you are. Just make sure that your tablet's power cable is compatible with your charger's output port.

Write, draw, create — why a stylus is a must-have

A stylus is a great accessory to have for your tablet. Here are a few ways you can use one of these devices.

- Tap on apps, text, and links with the stylus instead of your finger. The fine point on a stylus means you won't have to worry about opening the wrong app or clicking an incorrect link.

- Some apps let you use your tablet and stylus just like a notepad and paper. This is a great way to jot down a quick reminder or take handwritten notes during a speech. Some apps also convert these notes into typed text.

- Turn your tablet into a digital easel with art and drawing apps. Certain stylus devices are also pressure sensitive, so you can use them just like you would a pencil or paint brush.

When shopping for a stylus, make sure that it's compatible with the device you have. For example, the Apple Pencil will not work with an Android tablet.

Master the basics of your tablet with this user guide

In order to use your tablet effectively, you'll want to learn a few important terms. Here are some to know before you start using your device.

- Home screen. This is the screen on your tablet where apps are displayed. Tap an app's icon to open it. Your apps will automatically flow to a new screen if you have too may of them on a home screen. Swipe left or right to change home screens.

- Home button. This is the button that will take you back to your tablet's home screen. On some devices, it may be a physical button. On others, you might need to tap a virtual button or swipe up from the bottom of the tablet's touch screen.

- Favorites bar or Dock. This bar at the bottom of the home screen is called the Dock on an iPad, and the Favorites bar or Taskbar on an Android tablet. It stays in place no matter which home screen you're on. This way, you can quickly access your favorite apps.

Navigate your device with these gestures

You don't need a mouse and keyboard to work on a tablet. Instead, you can get around on this device with a series of swipes and taps. Here are some universal tips that can help you access all the features on your tablet.

- Place your thumb and forefinger tips together over an item, such as an image or a website, and slowly move them apart to zoom in.

- Pinch your thumb and forefinger back together to zoom out and make the item smaller.

- Double-tap on a photo to zoom in on the spot you tapped. Repeat to go back to the original view.

In addition to these universal controls, some tablets have unique gestures you'll need to know.

iPads. Here's how to get around on your iPad.

- Swipe up from the bottom of the screen to return to the home screen when you're in an app.

- Swipe up from the bottom of the screen and stop in the middle of the screen to open the App Switcher. This displays thumbnail windows of your open apps. You can tap on one to go to that app, swipe left and right to view more open apps, or press on an app and drag it to the top of the screen to close it.

- Swipe down from the top, right-hand corner of the screen to open the Control Center. You can use this screen to adjust features such as volume and screen brightness or quickly access certain apps.

- Swipe down from the top, middle of the screen to view your current notifications.

To change the way certain gestures work on your iPad, or to view more options, go the Settings app and tap *Multitasking & Gestures.*

Android tablets. Because Android tablets are made by a variety of companies, not all of them respond to the same swipes and taps. Here are a few to try.

- Swipe up from the bar at the bottom of the screen to return to the home screen.

- Swipe up from the bar at the bottom of the screen, hold, then let go to view all open apps.

- Swipe down from the top of the screen to access the Quick Settings panel. Tablets that use Android 13 or later versions may refer to this panel as the Control Center.

Tablet troubleshooting — smart tips to make it last for years

Tablets are expensive pieces of tech, so it makes sense to try to keep them in tiptop condition. Follow these tips to make sure your device stays in good working order.

- Keep it clean. Use a microfiber cloth, like the kind used to wipe reading glasses, to clean away fingerprints and smudges. It's the safest way to clean your tablet's screen without scratching it.

- Watch out for extreme temperatures. Avoid storing your tablet in the freezing cold or blistering heat for long periods of time. For example, you don't want to leave it in the garage during the winter or in a hot car during the summer. Doing so could damage the electronics.

- Use the 80/20 rule when you're charging your tablet. Over time, the lithium-ion battery in it can wear down and won't hold as much power as they did when they were new. But if you don't charge your battery to more than 80 percent and don't let the charge dip below 20 percent, you can slow down how quickly the battery degrades.

Harness your tablet's full potential

Why your device's Control Center matters

Want to tweak the volume of your tablet in a flash? Or maybe you want to access the music controls without leaving the app you're using? You can do these tasks and more by using the Control Center or Quick Settings. Here's how.

iPads. The Control Center has been a regular feature on iPads for many years, but the latest version of iPadOS has given it even more functionality. Follow these steps to access the Control Center's basic functions.

1. Swipe down from the top, right-hand corner of the screen to open the Control Center. It will open to the Favorites panel. Tap on an app or a control to open it and view more information.

2. Tap on the antenna icon on the right-hand side of the screen to open the network and communications controls. This panel will let you choose which Wi-Fi network you want to connect to, manage any devices connected to your iPad via Bluetooth, and turn Airplane Mode on or off.

3. Tap on the music note icon on the right-hand side of the panel to view more music controls. You can use this screen to start or stop music, skip to the next song, or adjust the volume of your music.

You can customize which apps and options appear in the Control Center with these steps.

1. Press the + button at the top left of the Control Center to begin editing.

2. Tap on the — icon to delete an item from the Control Center.

3. Drag the thick border on the bottom, right-hand corner of an icon to make it larger or smaller. When an icon is resized, the other icons will move to allow it to fit.

4. Tap on the Add a Control button at the bottom of the panel to access the controls gallery, which shows apps and other settings that can be added to the Control Center.

5. Tap on an item to add it to your Control Center.

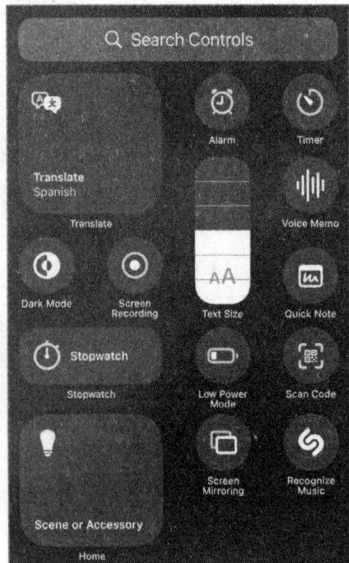

Android tablets. Most Android devices have a Quick Settings menu, which can be accessed by swiping down from the top of the screen. However, devices that use Android 13 or later versions have a Control Center which closely resembles the iPad's version. Here's how to use it.

1. Swipe down on the top, right-hand corner of the screen to open the Control Center.

2. Tap on an item to turn it on or off.

3. If there is an arrow on the bottom, right-hand corner of an item, tap it to view more options.

4. Swipe up from the bar at the bottom of the Control Center to close the Control Center. Tap this bottom bar to view more options.

The ABCs of typing on your tablet

Unlike computers, tablets don't have a physical keyboard. That means you'll need to use your tablet's touch screen to type on its virtual keyboard any time you want to write an email or go to a website. These tips and tricks can help you type on your tablet like a pro.

- Tap on a text field or box to access the default tablet keyboard.

- Tap the *shift* button to type a capital letter.

- Tap this button to access the numbers on the keyboard.

- From the numbers, tap on this button to access symbols.

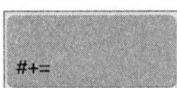

- Swipe from top to bottom on a letter to enter the number or symbol above it.

- Press and hold on a letter to view other options, such as accented characters.

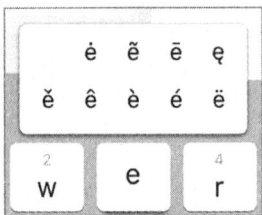

If you're typing on an iPad, you can move the keyboard around the screen so that you can type without adjusting the way you're holding your tablet. Here's how.

1. Tap on this button in the bottom, right-hand corner of the keyboard.

2. Tap on the *Floating* button to minimize the keyboard on the screen.

3. Press the bar at the bottom of the keyboard and drag it to any position on the screen.

4. To return the keyboard to its original size, press on the bar at the bottom of the keyboard and drag it to the bottom of the screen.

Would you rather type on your tablet with a physical keyboard? If so, you can pair a Bluetooth keyboard with your device.

Go to the Settings app and find the *Bluetooth* option. Make sure the keyboard you have is Bluetooth enabled and turned on, and that your tablet is searching for the device. When you see the keyboard pop up under the devices list, simply tap it to finish pairing.

Don't miss these app management tricks

Your tablet would be useless without apps. That's because you need these little programs to do everything from browsing the web to viewing your digital photos.

Follow these handy tips to manage your apps.

- Press and hold on an app's icon to view a menu with more options.

- Press and hold on an app and drag it on top of another to create a folder containing multiple items. This keeps your screen from being cluttered with apps, and lets you keep apps of the same type in one place. You can also drag folders onto the Dock or Favorites bar, which lets you access them from any home screen.

Depending on what type of tablet you have, you may need to follow a few more specific steps to manage your apps.

Find all your iPad apps. Every new app that gets added to your iPad automatically goes on a home screen. If you have dozens and dozens of apps, you don't want to have to search through all your screens just to find the one you're looking for. That's where the App Library comes in. This tool lists every single app on your device, making it easy to find one. To access the App Library, swipe left from the right-hand edge of the home screen until you reach it. All the apps are organized by categories. You can search for apps using the box at the top of the window.

If you want to remove an app from your home screen without deleting it from your iPad, press and hold on the app's icon. Tap *Remove App* then tap *Remove from Home Screen.* You will still be able to access this app from the App Library.

After you've cleaned up all your apps, you may want to consolidate your home screens so you don't have to swipe through so many to open the App Library. Here's how.

1. Press and hold on an empty space on the home screen.

2. Tap on the dots at the bottom of the window.

3. All of your iPad's home screens are displayed. If the circle below a home screen doesn't have a check mark, it won't be visible when you swipe between home screens. Press the — button to delete that home screen.

Keep track of Android apps. To view every app on an Android tablet, swipe up from the bottom of the screen to open the All Apps section.

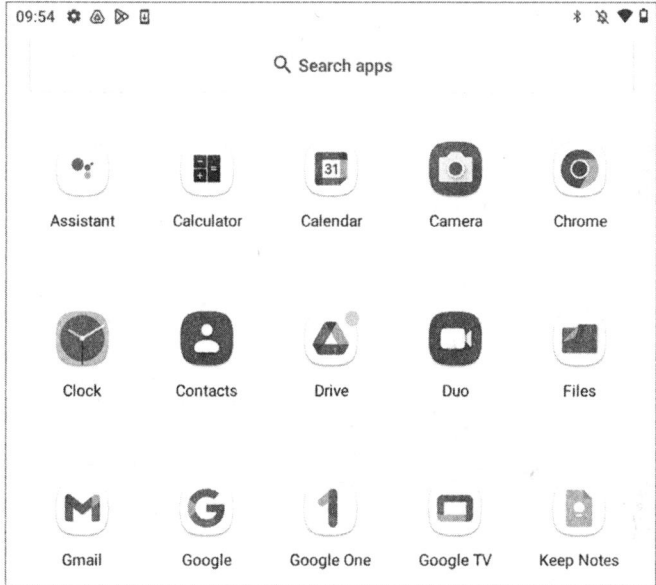

To add an app to your home screen from this view, drag it from this section onto the desired position of your home screen.

A step-by-step primer for mastering widgets

Widgets are a bit like mini apps. They let you display and interact with information from apps, such as the current weather or your to-do list, in a small window on your screen. Widgets also allow you to check off small tasks without opening an app. Here's how to set them up on your tablet.

iPads. Follow these steps to add widgets to your iPad's home screen.

1. Press and hold on an empty space on your home screen until the app icons begin to jiggle.

2. Tap the *Edit* button in the top, left-hand corner.

3. Tap the *Add Widgets* button.

4. Scroll through the list of available widgets. When you find the one you want, tap it and swipe left or right to see different sizes and layouts.

5. When you have selected the size you want, tap *Add Widget*.

6. While the apps are still jiggling, move the widget where you want it on the screen, then tap *Done*. You can also drag the widget on top of another equally sized widget to create a stack, which allows you to cycle through the widgets without changing screens.

You can also add widgets to your iPad's Lock screen. This lets you do tasks such as playing or pausing music without unlocking your tablet. Here's how.

1. Press the top button on your iPad twice to go to the Lock screen.

2. Touch and hold the screen until the *Customize* and + buttons appear.

3. Tap *Customize* and then tap *Add Widgets*.

4. Choose from the available widgets and tap on one to add it to the Lock screen.

5. Tap the X icon to close the Widgets panel.

Android tablets. Use this guide to add widgets to your Android tablet's home screen.

1. Press and hold an empty space on your home screen.

2. Tap the *Widgets* button.

3. Find the app that has the widget you want. To see all the available widgets for that app, tap on it.

4. Touch and hold the widget you want to add to your home screen. You will see images of your tablet's different home screens.

5. Drag the widget to the spot on your home screen where you want to place it and lift your finger.

If you want to change the size of a widget, follow these steps.

1. Press and hold the widget you want to resize.

2. Lift your finger. If the widget can be changed, an outline with dots on the side will appear.

3. Drag the dots to resize the widget.

4. When you're happy with the size, tap outside of the widget.

Find answers to anything, anytime

Maybe you want to quickly find the answer to a question. Or perhaps you're looking for a file but can't remember where you stored it. Either way, your tablet has got you covered. These devices have their own intelligent search functions that let you use voice queries or a text search to easily find what you're looking for.

Use Siri to search your iPad. Apple's digital voice assistant, Siri, is used on all of the company's electronics. It can be activated with a voice command, such as saying "Hey Siri." After that, it will respond to questions or searches. Here's how to set up Siri on your iPad.

1. Go to the Settings app and tap *Siri*.

2. Tap *Talk to Siri.*

3. Choose *Hey Siri* or *Siri.*

4. When you say "Siri" or "Hey Siri," your iPad will begin listening for a question or search.

You can also activate Siri by pressing and holding the home or top button on your iPad until your device indicates that Siri is listening.

Searching on Android tablets. You can use the Google Search box on your home screen to search the web, as well as your device's files, apps, and images. Tap on the box and enter your question, or tap the microphone icon to start a voice search. You can also turn on a feature that lets you activate your Google Assistant app by saying "Hey Google." Follow these steps to turn it on.

1. Open the Google Assistant app on your tablet. If you do not have this app, download it from your device's approved app store.

2. Select *Assistant settings.*

3. Go to *Popular settings* and tap *Hey Google and Voice Match.*

4. Turn on *Hey Google*. If you don't see this option, turn on *Google Assistant*.

5. Follow the on-screen prompts to train your device to recognize your voice.

6. After you've completed the setup, saying "Hey Google" will activate the digital assistant. You can ask it to perform searches or give it other commands, such as opening an app.

Sync your tablet and smartphone for seamless communication

If you pair your smartphone with your tablet, you may be able to use your tablet to send and receive text messages. You'll need to share the same account on both devices. That means you'll have to have an iPad and an iPhone, as well as an Apple ID, or a Google Account and compatible Android tablet and smartphone. Follow these steps to set up text messaging on your tablet.

iPads. You'll need an iPhone in order to receive and send texts on your iPad. Here is how to pair these devices.

1. Go to the Settings app and make sure you're signed into the same Apple ID on both your iPhone and iPad. You should see your name and initials at the top of the Settings app when it is opened.

2. Got to the Settings app on your iPad and go to *Apps*.

2. Tap on *Messages*.

3. Toggle *iMessage* to *On*.

4. Go to the Settings app and select *Messages*.

5. Tap on *Send & Receive*.

6. Choose from the available options below *You can receive iMessages to and reply from.*

After this process is complete, any texts you receive or send on your phone will also appear on your iPad and vice versa.

Android tablets. Before you can pair your Android tablet with your smartphone, make sure that both devices have the latest version of Google Messages and are running Android 5 or later. You'll also need to be connected to Wi-Fi on both devices.

1. Open Google Messages on your smartphone.

2. At the top right, tap your account menu and then select *Device Pairing.*

3. If you get a prompt to sign in with your Google Account, select the account that you want to use with Google Messages.

4. On your tablet, sign in to Google Messages with the same Google Account that you chose for your smartphone.

5. Your smartphone will get a message in Google Messages with three images. Tap the image that matches the one shown on your tablet's screen.

6. Your phone will vibrate when the pairing is complete.

Schedule texts with this hack

A new feature in iPadOS 18 allows you to schedule text messages to be sent at a certain time. Here's how.

1. Open the Messages app and write out a text message.

2. Tap the + button to the left of the text box.

3. Tap *Send Later*.

4. Tap on the time option, and select the time and date you want the text to be sent.

Email setup 101: What you need to know

Email is one of the most important communication tools in the digital world. And your tablet is equipped to send and receive this information. Here's how to set up your account.

iPads. These tablets come with the Mail app already installed. Follow these steps to add any existing email accounts you have to this app.

1. Go to the Settings app and select *Apps*.

2. Go to *Mail* and tap *Mail Accounts*.

3. Tap *Add Account*.

4. Select your email provider and follow the on-screen instructions to sync your accounts.

If you prefer to use a different email app, you can download one from the Apple App Store. Open the App Store and type "email" into the search box to view more options. Tap on an app to begin the downloading process. After it is installed on your device, follow these steps to make it your default email option.

1. Go to the Settings app and select *Apps*.

2. Go to *Mail* and tap *Default Mail App*.

3. Tap the app you want to set as the default.

Android tablets. Android devices use different default email apps depending on the manufacturer of the tablet. You can also download other options from your device's App Store. Follow the app's instructions to sync your accounts. Once you have found an app you want to use, here's how to make it the default option.

1. Go to the Settings app and select *Apps*.

2. Select *Manage apps*.

3. Find the old email app that came pre-installed on the tablet. Tap on it.

4. Scroll down and tap on *Open by default*.

5. Select the *Clear default preferences* button.

6. The next time you attempt to send an email, say by clicking the *email* option from your tablet's contact list, your tablet will ask you which app you want to use. Select the new email app and hit the *Always* button.

Protect your privacy with a Lock screen

Tablets are a great alternative to laptops. But if you use your tablet to do all the tasks that you used to do on a computer, chances are it's full of sensitive information that thieves and hackers would love to get their hands on.

That's why you'll want to set up a Lock screen, which will prevent access to your tablet without a passcode, PIN, fingerprint, or face scan. Here's how to add this feature to your iPad.

1. Go to the Settings app.

2. Depending on your device, tap on *Face ID & Passcode, Touch ID & Passcode,* or *Passcode.*

3. If this is your first time setting up the Lock screen, select the option *Turn Passcode On.*

4. If your device has face-scanning technology or a fingerprint reader, you'll see the additional option to set up *Face ID* or *Touch ID.*

Here's how to set up Lock screen on most Android tablets.

1. Open your Settings app.

2. Tap *Security.*

3. Tap *Screen Lock.*

4. Choose a lock type. You can use a numeric PIN, a pattern that you draw with your finger, or a passcode of four or more letters and numbers. Your device may offer additional options depending on the make and model.

5. Follow the on-screen instructions.

Innovative ideas for Lock screen customization

Your Lock screen can do more than keep strangers from using your tablet. You can add a personal touch to this screen, check the time, and even see the weather forecast — all without unlocking your tablet.

iPads. Here's how to edit your Lock screen on an Apple iPad.

1. Press the top button of your iPad twice to go to the Lock screen.

2. Touch and hold the screen until the *Customize* and + buttons appear at the bottom of the screen. If they don't appear, touch and hold the screen again and then enter your passcode.

3. Tap the *Customize* button to edit the options on the current Lock screen. If you have more than one Lock screen, you can cycle between them by swiping left or right. Or tap the + button to create a new Lock screen.

4. Tap the *Lock Screen* option.

5. Tap the date or time boxes to change the font size, style, and color of these boxes.

6. Tap the *Add Widgets* button to add widgets that can display info such as the weather, calendar events, or news headlines.

7. Tap the buttons at the bottom of the screen to change the color theme of the Lock Screen.

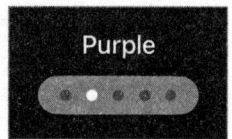

8. Tap the *Done* button to apply your changes.

Android tablets. Follow these steps to change the Lock screen on an Android.

1. Press and hold on an empty area of your tablet's Lock screen.

2. Tap the *Customize lock screen* button at the bottom of your screen and then unlock your tablet.

3. Pick a clock type, color scheme, and wallpaper for your Lock screen.

4. Scroll down to adjust your Lock screen notification settings and shortcut options.

Stay a step ahead with security and privacy settings

The privacy and security settings on your tablet can help you keep your identity and data safe while you use your device. Getting them set up properly is a great way to make sure you're protected from hackers and other digital dangers.

iPads. Apple has overhauled its privacy options in iPadOS 18. The changes make it easier for you to protect your device and the data on it. Here's how to access and change the settings.

1. Go the Settings app and tap *Privacy & Security.*

2. Tap on *Location Services* to choose which apps can track your iPad's current location and how frequently they are able to do so. For example, you may want to allow a map and driving app to have access to your location, but prevent a shopping app from being able to track where you go.

3. Tap on the *Tracking* option to edit which apps are able to track your activities and browsing habits when you're online. This data may be used by advertisers to send you targeted ads.

4. To view more privacy and security options about a specific app, tap on its name and icon beneath the *Applications* heading.

5. Scroll down the page and tap on *Sensitive Content Warning*. Your iPad will warn you before you see explicit photos or videos through messaging apps.

6. To see what sort of data your apps are collecting, tap on *App Privacy Report*. You will see a snapshot of what information your apps gathered over the past week.

Android tablets. To adjust the settings on your device, go to the Settings app and look for the *Security and privacy* option. Depending on which version of Android your tablet is running, your tablet may have separate options for privacy and security settings.

You can use these settings to enable alerts that will notify you of potential risks for your tablet, find recommendations on how to improve your tablet's security, and view an overall assessment of how secure your data is.

Make the most of your tablet's bells and whistles

Express yourself — how to personalize your device

Customizing your tablet's appearance gives it a personal touch. Most devices offer a number of ways to change the background of your home screen, add accent colors, and even personalize app icons. Here's how you can do this.

iPads. Apple has introduced a number of exciting ways to customize your home screen in iPadOS 18. Follow these steps to get started.

1. Press and hold an empty space on the home screen until the app icons begin to jiggle.

2. Tap the *Edit* button in the top, left-hand corner of the screen.

3. Tap on *Customize*.

4. By default, the *Light* option is selected. You can tap the *Dark* option to use a darker theme for the home screen and app icons. Or you can tap the *Automatic* option to switch between *Light* and *Dark* depending on the time of day.

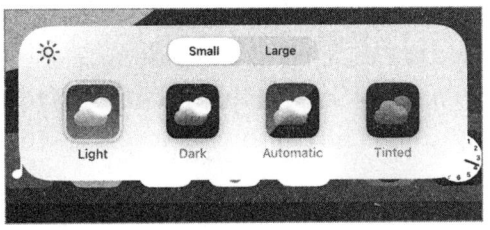

5. Tap *Tinted* to view customizable options for the app icons.

6. Change the color of the app icons by dragging the sliders.

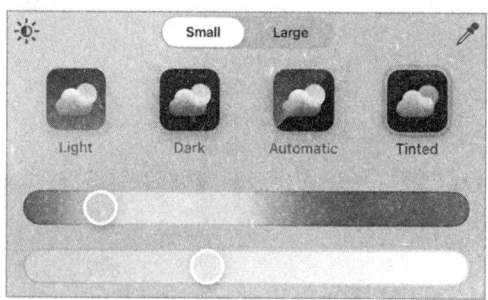

7. You can also use the eyedropper to select a color from your wallpaper and apply it to the app icons.

It's also possible to change the size of the iPad icons on the home screen. There are two different ways to do so.

- When following the above steps to customize the home screen background, tap the *Large* button in the customization panel.

- Go to the Settings app and tap *Home Screen & App Library*. Toggle the button next to *Use Large App Icons* to *On*.

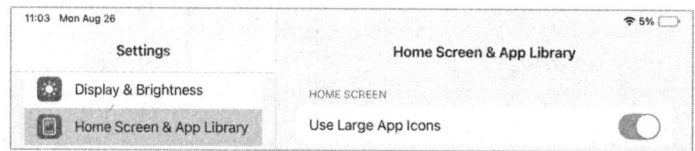

Android tablets. Depending on which version of Android your device uses, you may have different options for customizing the background. If your tablet uses Android 12 or an earlier version, go to Settings and tap on *Display* to customize the home screen. Tablets that use Android 13 or later versions have a wider range of customization options. Here's how to access them.

1. Go to the Settings app and select *Personal customization*. This menu option may be slightly different depending on the brand of your tablet. You can also access this menu by pressing and holding on the home screen and tapping the *Personal customization* button.

2. A menu will display your home screen settings.

3. Tap on *Theme*.

4. Select an option for the wallpaper and the appearance of the app icons. Certain selections will change the app icon's colors to match the background color. Once you have selected a new theme, tap *Apply*.

5. Go back to the Personal customization page and tap the *System theme color* option.

6. Select an option from the menu. You can choose a color scheme that is based on your tablet's *Wallpaper color* or use a *Basic color*.

7. Toggle the *System theme color* button to *On* to apply the selected color scheme to the tablet's interface.

8. Toggle the *Apply system theme color to home screen icons* button to *On*. This will apply the selected color scheme to the app icons.

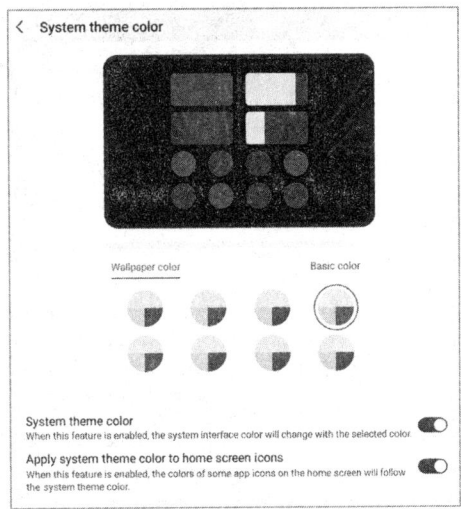

Customize your iPad background

The background image on your tablet's home screen is known as wallpaper. You can change its appearance on your iPad. Here's how.

1. Open the Settings app and tap *Wallpaper*.

2. Tap the *Add New Wallpaper* button.

3. Use the buttons on the top toolbar to view the different categories of wallpaper.

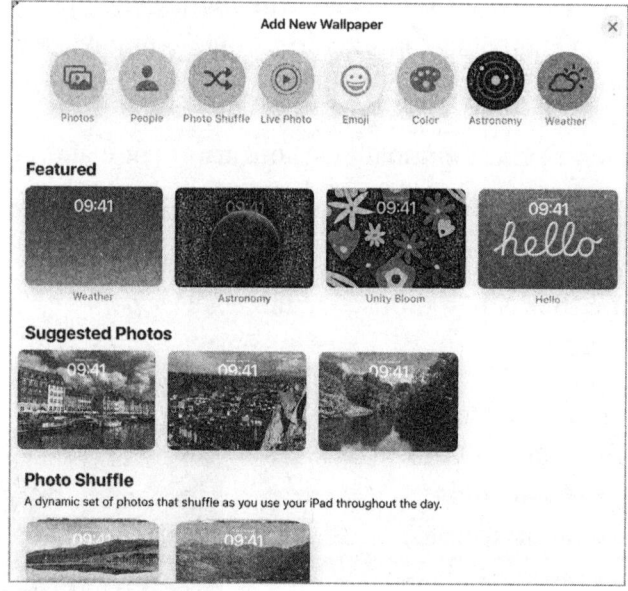

4. Select an image to use as your tablet's wallpaper.

5. Tap the *Add* button.

6. If you want to use the same wallpaper for both your home screen and Lock screen, choose *Set as Wallpaper Pair*. Tap *Customize Home Screen* if you only want to set the image as the home screen wallpaper.

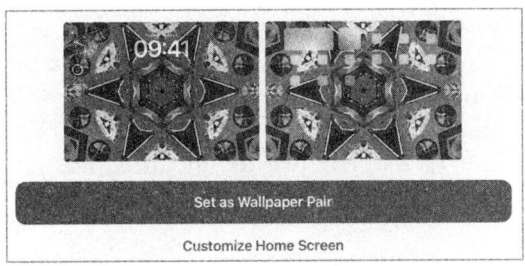

7. If you selected *Customize Home Screen*, you can change the background settings. You can add a color, change the image, and blur the background. Tap *Done* to apply your changes.

You can also use one of your own photos for the wallpaper on your home screen. Follow these steps to create a custom background.

1. Open the Settings app and tap *Wallpaper*.

2. Select the *Add New Wallpaper* button and tap on the *Photos* button at the top of the screen.

3. Your photo library will be displayed. Use the left-hand side-bar or the buttons at the top of the screen to scroll through your pictures.

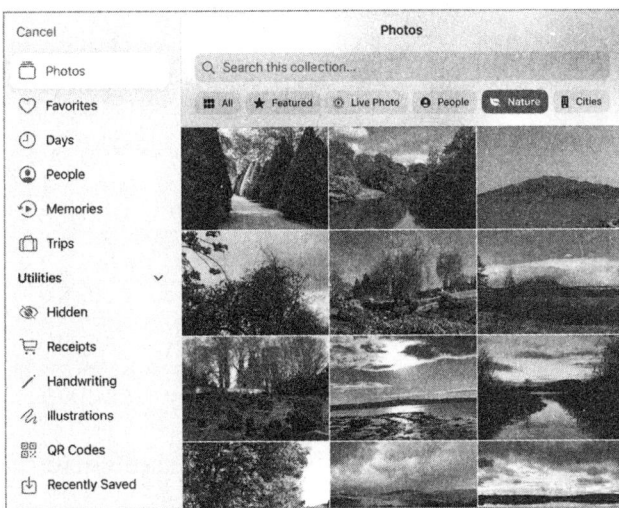

4. Tap on a photo to select it.

5. Tap on the *Add* button.

6. Select whether to use the photo on the Lock screen and the home screen or only on the home screen.

Alternatively, you can add a photo directly from your photo library to your home screen. In the Photos app, tap *Library*, select a photo, then tap the share button. Scroll down and select *Use as Wallpaper*, tap *Add*, then choose whether to show it on both your home screen and Lock screen or only your home screen.

Make your Android tablet unique

On devices using Android 12 or earlier versions, you can change the wallpaper by pressing the home screen until the menu appears. Then select the *Wallpapers* option to view more backgrounds. Tap on one to set it as your new wallpaper. You can also find this menu by going to the Settings app, selecting *Display,* and tapping on *Wallpaper*.

You can find the default wallpaper options on a tablet using Android 13 or later versions by going to the Settings app and selecting *Personal customization*.

If you want to use your own pictures to create a unique wallpaper for your tablet, follow these steps.

1. Open the Photos app on your tablet.

2. Select the picture you want to use as your wallpaper.

3. Tap the menu button in the top, right-hand corner and select the *Use as* option.

4. Tap the *Photos Wallpaper* icon.

5. Choose the *Set wallpaper* option.

Photos
Wallpaper

6. Select whether to use the photo as the home screen wallpaper, the Lock screen wallpaper, or both.

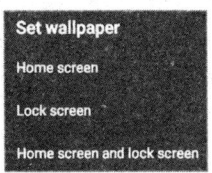

Set wallpaper

Home screen

Lock screen

Home screen and lock screen

Get more done with these multitasking features

Many tablets let you view multiple apps at the same time. This can make it easy to, say, take notes while watching a cooking video online. Or, for example, you could track and record your income and spending in a budgeting app while reviewing your bank statement.

Multitasking on an iPad. You can use either the Split View or Slide Over feature on devices that run iPadOS 18 or later versions. Split View lets you look at two apps side by side. The Slide Over feature lets you view one app in a smaller, floating window while another app is in full-screen mode.

Here's how to open multiple apps on your iPad.

1. Open an app and tap the three dots at the top of the screen.

2. Choose the *Split View* or *Slide Over* button. The current app will move aside and your home screen will appear.

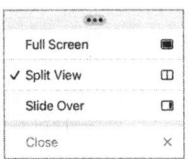

Full Screen	▣
✓ Split View	▥
Slide Over	▢
Close	✕

3. Select the second app that you want to open. If you opted for *Split View*, the second app will appear in a window next to the one you opened. You can resize the apps by dragging the slider that appears between them. If you selected *Slide Over*, the second app will open to full screen. The first app you

opened will move to a smaller window that you can move to the right or left side of your screen.

Multitasking on an Android tablet. Certain Android tablets allow you to open two apps side by side in the Split Screen mode, or let you have one app in a smaller window using the Floating Window mode. Here's how to use Split Screen to multitask.

1. Open an app.

2. Tap the three dots at the top of the screen.

3. Select the *Split Screen* option.

4. The app's window will move to the left side of the screen. All your tablet's apps will be displayed on the right.

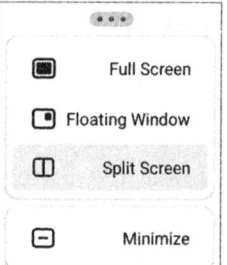

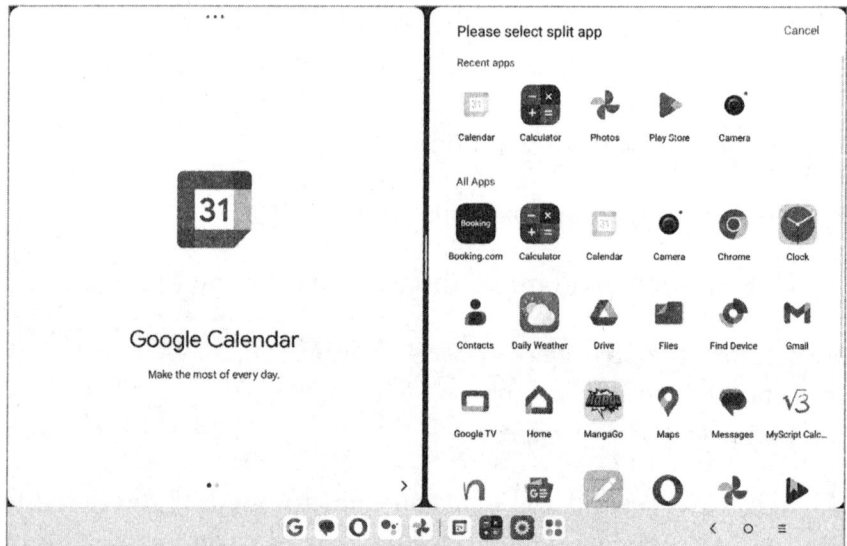

5. Select one of the apps on the right side of the screen to open it. Both apps will take up half of the screen. You can drag the middle bar to resize the windows.

6. To exit Split Screen mode, tap the three dots at the top of the screen. Select the *Full Screen* or *Minimize* option.

Here's how to use Floating Window.

1. Open an app and tap the three dots at the top of the screen.

2. Select the *Floating Window* option.

3. The app will be displayed as a Floating Window on your home screen. Drag the top of the window to reposition it.

4. Tap on another app to open it in full screen. The Floating Window will remain in front of the new app so you can view both.

5. To exit Floating Window mode, tap the three dots at the top of the screen and choose the *Full Screen* or *Minimize* option.

These features may not be available on every Android tablet. Check your device's options to see if it offers multitasking.

Let Stage Manager take center stage

Certain iPad models have a feature called Stage Manager that lets users multitask with ease. When it's activated, the apps you're working on will go to the center of the screen. The rest of your recently used apps will move to the left of the screen. You can organize these apps by type so you can switch between them with ease.

Here's how to set up this feature and use it on some iPads.

1. Go to the Settings app and select *Multitasking & Gestures*.

2. Tap the button under *Stage Manager*.

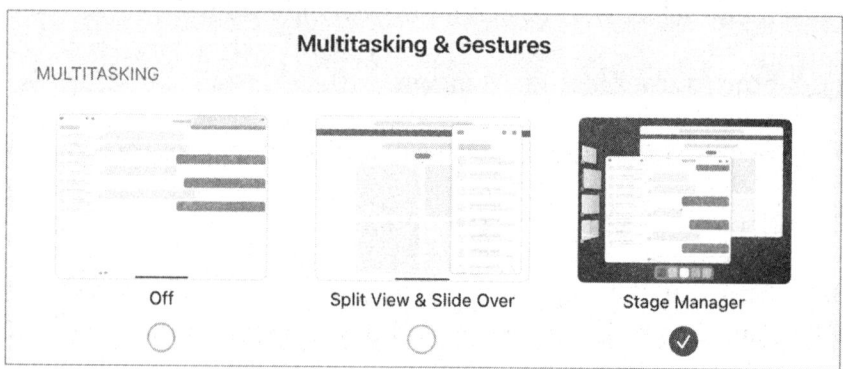

3. Open an app.

4. The app will open on the home screen. There will be a border around it to show that Stage Manager is currently active.

5. Resize the app by dragging the bottom, right-hand corner of the app's border.

6. Tap on another app to make it the active app. The app you were originally using will be minimized into a thumbnail on the left-hand side of your screen. If you want to switch back to this app, tap on it.

7. Drag app thumbnails from your sidebar to the center of the screen to open them in Stage Manager. You can have up to four apps open at the same time. Drag an app back to the sidebar to minimize it.

8. To turn Stage Manager off, go back to the Settings app and tap *Multitasking & Gestures*. Toggle the button next to *Stage Manager* to *Off*.

You can also activate Stage Manager from the Control Center. Swipe down from the top, right-hand corner of the screen and select the *Stage Manager* button.

How to share files with family and friends

Your tablet is probably loaded with photos and videos. And chances are, you'll want to share them with your loved ones. Here's how to send files straight from your tablet.

iPads. These devices have several options for sharing content.

- The Mail app. You can attach files to emails to send photos, videos, and documents to your contacts. To do so, create a new email and tap in the main text field. Select the page icon above the keyboard to add a document to the email. Tap the camera icon, select *Photo Library*, and tap a picture or video to add it to the message. You can also tap the camera icon and select *Take Photo or Video* to take a photo or record a video. Select *Use Photo* or *Use Video* to insert it into your email, or tap *Retake* if you want to reshoot it.

- The Messages app. If you've synced your smartphone and iPad, you can use your tablet to share content in text messages. To do so, create a new message and tap the + button. Tap

Photos to browse recent photos and videos, then select one to add it to the text. Press the up arrow to send the message.

- The Photos app. This app can be used to create a Shared Library, which allows you to share entire photo albums. To set this up and limit who can see the albums, go to Settings > Apps > Photos > Shared Library > Get Started. Tap on the *Add Participants* button to enter the email addresses of the people who will have access to the Shared Library.

- The Share button. Many apps have a button that you can use to share items. For example, you can send a link to a song from the Music app, or you can share the address of a restaurant from the Maps app. To do so, tap on this button while you are using an app. Select the method you want to use to send the information to another person. You can choose from the Messages app, the Mail app, or any other of your installed apps that allow you to send messages or emails.

Android tablets. These devices have a Quick Share function that can be used to send and receive content on compatible devices close to your location. This is also known as Nearby Share on some Android tablets. Before others can receive content from you, they'll need to set up their Android device. Here's how you can help them on their tablet or smartphone.

1. Go to the Settings app and select *More connections.*

2. Tap on *Quick Share.*

3. Tap the *Who can share with you* button.

4. Toggle the *Visible to nearby devices* button to *On* and select who they want to receive content from. *Contacts* will let them receive data like photos and videos from their nearby contacts. The *Everyone* option lets any Android user close to their location send them files. This is the least secure choice, so it should be used sparingly. If you decide to tap *Everyone,* you should consider also selecting the *Only for 10 minutes* option. This will cause their device to revert to the previous privacy setting after 10 minutes.

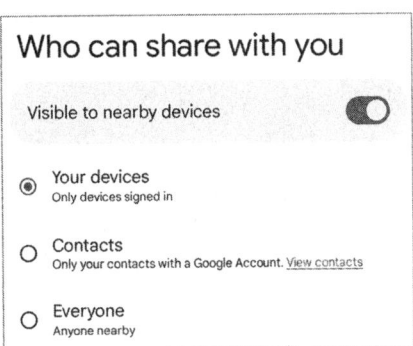

5. There's also the *Your devices* option. They can use this to send content between their Android devices as long as both of them are signed into the same Google account.

Once everything is set up, it's time to focus on your tablet.

1. Open an app on your tablet and select the content you want to share.

2. Tap on the *Share* button.

3. Tap on the *Quick Share* option.

4. Select the device you want to send the selected content to.

Sync your tablet in seconds

If you own a compatible smartphone or computer, you can link them with your tablet. That makes it easy to do tasks like sharing photos or syncing your calendar between multiple devices. Here's how.

iPads. You'll need an iPhone or a Mac computer to share content between devices if you have an iPad. You'll also need to be signed in to the same Apple ID on your tablet and your phone or computer. Once you are signed in, follow these steps.

1. Go to the Settings app and tap *General*.

2. Choose *AirPlay & Continuity*.

3. Toggle the *Handoff* button to *On*.

4. Once *Handoff* is turned *On*, apps being used on your other device can be viewed on your iPad. For example, if you're browsing a website in Safari on your iPhone, you can see the page on your iPad instead. When that option is available, you'll see this icon in the Dock. Tap on it to open the app.

Android tablets. You can sync an Android tablet with an Android smartphone. You'll need to be signed in to the same Google account on both devices.

1. Go to the Settings app and tap *Google*.

2. Tap *Devices & sharing* and select *Cross-device services*.

3. Make sure *Use cross-device services* is toggled to *On*.

When this feature is enabled, you'll be able to switch between devices on video calls in apps like Google Meet and Gmail, share information between apps, and turn on your phone's Wi-Fi hotspot from your tablet.

From tablet to TV — it's easy to stream your favorite shows

Did you know that you can connect your tablet to most smart TVs and streaming devices? Then you can watch videos from your tablet on the big screen. It's easy to do.

iPads. You can connect iPads with compatible devices using a feature called AirPlay.

1. Open the Settings app and tap on *General*.

2. Go to *AirPlay & Continuity*.

3. Tap the *Automatically AirPlay* option.

4. Choose a setting. If you select *Ask*, your tablet will suggest devices that you can connect to with Airplay. You can tap the notification to connect, or dismiss it and manually choose a different device for AirPlay. If you choose *Automatic*, your

tablet will automatically connect to any frequently used streaming devices or smart TVs when playing content from apps that you regularly use with AirPlay. If you choose *Never*, you must manually hit the AirPlay button to connect to a device with AirPlay.

Android tablets. These tablets can connect to compatible smart devices using the Cast feature.

1. Go to the Settings app and tap *More connections*.

2. Tap on *Cast*. If you don't see this option, search for "Cast" in the Settings search box.

3. Toggle the *Enable wireless display* button to *On*.

4. If there is a compatible device that can be used with the Cast function, it will be shown below the *Enable wireless display* heading.

5. Open the Google Home app.

6. Select *Devices* and tap *Add*.

7. Tap on the Cast screen icon to play the content from your tablet on your smart TV.

Smart hacks to keep tabs on your screen time

Think you're spending too much time on your tablet each day? There's a way to limit that. You can set up your device to monitor and restrict how long you use it every day. Here's how.

iPads.

1. Go to the Settings app and tap *Screen Time*.

2. Tap on the *App & Website Activity* option.

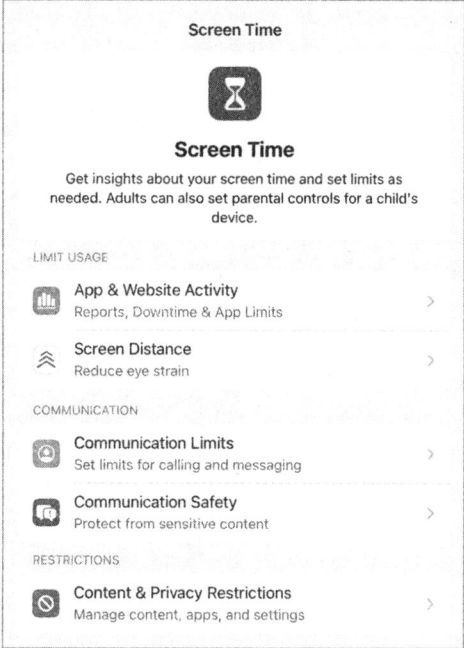

3. Tap the *Turn On App & Website Activity* button.

4. You will see a report showing how much time you spend on apps and surfing the web.

5. To manage your screen time restrictions, select a category under the *Screen Time* menu and tap it. You can limit when certain apps are allowed to be used and set up prompts to remind you to take breaks from using your tablet.

Android tablets.

1. Go to the Settings app and then select *Digital Wellbeing & parental controls*.

2. The graphic at the top of the window will display general information about the tablet's usage.

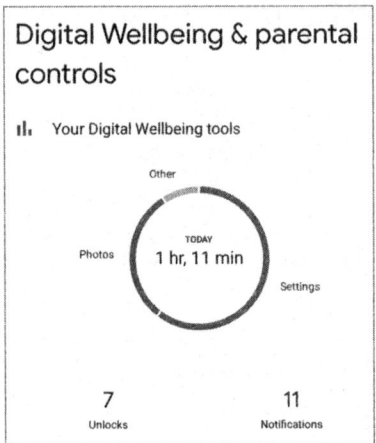

3. Tap on the graphic to view more detailed information and display the dashboard.

4. Select a day on the graph to view screen time information for that day.

5. Choose an app below the dashboard graph to view more details about its usage.

You can also manage the amount of time that your grandchildren spend on your tablet. On the main Digital Wellbeing & parental controls page, choose *Set up parental controls* to limit how long they can use the tablet each day. You can also create filters for age-appropriate content.

Navigate the smartphone maze

Ask yourself these 7 questions before buying a new device

Most smartphone manufacturers introduce a brand-new model every year. These devices are packed with the latest and greatest tech, but they cost an arm and a leg. So before you shell out a lot of money, ask yourself these questions to decide whether or not you really need a new device.

1. Is your current phone obsolete? If your smartphone is no longer able to receive important security updates or run the latest versions of your favorite apps, you may need to upgrade. Your device could be vulnerable to hackers and other fraudsters. Go to your phone's Settings app and search for *System Update* or a similar option. Look for the latest security patch listed and check the date. If it's recent, chances are you don't need to upgrade.

2. Is there a different problem at play? Perhaps your smartphone is slow and buggy. But before you buy a new one, you'll want to check to see if there's a quick fix. For example, deleting unused apps could help free up storage so that your smartphone runs better.

3. Is your phone worth fixing? If your device has been acting up, it may need repairs to get it back on track. Maybe you need to get the cracked screen replaced. Or perhaps your smartphone just needs a new battery. Compare the cost of the repair to the price of buying a used version of the same device from eBay or Walmart. If the cost of the repair

exceeds what your current smartphone is worth, it may make more sense to buy a new phone.

4. Will you make use of all the new features? Companies always boast about big upgrades to their new phones. But think carefully about whether these features are worth the money. You may find that you don't really need a slightly better camera or a moderately brighter screen.

5. Can you get new features from a software update? Companies often debut new capabilities for their phones around the same time that they announce major software updates. If you hold off on buying a new device, you may discover that your phone will get a refresh when you update its operating system.

6. Will a refurbished phone meet your needs? Companies often buy used smartphones and fix them up before selling them at a discount. These refurbished electronics are a great way to get a new device without paying premium prices. Check to see what options are available and whether or not they have all the features you need.

7. Can you buy an older model phone at a discount? When new electronics hit the market, stores often offer deep discounts on last year's model. That means you can pick up a smart-phone packed with relatively new features for a fraction of the original price.

Discover the top 5 phones for seniors

Shopping for a new phone can be overwhelming. After all, there are dozens of devices to choose from. Here are a few of the best options.

- Jitterbug Smart4. Ever wondered why someone doesn't design smartphones for folks who didn't grow up with high-tech devices? Believe it or not, they do. This phone has a large screen, big buttons, and simple menus.

- iPhone 16. The latest version in Apple's smartphone lineup is a pricey pick, but it's packed with great features like a long battery life and a friendly user interface.

- Samsung Galaxy. This is one of the top-of-the-line picks for Android users. This phone has a great camera and a fast-charging battery.

- TCL Flip2. This compact phone has a flip cover, which can help protect it from drops, falls, and other damage. Plus it has Wi-Fi connectivity so you can use it for basic web browsing and sending emails.

- Consumer Cellular IRIS Flip. Consumer Cellular specializes in providing affordable phone and internet plans, but the company makes an easy-to-use and affordable phone, too.

Cut your bill in half with these secret tricks

Looking to save money on your phone bill every month? If so, you'll want to check out the following ways to slash your spending.

- Consider what you need in a service plan. Think about how much data you use each month, how many phones your household has, and if there are other devices — like tablets or smartwatches — that need to be covered. Once you know what you need, shop around to find the best price.

- Keep tabs on your data usage if you don't have an unlimited plan. You may be charged a hefty penalty if you go over the monthly limit. To see how much data an iPhone is using, go to Settings > Cellular or Settings > Mobile Data. You can also toggle the button next to an app to *Off* to prevent it from automatically connecting to cell service. On an Android, check your data usage by going to Settings > Network & internet > Mobile network > App data usage. Enter a date range to view your usage.

- Look into alternate plans. Mobile virtual network operators, such as Boost Mobile and Cricket Wireless, lease the infrastructure that provides cell service. Other providers own and operate this equipment, which means they charge more for their plans to cover higher costs.

Dropped your smartphone and cracked the screen? It could cost hundreds to get it fixed. Instead of risking a big bill down the road, spend a few dollars to protect your device and buy a case.

Look for one that is made of shock-absorbing material, such as silicone or rubber. Make sure that the case covers the corners of your device. You may also want to get a screen protector. They are thin sheets of plastic or tempered glass that will keep your screen safe from scratches.

A simple user guide for mastering the basics

Smartphones are the single most frustrating device for seniors. But don't worry — it's easy to learn how to use them. Just follow these tips.

Here are a couple of basic terms to know.

- The Lock screen is the first thing you'll see when you turn on your smartphone. Because you need to use a password, PIN, fingerprint, or face scan to get past this screen, it keeps others from gaining access to your phone. The Lock screen also shows the time and date, as well as other basic information, including the amount of charge on your phone and the strength of your cell signal.

- The home screen shows all the app icons that are on your phone. You can swipe from left to right to move between home screens if you have too many apps to fit on a single screen. Tap on an app from this screen to open it.

iPhones. These tricks will help you with your iPhone.

- Swipe left from a home screen until you reach the App Library. This displays every app installed on your device. You can use the search box at the top of the screen to find an app that you've downloaded.

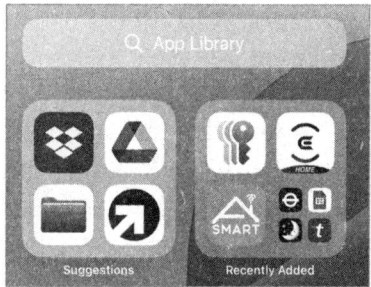

- Press on the home screen until the apps jiggle. Tap on the dots at the bottom of the screen to manage your home screens. You can hide ones that you don't use by making sure that the button beneath the home screen doesn't contain a check mark.

- Swipe down from the top, right-hand corner of the screen to open the Control Center. This feature contains a number of useful settings and app shortcuts. For example, you can use the Control Center to connect to Wi-Fi or open your phone's camera.

- Swipe down from the middle of the top of any screen to view notifications about unread messages and app updates.

- Swipe up from the bottom of the screen while you're using an app to return to your home screen.

Android smartphones. If you have an Android phone, you may be able to activate swipe gestures so that you can navigate the phone using a serious of swipes and taps instead of the device's buttons. Here's how to activate this feature.

1. Open the Settings app on your phone and tap on *System*.

2. Select the *Gestures* option and tap *System navigation*.

3. Make sure the button next to *Gesture navigation* is toggled to *On*.

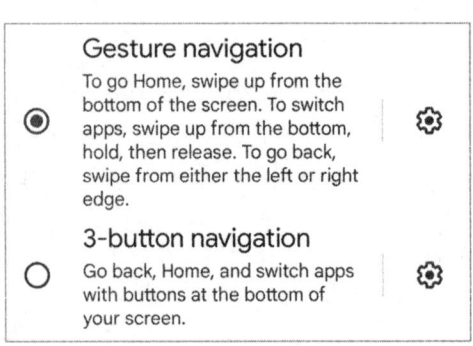

Once this is turned on, here's how to navigate your device.

- Swipe up from the bottom of the screen to return to your home screen.

- Swipe halfway up from the bottom of the screen until you see your recently used apps.

- Swipe up on the Google Search box at the bottom of the screen to view the All apps page. This page shows every app that's installed on your smartphone.

- Drag down from the top of the screen to access the Quick Settings panel, which can be used to easily adjust things like your device's screen brightness and volume.

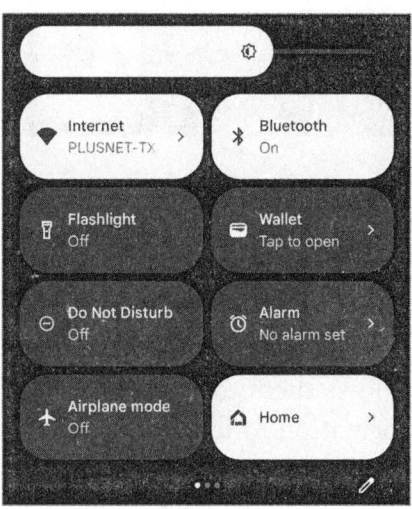

The fundamentals of apps

You can't do much on a smartphone without apps. You'll use these programs to do everything from making calls and sending messages to playing games. Here are a few things to know about using them.

- Press and hold on an app's icon to view more menu options.

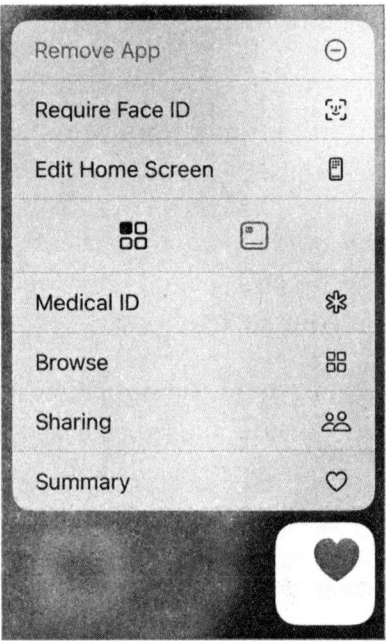

- Press and hold on an app to move it around your home screen. Drag it to the left or right of the screen to move it to a new home screen.

You can leave apps open in the background when you're using another app. This allows them to refresh more often, so you don't have to wait for information to load when you return to them. However, leaving apps open may cause your phone to slow down.

Sometimes you may want to switch between apps quickly. Here's how to do this on an iPhone.

1. Swipe halfway up from the bottom of the screen to open the app switcher. You'll see all of your open apps as thumbnails.

2. Swipe left or right to view all your open apps.

3. Tap on an app's thumbnail to make it full screen.

4. To close an app, return to the app switcher, press on a thumbnail, and swipe up to the top of the screen.

To quickly cycle between apps on an Android, tap this button on your screen. If you don't see this button, you may be able to swipe halfway up from the bottom of the screen to view all your open apps. Swipe left or right to view different apps. Select an app to make it full screen.

Fun ways to refresh your phone's appearance

Almost every smartphone looks the same these days. But yours doesn't have to. Fortunately, it's easy to personalize your device with these steps.

Change the iPhone wallpaper and app icons. Apple has introduced new ways to customize the appearance of your home screen in iOS 18. In addition to modifying your wallpaper, you can also tweak the appearance of your app icons. Here's how to alter your phone's background.

1. Press and hold an empty spot on your home screen until the app icons begin to jiggle.

2. Select the *Edit* button in the top, left-hand corner.

3. Tap the *Customize* button.

4. Choose one of the options for the home screen. By default, the *Light* option is selected. You can tap the *Dark* option to use a darker theme for the home screen and app icons. Or you can tap the *Automatic* option to switch between *Light* and

Dark depending on the time of day. Tap the tinted option and drag the sliders to change the color of the app icons.

You can also customize your iPhone's Lock screen. Follow these steps to do so.

1. Press your phone's Lock screen until the *Customize* button appears.

2. Tap the *Customize* button, then choose the *Lock Screen* option.

3. Tap the wallpaper icon in the lower, left-hand corner to change your background picture.

4. Tap in the time and date field to change its text color, size, and font.

5. Tap the widget boxes to add widgets to your home screen. You can use this field to view information, including the weather and notifications, at a glance.

Customize an Android's wallpaper and app icons. The steps to change an Android's appearance will vary depending on the device's manufacturer and the version of Android your phone is using. Follow these steps to change the appearance for most phones using Android 13 or a later version.

1. Press and hold on the home screen, then tap the *Wallpaper & style* option.

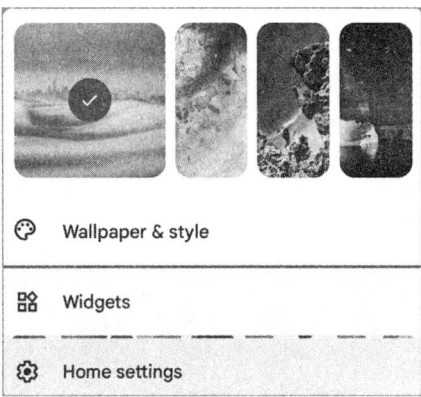

2. Tap the *Change wallpaper* option to select a new background image.

3. Toggle the *Themed icons* button to *On* to change the appearance of the app icons.

4. Tap the *Wallpaper colors* button to make the app icons match the colors of your phone's background. Tap the *Basic colors* button to select a different color for the app icons.

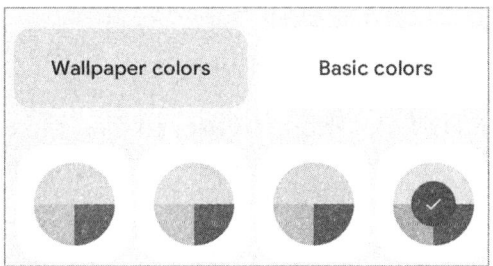

Did you know that your phone is probably dirtier than most toilet seats? Many people bring their phones with them wherever they go, and that could mean carrying a lot of gross bacteria around with them. Here's how to properly clean a phone without damaging it.

Avoid using any harsh cleaners that contain bleach or abrasives, and never spray cleaning products directly on your phone. Instead, use a lint-free cloth that has been lightly dampened with soap and water to gently wipe down your phone. Avoid getting moisture in any openings on the device, such as the charging port.

Can't find your phone? Here's how to locate it fast

Uh-oh. Your smartphone is lost or stolen. Never fear. Most modern phones have a feature — called Find My or Find My Device — that helps you locate them. But you'll need to set up the app before your device goes missing. Follow these steps to do so on an iPhone.

1. Go to the Settings app and tap your name at the top of the screen to open your Apple Account.

2. Tap on *Find My*.

3. Select the *Find My iPhone* option.

4. Toggle the *Find My iPhone* button to *On*. This will record your phone's location so that you can search for it if it's missing.

5. To find your phone — even when it's offline — toggle *Find My network* to *On*. To have the location of your device sent to Apple when the battery is low, toggle *Send Last Location* to *On*.

6. If your iPhone is ever lost or stolen, go online to *icloud.com* and sign in with your Apple Account details.

7. Click the *Find My* icon.

8. Enter your Apple Account details and click on your smart-phone's name to view its current location on a map.

9. Once you've located your smartphone, click on it again to view more options. Select *Play Sound* to make the speakers on the device make a noise so you can find the phone. This can help you locate your device if it's nearby. Select *Mark As Lost* to cre-ate a custom message on your phone's Lock screen that says your device is lost and how to contact you. Doing so will also disable any credit cards or other payment methods stored on your phone. Select *Erase This Device* to lock the phone and pre-vent anyone from using it without a passcode. Select *Remove This Device* to delete the phone from your list of devices.

Follow these steps to set up the Find My Device feature on an Android smartphone.

1. Open the Settings app on your phone and tap *Google*.

2. Go to *Find My Device* and toggle the *Use Find My Device* but-ton to *On*.

3. To locate your smartphone, go online to *google.com/android/find*. Sign in with the same Google Account credentials that

you use on your phone. Click on your smartphone to view your options. *Play sound* will activate your device's speakers so you can locate it if it's nearby. *Secure device* prevents anyone from using the phone without a PIN or passcode. You can also add a message and contact information to the Lock screen so that anyone who finds the phone knows it is lost and can return it to you. *Factory reset device* will remove all your information from your phone and restore the device to its original settings. This will prevent a thief from accessing your passwords or payment information if the phone is stolen.

Unlock convenience with mobile payments

Sarah was in line to pay at the grocery store when she realized that she had forgotten her wallet at home. Fortunately, though, she had already set up mobile pay on her smartphone. That meant she could check out with her credit card even though it wasn't in her hands.

Sarah had simply added her card's details to her phone's digital wallet. So when she went to pay with her smartphone, she only had to enter her phone's passcode and tap the device to the payment terminal. Voila — transaction completed! Not only is this payment method convenient, the added identity verification makes it safer than using a physical card. Here's how to set up mobile pay on your smartphone.

Apple Pay. Follow these steps to add credit or debit cards to your iPhone.

1. Open the Wallet app and tap the + button.

2. Tap *Debit or Credit Card* to add a new card.

3. Tap *Continue*.

4. Position your card in the frame to scan and automatically enter its information. Or tap *Enter Card Details Manually* and follow the on-screen instructions.

5. Verify your information with your bank or card issuer. You may need to provide more information or download an app before getting approval to use your card with Apple Pay.

To make a purchase with Apple Pay, open the Wallet app or double-tap the lock button on the side of your phone. Select a card, enter your passcode, fingerprint, or FaceID, and tap the phone to the payment terminal when prompted.

Google Wallet. Android phones can use Google Wallet to store their credit and debit card info. If it's not already installed on your device, go to your approved app store to download Google Wallet. Here's how to add your cards to this app.

1. Open the Google Wallet app.

2. Tap the *Add to Wallet* button.

3. Select *Payment card*.

4. Tap *New credit or debit card*.

5. Use your phone camera to scan the card details or tap *Enter details manually*.

6. Tap *Save and continue*.

7. Read the issuer terms before tapping *Accept*.

8. You may be asked to verify your payment method. If so, choose an option from the list and follow the on-screen instructions.

To pay with Google Wallet, turn on your screen and unlock your phone. Hold the back of your phone to the card reader and enter your PIN or signature if you are asked to do so. A blue check mark will appear on your screen when the payment is complete.

With both Apple Pay and Google Wallet, you may notice a small transaction fee after adding a card to your digital wallet. This charge is used to check that the card and account are valid. It should soon disappear and won't affect your balance.

4 signs that your phone has been hacked

Phones contain a lot of personal information. That makes them a prime target for hackers. Cybercriminals may use fake apps, phishing attacks, or other high-tech ways to infiltrate your smartphone. And once they do, they can sell your data on the dark web, steal your identity, or even listen in on your calls. So watch out for these warning signs that your device may be infected.

- High data usage. If you notice that your phone is using more data than usual, it could be an indication that there's a malicious app running in the background. Review your apps and look out for any you don't recognize.

- Poor battery life. Charging your phone more and more than you used to? While the battery may simply be getting older, it could also be a sign that hackers are running programs and apps that eat up battery life without you knowing.

- Reduced performance. Frequent dropped calls, text messages that aren't going through, and crashes are all signs that a virus or malware has infected your smartphone.

- Changes to your settings. Hackers may alter your device's privacy settings and grant apps permission to track your phone's location, use its camera, or turn on its microphone. Review your settings regularly so you can catch any suspicious activity.

If you suspect that your phone has been hacked, here's what you can do about it. First, start by deleting any unknown apps that you find. Next, install and run trusted antivirus software on your phone. You can find good options on your device's approved app store.

You can also do a factory reset on your phone. This step can remove most malware, but it will delete the data on your phone. That means you can lose access to all your pictures, videos, and apps if you don't have them saved elsewhere. So use this step as a last resort. Here's how to perform a factory reset on an iPhone.

1. Go to Settings > General > Transfer or Reset iPhone.

2. Tap *Erase All Content and Settings.*

3. If prompted, enter your iPhone passcode or Apple Account password.

4. Tap *Continue* to confirm.

Here's how to do it on an Android phone.

1. Open the Settings app and go to *Backup and reset.*

2. Tap *Factory data reset.*

3. Tap *Reset Device.*

4. Tap *Erase Everything.*

Power up: How to maximize your device's battery life

When you're out and about, you shouldn't have to stop and charge your smartphone so it doesn't die. These simple hacks can help make your battery last longer.

- Turn your screen brightness down. To do this on an iPhone, swipe down from the top, right-hand side of the screen to open the Control Center. Drag the slider with the sun icon down to dim the screen. On an Android, swipe down from the top of the screen and look for the sun icon. Tap on it and move the slider to change your screen's brightness.

- Disable push notifications for apps you don't use regularly. Every time an app sends an alert, like a breaking news headline or an email notification, it has to connect to the internet using Wi-Fi or cellular data. That can eat up a lot of battery power over the course of the day, so it's best to turn off notifications you don't immediately need. To do so, go to the Settings app and tap *Notifications*. Select specific apps to toggle notifications *On* or *Off*.

- Turn off keyboard sounds and vibrations. While this feature can help you know when you've keyed in a letter or number on your phone, it also uses a lot of power. To turn it off on an iPhone, go to Settings > Sounds & Haptics > Keyboard Feedback. Toggle the buttons next to *Sound* and *Haptic* to *Off*. On an Android phone, go to the Settings app > System > Languages & input. Tap on *Virtual Keyboard* and select *Gboard*. Select *Preferences* and toggle *Sound on keypress* and *Haptic feedback on keypress* to *Off*.

The ins and outs of staying in touch

Ring, ring — make and receive calls on your smartphone

Smartphones are packed with tons of fancy features. But they still have to perform basic duties like placing and receiving calls. Here's how to do so on an iPhone.

1. Tap the Phone app in the Dock at the bottom of the screen.

2. Tap the keypad icon in the bottom toolbar.

3. Enter the number you want to call and tap the phone icon.

4. If you have already added somebody to the Contacts app, open it and select their name. Tap the *Call* button.

When you receive a call on an iPhone, the caller's name and phone number are displayed in a banner at the top of the screen. Tap the green phone icon to accept the call. Select the red icon to decline it. If the phone is locked when a call comes in, the whole screen will display the caller ID. Swipe the phone icon to the right to accept the call.

Follow these steps to make a call and receive a call on an Android smartphone.

1. Tap the Phone app in the Favorites Bar at the bottom of the screen.

2. Tap the keypad icon, enter the number you want to call, and tap the *Call* button.

3. If the number you wish to call is already stored in your phone, tap *Contacts* at the bottom of the screen instead of the keypad. Select a name to view that person's information and tap the phone icon.

To accept a call on an Android, tap on the green button. If you want to reject the call, select the red button. If your phone is locked, swipe up to accept the call, or swipe down to send the call to voicemail.

Oh no — you accidentally deleted an important voicemail on your phone. Don't panic. You can get it back with these simple steps.

Open the Phone app and tap the *Voicemail* button. It should be at the bottom of the screen in the toolbar. Look for a *Deleted Messages* or *Trash* option. Tap it, and select the voicemail you want to recover. Tap the *Save* option on an Android, or tap the trash icon with a slash through it on an iPhone to recover the voicemail.

Boost the volume of your calls

Can't hear the person on the other end of the phone? Or perhaps he constantly asks you to repeat yourself. Either way, these cheap and simple hacks will make your conversation clearer and louder.

- Turn on voice isolation features. Apple's iPhones have a feature that blocks background noise as you speak into the phone. To turn it on while you're on the phone, swipe down from the top, right-hand corner of the screen to open the

Control Center. Tap on *Mic Mode* and select *Voice Isolation*. Some Android phones offer similar features. To activate it, open the Settings app, select *Sounds & vibration*, and tap *Clear calling*.

- Check to see if your hearing aids have Bluetooth. Some of these helpful devices can pair with your smartphone. If you don't use hearing aids, a pair of Bluetooth headphones may help you block out background noise and hear phone conversations better.

- Use your phone's speakers. Your device's speakerphone feature can raise the volume of your conversations. Plus, you won't have to hold the phone to your ear. To activate your speakerphone, tap the speaker icon on the call screen.

Do you hate getting calls from telemarketers? What about those annoying robocalls? Fortunately, you can stop them. Just sign up for the Do Not Call registry. All you have to do is go online to *donotcall.gov* and enter your phone number and email address.

If you continue to receive unwanted calls after enrolling in this service, you can report the caller's number to the Federal Trade Commission by going to *donotcall.gov/report.html*.

Keep track of your contacts

You don't need to enter someone's phone number every time you want to call or send a text. Instead, you can use your phone's Contacts app to store their name, number, and other details. Here's how to do this on an iPhone.

1. Open the Contacts app. If you don't see it on your home screen, open the Phone app and tap the *Contacts* button in the bottom bar.

2. Tap on the + button in the top, right-hand corner of the screen to create a new contact.

3. Enter the new contact's name, number, and other details. Tap the *Done* button to save the contact to your phone.

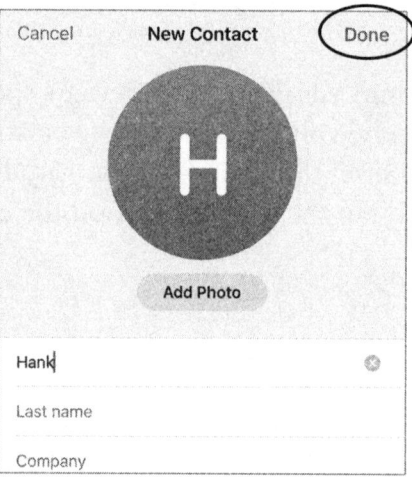

Follow these steps to quickly reach out to someone in your Contacts app.

1. Open the Phone app and select the *Contacts* button.

2. Tap on the person you want to reach out to. You can use the search bar to type in a contact's name instead of scrolling through the list.

3. Tap the buttons below the contact's name to send a text, place a call, start a video chat, send an email, or send and request money using Apple Cash.

4. You can also quickly find contacts from the Messages or Email app. When you're composing a text or email, type the recipient's name into the bar at the top of the screen. Their contact information should pop up in a drop-down menu. Tap their name to add them to the message.

Follow these steps to us the Google Contacts app to manage contacts on an Android smartphone.

1. Open the Google Contacts app. If you don't have this app on your phone, download it from your device's approved app store.

2. Tap the *Contacts* option on the bottom toolbar.

3. Tap + button to add a new contact.

4. Select where you want the contact to be saved. You can save it on your smartphone. Or you can save it to your Google Account, which will sync with your phone as well as any other devices signed into that account.

5. Enter the details for the contact and tap the *Save* button at the top of the screen.

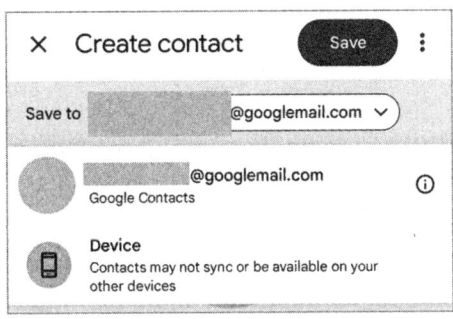

You may not want to answer your phone if a strange number shows up on your caller ID. After all, there's a chance that it could be a scammer trying to contact you. But you don't want to miss an important conversation either. So instead of picking up the phone, use this easy way to find out who's been calling you.

Start by going online and searching for the caller's phone number. You may find that it's linked to a business, or that it's a number used by scammers. You can also try a phone lookup service, such as *usphonebook.com* or *detectico.com*. These websites can tell you basic information about the caller, but they may charge a small fee.

A step-by-step guide for personalizing your ringtone

Most smartphones have a similar default ringtone. That can make it difficult to know if your phone is the one that's ringing when you're in a public place. Fortunately, you can customize the sound or tune that your phone makes when someone is calling. Here's how to do it on an iPhone.

1. Open the Settings app and select *Sounds & Haptics*.

2. Tap on the *Ringtone* option.

3. Select one of the options to play a sample tone. Doing so will make that choice your current ringtone.

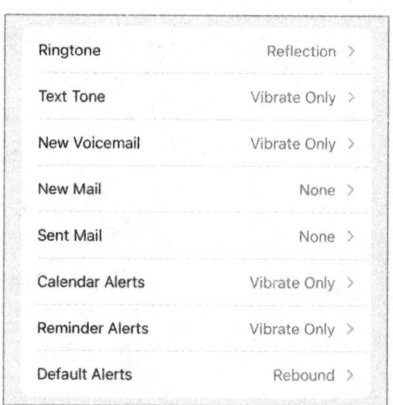

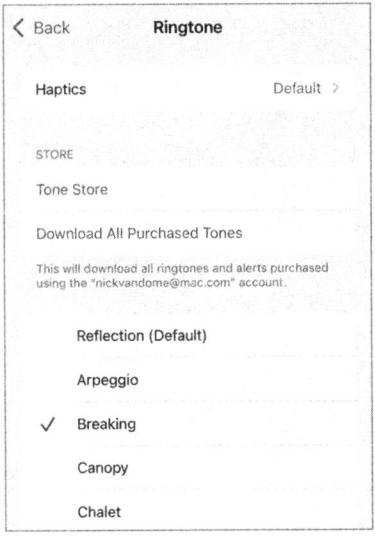

4. To view more options, tap the *Tone Store* option. You may need to download the iTunes Store app to use this feature if you don't already have it.

5. The Tone Store contains musical ringtones and sound effects that, for a price, you can download to your phone. Once you download an item, it will be added to your list of ringtone options.

You can also alter the sounds your phone plays when you receive a text, voicemail, or other alert. Tap on any of the categories below the *Ringtone* option in step 2 to select a new sound.

Follow these directions to change your ringtone on an Android phone. The steps may be slightly different depending on the version of Android your phone is using.

1. Go to the Settings app and tap on *Sounds and vibration*.

2. Select *Phone ringtone* and tap on *My Sounds*.

3. Select one of the sound categories.

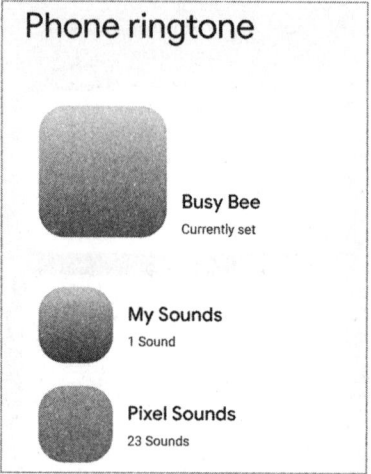

4. Select the button next to an item to set it as your ringtone.

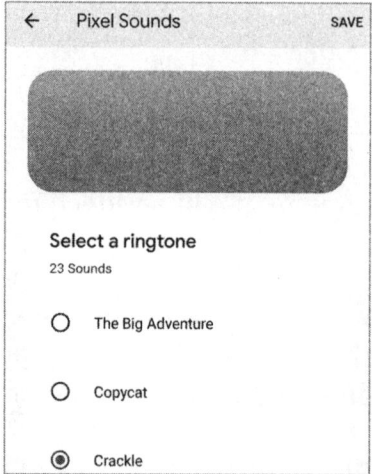

5. Tap the *Save* button at the top of the screen.

You can download additional ringtones for Androids from the Google Play Store. Open the app and type "ringtones" into the Play Store search box to view the available options.

Create a custom iPhone contact card

Want to share your contact info with someone quickly? If so, you can create a virtual contact card on an Apple iPhone. Along with your name, this card can feature your number, address, and even a photo so that the other person will always recognize your calls or texts. Here's how to create one and send it to another person.

1. Go to the Contacts app on your phone.

2. Tap on the *My Card* option at the top of the screen. If you don't see this option, tap the + button and enter your information. Return to the contact list, tap and hold your contact's name, and select *Make this My Card*.

3. Tap the *Edit* button.

4. Enter the contact information that you want to share, such as you number or address.

Here's how to add a photo that will appear on someone else's iPhone when you call or text them.

1. Go to the Contacts app and tap *My Card*.

2. Tap *Contact Photo & Poster* and select the *Edit* button.

3. Tap the *Customize* button. Choose *Contact Photo* to select a photo that will accompany your number and other details. Choose *Call Poster* to edit the screen that people will see when you call them.

Here's how to share your contact card with others.

1. Open the Contacts app and tap on *My Card*.

2. Select *Contact Photo & Poster*.

3. Toggle the button next to *Name & Photo Sharing* to *On*. You can share automatically with *Contacts Only*, or select *Always Ask* to be prompted before your name, photo, and information are shared with anyone you're communicating with.

Smartphone keyboards made simple

Follow these tips to use your smartphone keyboard like a pro.

iPhone keyboards. The iPhone has a feature called predictive text, which can help you text faster or respond to messages with only a few taps. Here's how to turn it on and use it.

1. Go to the Settings app.

2. Tap on *General* and select *Keyboard*.

3. Toggle the button next to *Predictive Text* to *On*.

When this feature is activated, suggestions appear in a box above the virtual keyboard. These words will change as you begin to type. If you see a word you wish to add to a message, tap on it.

Here are a couple of other iPhone keyboard settings that will help you text.

- Tap on this icon at the bottom of the keyboard to access the emoji library. You can find specific emojis by typing moods, images, and other keywords into the search box. Tap an emoji to add it to a message.

- Tap the microphone icon to dictate text messages instead of typing them out.

- Press and hold the space button on the keyboard to transform it into a trackpad. Slide your finger across the trackpad to move your cursor through text quickly.

Android keyboards. Some Android phones also feature predictive text. Follow these steps to turn this option on if you're using the Google Gboard keyboard.

1. Open the Settings app and select *System*.

2. Tap *Keyboards* and select *On-screen keyboard*.

3. Tap *Gboard* to view more settings.

4. Select *Text correction.*

5. Toggle the button next to *Show suggestion strip* to *On*, then enable *Next-word suggestions* to get predictive text suggestions.

Try these other tips on your Android keyboard.

• Tap the three dots on the top, right-hand side of your keyboard and select the *One-handed* button to make the keyboard more compact. This way you can type without using both hands.

• Combine two emojis to make a custom image by tapping on the emoji button on the keyboard. Select two emojis, then tap the new image at the top of the keyboard.

• Tap the spacebar twice to insert a period at the end of a sentence.

Make your messages pop with files and photos

Text messages aren't limited to only words. You can use your smartphone's messaging app to share pictures, videos, or files. Here's how to do so on an iPhone.

1. Tap this icon to open the Messages app.

2. Tap this icon on the upper, right-hand side of the screen to begin a new message.

131

3. Enter the contact information for the person you want to text.

4. Use the keyboard to type a message into the text box. To add other content to a text, tap on the + button next to the text box.

5. Select an item from the list to send content. For example, you can select the Photos app to send pictures saved in your phone's library. Or you can choose the Camera app to take a picture and send it.

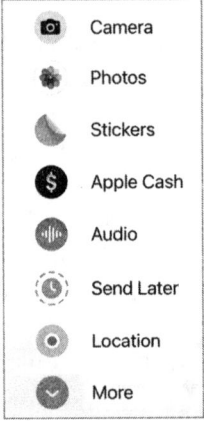

Here's how to add photos and other files to texts on an Android smartphone.

1. Tap this icon to open the Messages app.

2. Press the *Start chat* button to begin a new message.

3. Enter the name or number for the person you wish to text.

4. Use the keyboard to type a message into the text box. To add emojis to your text, tap on this icon to the right of the text box.

5. Tap on this icon to the left of the text box to add a photo from your phone or to take a photo.

6. Tap on the + icon to add more content, such as stickers, files, or your current location.

Want to unsend a text? Here's how

Yikes! You sent a text message before you noticed that there was a typo in it. If you have an iPhone and are messaging another Apple user, you may be able to take that message back before it is seen. If your device has iOS 16 or a more recent version, here's how to unsend messages.

1. In the Messages app, touch the message you want to unsend until the menu appears. The message must have been sent within the last two minutes.

2. Tap the *Undo Send* button.

Even if you unsend a message, it may still be read by the recipient if they saw it before the two minutes passed.

Voice notes 101: How to add audio to your text messages

Smartphones have introduced a feature that allows people to attach a short audio clip to their texts. This way you can send a personalized message instead of calling and leaving a voicemail. Here's how to record and send a voice note on an iPhone.

1. Open the Messages app and tap on the new text message icon at the top, right-hand side of the screen.

2. Enter the contact information of the person you want to send the voice note to.

3. Tap on the + icon to the left of the text box and select the *Audio* option.

4. Speak into the phone to record your voice message.

5. Tap this icon to stop recording.

6. Tap on the send icon. The recipient will receive an audio file that they can listen to by tapping on it.

7. After you have sent one voice message to a contact, you can use this button on the right-hand side of the text box to send another to the same person. Tap it to begin recording.

Here's how to send voice notes using the Messages app on an Android smartphone.

1. Open the Messages app and create a new text message.

2. Enter the contact details for the person you want to send a voice message to.

3. Press and hold the microphone icon on the right-hand side of the text box.

4. Speak into the phone to record a voice message.

5. Release the microphone icon to stop recording.

6. The voice note is embedded in a message. You can also add text by typing into the text box. Press the send button to deliver the message.

Dial in to all that your smartphone offers

Mobile browsing — everything you need to know

Smartphones allow you to surf the web from anywhere in the world. As long as you're connected to mobile data or Wi-Fi, all you'll need to search the internet is a web browsing app.

iPhones. The default web browser for Apple's smartphones is Safari. It comes pre-installed on iPhones.

1. Tap the Safari icon in the Dock to open the app. If you don't see it there, find it by swiping right on your home screen until you see the App Library. Type "Safari" into the search bar.

2. Tap the address bar to enter a website address or search terms. Typing in a URL will take you directly to that page, otherwise the search results will be displayed in Google.

3. Use the bottom toolbar to navigate web pages. You can use these buttons to go back or forward between pages you have previously viewed, share your current web page, view your favorite pages or reading list, and see all your open tabs.

4. While viewing all your open tabs, tap the + button in the bottom toolbar to open a new tab. Select the middle button to manage your tabs, and tap the *Done* button to close the view. Tap the *Private* button to begin a private browsing

session. Your browser will not save your history or other browsing data.

Private	15 Tabs	
+	≔	Done

5. While viewing your open tabs, tap the X in the top, right-hand corner of a tab to close it. You can also swipe the tab to the left side of the screen. That will also close it.

Safari is the default web browser for iPhones. That means any URL you select in a text message or email will open in Safari. However, you can download and use a different web browser if you wish.

1. Go to the App Store and download a different web browsing app, such as Google Chrome or Firefox.

2. After the app is downloaded, go to your Settings app and select *Safari*.

3. Tap *Default Browser App*, then choose the browser you want to set as the default browser.

Android smartphones. Because lots of companies make Android phones, they don't all come with the same default browser. However, many use Google Chrome. If it isn't pre-installed on your phone, download it for free from the Google Play Store. Once it's downloaded, use these steps to navigate the web.

1. Tap this icon to open Chrome.

2. Tap the address bar to enter a website address or search terms. Entering a website address will take you directly to that page. Otherwise the search results will be displayed in Google.

3. Select this icon at the top of the page to return to your starting screen.

4. Tab this icon at the top of the screen to view your open tabs.

5. Select the *New tab* button to open a new web page.

6. Tap the X in the top, right-hand corner of a tab to close it.

Keeping files — smart ways to download and save

You may want to download certain files from the internet and save them on your smartphone. Follow these steps to do so on an iPhone.

1. Locate the file you want to download using the Safari browser. Tap the share icon in the bottom toolbar.

2. Swipe up on the page and tap *Save to Files*.

3. Choose where the file will be saved in the Files app.

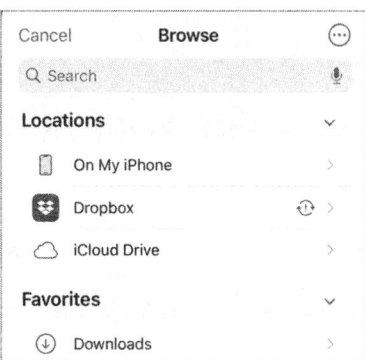

After downloading a file, follow these steps to view it.

1. Open the Files app.

2. Select the folder that you chose for the document you downloaded. You can also use the search bar at the top of the screen to find files or folders.

3. Tap on the document to open it.

Here's how to download files to an Android smartphone.

1. Go to the file you want to download in the Chrome browser or another web-browsing app.

2. Tap the menu icon on the top, right-hand corner of the screen.

3. Select *Download*.

After you've downloaded a file, use the Google Files app to view them.

1. Open the Google Files app.

2. Recently downloaded items are shown at the top of the window. Tap one of the categories to view other documents or files that you've saved to your phone.

3. Select a file to open it on your phone.

Never miss a story with built-in news apps

You don't need to use your smartphone's internet browser to read the news. You can use your phone's built-in news apps to find the latest stories in one convenient place.

iPhones. These smartphones come pre-loaded with the News app. Before you can start using it, you'll need to set it up so it displays the types of stories that interest you.

1. Open the News app.

2. Tap the *Today* option in the bottom toolbar to view a collection of recent headlines. Swipe down on your page to refresh your news feed manually.

3. Tap the *Following* option in the bottom toolbar to select which types of stories you'd like to read.

4. Scroll down to the bottom of the page and tap the *Discover Channels* option to view more news sources.

5. Tap the + button on a news source to add a channel to your news feed.

6. Tap the *Done* button.

7. When you follow a channel or topic, related stories appear more often in your news feed. The channel or topic appears under the *Following* tab.

8. To stop content from appearing on your page, swipe from left to right on an item and tap the *Unfollow* button.

Android smartphones. You can use the Google News app on an Android smartphone to create a news feed with the latest stories. All you have to do is follow these steps.

1. Open the Google News app. If it isn't already installed on your phone, download it from your device's approved app store.

2. Tap the search box at the top of the page and enter a topic, location, or interest.

3. Tap the *Follow* button to add that story and similar ones to your news feed.

Here are a few tips to help you use the app.

- Filter out content you don't want by tapping the *More* button under a story that doesn't interest you. Select *Fewer stories like this* to see less content similar to that story. Select *Fewer stories about a topic* to limit content about that subject in your news feed.

- Remove a news source from your news feed by tapping the *More* button and selecting *Hide all stories from [source]*.

- Tap the *Headlines* button to read the latest news.

- To get more coverage of a topic or read stories from another perspective, tap *Full coverage of this story*.

Easy steps for managing noisy push notifications

With smartphone notifications, your device will alert you when an app has an update or you get a new text or email. But sometimes these alerts can be noisy and bothersome. You can use these tips to manage them.

iPhone notifications.

1. Go to the Settings app and select *Notifications*.

2. Tap on an app to manage its notifications.

3. To enable the app to send notifications to your phone, toggle the *Allow Notifications* button to *On*. If you want to prevent the app from sending alerts to your phone, toggle the button to *Off*.

4. Under the *Alert* heading, toggle the buttons under *Lock Screen*, *Notification Center*, and *Banners On or Off* to change whether or not these alerts will appear on those screens. Selecting *Lock Screen* will allow this app to display alerts when your phone is locked. Selecting *Notification Center* will store unread alerts in

your phone's current notifications list. To view your phone's Notification Center, swipe down from the top, middle of the screen. Selecting *Banners* will allow the phone to send an alert while you're on the home screen or using another app.

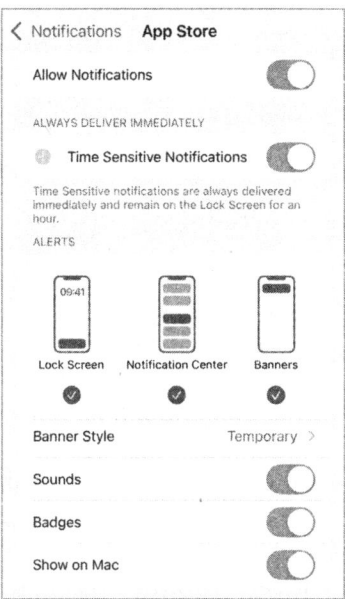

5. Toggle the button next to *Sounds* to *On* if you want alerts to play an audio notification.

6. Toggle the button next to *Badges* to *On* if you want the app's icon to change when you have unread notifications. For example, if this feature is enabled on your Mail app, the number of unread messages you have will appear above the Mail icon on your home screen.

Apple's iPhones also have a feature that lets you hide certain alerts until a specific time of day. This could be used, for example, to show you all your new emails at nightfall. That way you won't be distracted by constant notifications until you're ready to sit down and review them. Here's how to turn this feature on.

1. Go to the Settings app and select *Notifications*.

2. Tap the *Scheduled Summary* button.

3. Toggle the *Scheduled Summary* button to *On*.

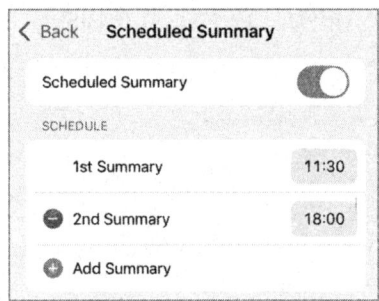

4. Set a time for your summary to appear. If you want to receive more than one, tap *Add Summary*.

5. Select the apps to include in your summary.

6. Tap *A to Z* below *Apps in Summary*. Make sure the apps you want to include in your summary are toggled to *On*.

Android smartphone notifications.

1. Go to the Settings app and select *Notifications*.

2. Tap on *App settings*.

3. Go to *Most Recent* to find apps that recently sent you notifications. To find more apps, tap *All apps* in the drop-down menu.

4. Tap the app you want to enable or disable notifications for.

5. Toggle the app's notifications to *On* or *Off*. You can turn off all notifications for an app or choose specific categories.

The settings for changing an app's notifications can vary depending on your phone's manufacturer.

Stay on task with Focus mode

Ever sit down to read an e-book on your smartphone and get interrupted by notifications every few minutes? If this has happened to you, you can tune out these distractions with your phone's Focus mode. It lets you temporarily block notifications and limit certain apps from opening. Follow these steps to start using your iPhone's Focus mode.

1. Go to the Settings app and select *Focus*.

2. Tap on one of the options under Focus, such as *Do Not Disturb*, *Personal*, or *Work*.

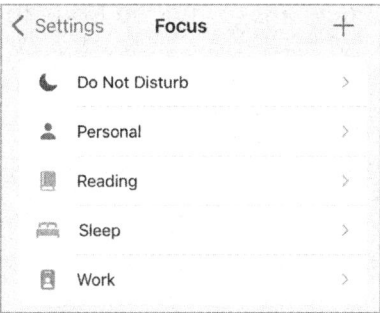

3. To specify contacts that you can receive calls and messages from during a focus session, tap *People*, then select *Allow Notifications From*. Tap the + button to add contacts, tap *Done*, and tap the < button to return to the previous page.

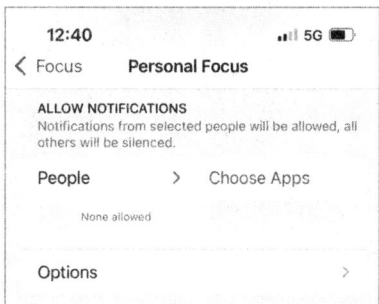

4. To allow certain apps to send notifications, tap *Apps*, then select *Allow Notifications From*. Choose the apps you want to

receive notifications from, select *Done*, and tap the < button to return to the previous page.

5. Tap *Options* under the *Allowed Notifications* heading to change additional settings for Focus mode, such as whether or not badge notifications can still appear on app icons. When you're finished selecting your options, tap the < button on the top, left-hand side of the screen.

6. Tap the images under the *Customize Screens* heading to change your wallpaper on the home screen and Lock screen while a Focus mode is active. You can also choose a new face for an Apple Watch if you have one that is paired with your smart-phone. Select a new image and tap *Done* to save your choice.

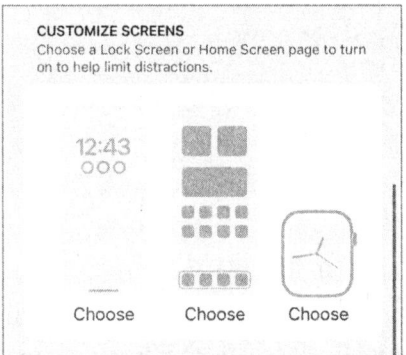

7. Tap the *Add Schedule* button to automatically start Focus mode when certain conditions are met. Tap *Time* to schedule a time of day that Focus mode will begin, select *Location* to have Focus mode trigger when your phone's GPS detects the phone's location, or tap *App* to have the mode begin when you open a specific app.

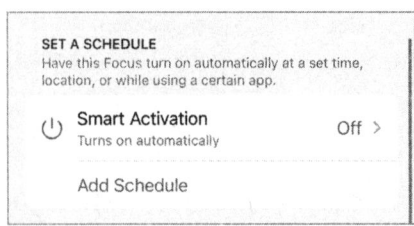

8. You can manually turn a Focus mode on or off from the Control Center. Swipe down from the top, right-hand side of your screen and tap the *Focus* button. Select the Focus mode you wish to turn on or off.

You can also create your own, custom Focus modes on iPhones.

1. Go to the Settings app and tap *Focus*.

2. Tap the + button and select *Custom*.

3. Enter a name for this Focus mode and tap *Next*.

4. Choose a color and icon and tap *Next*.

5. Tap *Customize Focus*, then follow steps one through eight for customizing and setting up a Focus mode.

Some Android smartphones also have a mode you can enable to block app notifications and other distractions. The name and instructions vary depending on the manufacturer. For example, Google's Pixel devices call their mode Focus, and it allows you to choose which apps to silence. Here's how to enable it.

1. Open the Settings app and go to *Digital Wellbeing & Parental Controls*.

2. Tap *Focus mode*.

3. Select the apps you'd like to silence when Focus mode is turned on.

4. Tap *Set a schedule* to set up a time of day when this mode is automatically enabled. Or tap *Turn on now* to immediately start using Focus mode.

Samsung devices, on the other hand, allow you to create multiple Focus modes and choose which apps are allowed to send notifications while active.

1. Open the Settings app and go to *Modes and Routines*.

2. Tap *Add Mode*.

3. Enter a name and select an icon for the Focus mode.

4. To restrict notifications and app usage while Focus mode is running, toggle the *Restrict app usage* button to *On*.

5. Select the apps you wish to allow. All others will be silenced and you'll be blocked from using them while the Focus mode is active.

6. Tap *Turn on automatically* to set a daily schedule for when your Focus mode will start and end. Or tap *Turn On* to begin using Focus mode immediately.

Jot ideas down and never forget them

Note taking apps are perfect tools for logging your ideas and thoughts. Not only that — these apps can include more than text. In fact, you can add photos, videos, and even voice messages.

iPhones. Apple's iPhones come with the Notes app pre-installed. Here's how to use it.

1. Open the Notes app.

2. Tap this icon in the bottom toolbar to create a new note.

3. Enter text to start the note. The first line of text becomes the note's title.

4. Tap the paper clip icon in the bottom toolbar to add photos, videos, documents, or a voice message to your note.

5. Tap this icon to create a checkbox. Tap in the box to check it off. This is a great way to create a to-do list or a packing list.

You can also add items from other apps to an entry in the Notes app, such as an address from the Maps app or a picture from your Photos app. Here's how.

1. Open a compatible app and tap the share icon.

2. Tap the *Notes* option.

3. The item will be added to a new note. If you want to save the item to an existing note, tap the *New Note* option and select *Save to Location*. Select the folder and tap the note you want to add the item to, then tap the *Save* button on the top, right-hand side of the screen.

Android smartphones. Here's how to use Google's Keep Note app. If you don't have it on your phone, download it from your device's app store.

1. Open the Keep Note app.

2. Tap the + icon to start a new note.

3. Enter a title, then enter text in the main body of the note.

4. Tap on this icon in the bottom toolbar to add photos, videos, and other files.

5. Tap the left-pointing arrow at the top of a note to go back to the Keep Note home page.

6. The newly created note is shown at the top of the window. As more notes are added, the most recent ones will be displayed at the top.

7. Select a note to open it.

How to set up a calendar on your device

Your smartphone has a built-in calendar app that you can use to keep track of appointments, birthdays, and other important events. Here's how to set up a calendar on your iPhone.

1. Open the Calendar app.

2. Tap the + button at the top of the screen to create a new calendar entry.

3. Enter details for the calendar entry. If it's a medical appointment, for example, you can include the address of your doctor's office and the time you should arrive.

4. If the calendar entry is for a regular occurrence, such as a birthday, tap *Repeat* and select how often you want it to repeat.

5. To be reminded of the calendar entry, tap the *Alert* option and choose when you want your phone to notify you of the event.

Follow these steps to set alerts on your Android smartphone using the Google Calendar app.

1. Open the Google Calendar app.

2. Tap the + button at the bottom of the screen to add a new event.

3. Tap the *Event* option.

4. Enter details for the calendar entry.

5. To schedule a recurring entry, such as a birthday, tap the *Does not repeat* option.

6. Select how often the event repeats.

7. To add an alert, tap on the *Add notification* option on the entry.

8. Select when you want to be notified about the event.

Some Android smartphones may come with different default calendar apps. If your phone doesn't have Google Calendar, you can download it from your device's approved app store.

Simplify your life with smartphone reminders

A virtual assistant that reminds you to pick up your dry cleaning may sound like something in the distant future. Not so — your smartphone can help you stay on top of daily chores. Here's how.

iPhones. Apple's smartphones use the Reminders app to help you stay on top of your to-do list. Here's how to use it.

1. Open the Reminders app.

2. Tap the *New Reminder* option.

3. Enter details about what you want to be reminded of.

4. Tap the i icon.

5. Toggle the *Date and Time* buttons to *On* if you want your phone to send you an alert to remind you of the task.

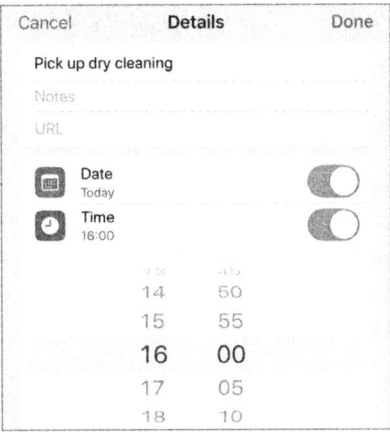

6. Tap on the *Done* button.

7. Your reminder will be displayed in a list. Once you've completed the task, tap the checkbox next to it to mark it as completed and remove it from the list.

8. Tap the *Lists* option at the top of the page to view more categories. Tap on a list to view your tasks or items saved in that list. Tap *Add List* to create a new category.

Android smartphones. You can use the Google Assistant App to create reminders on an Android smartphone. If you don't already have this app installed on your phone, get it from your device's app store. Follow these instructions to create reminders.

1. Touch the Home button on your phone until the Google Assistant app opens and begins listening for a voice command.

2. Ask Google Assistant to set a reminder, along with a time and date. For example, you could say "Remind me to call the doctor tomorrow at noon."

3. You will receive a notification on your phone with the reminder at the specified date and time. To mark a notification as completed, repeat step one and then use your voice to mark a task completed. You can also go to Settings > Apps > Assistant > Tasks and tap on the circle next to a reminder to close it out.

Here's how to view and edit your existing reminders.

1. Open the Settings app and tap *Apps*.

2. Select *Assistants* and tap *Tasks*.

3. Choose the task you wish to edit and change the preferences.

It's time to get more from your smartwatch

Buying tips: Features you shouldn't overlook

In the market for a smartwatch? If so, you might get a bit over-whelmed by all the different brands to choose from. Then there's the pricing — these devices can cost under $100 or over $1,000, and each seems to be packed with dozens of different features.

So before you start shopping, ask yourself a few questions to help narrow down your choices.

What kind of phone do you have? Smartwatches are closely integrated with smartphones, so you need to make sure that these two devices are compatible if you want to get the most out of a smartwatch.

For example, if you have an iPhone, you may want to consider purchasing an Apple Watch. However, if you have an Android smartphone, you'll be able to access more features if you buy a Samsung Galaxy Watch or a Google Pixel Watch. Or you could shop for a third-party smartwatch that works with both Androids and iPhones equally well.

What kind of features are most important to you? Think carefully about how you want to use your smartwatch. If you like to take long walks and exercise every day, you'd probably want a device with a good fitness tracker. Or you may decide that you want a smartwatch that offers more health and safety features, like fall detection and emergency calling. And if you don't want to worry about charging your device every day, look for one with a long battery life.

How big do you want the watch to be? Go to a local electronics store and see if they'll let you try on different smartwatches. You'll want to get a good sense of how big and heavy these devices can be. You may find a certain model is too big and bulky, or that it has a screen that's too small and difficult to use.

Want to stay safe? Don't miss this important tech

Wearable technology for seniors isn't just for fun activities like calling and texting friends and family. Many smartwatches have powerful safety features that can save your life. In fact, the days of wearing a life-alert necklace may soon be over. Here's why you might want to opt for a smartwatch instead.

- Fall detection. This feature can detect if you've fallen and remain immobile for a period of time afterwards. The watch will then alert authorities or your chosen emergency contacts so that you can get help.

- Crash detection. Some watches will detect when you come to a sudden stop after moving at a high speed and will automatically call 911 if you're unable to do so.

- Emergency SOS. If you can't get to your phone and need to dial the police or an ambulance, certain watches can send an alert to emergency services.

- Health alerts. Some smartwatches can monitor your health and vital stats, and will alert you if they detect problems such as an irregular heartbeat.

When looking for a smartwatch that can double as a medical alert system, carefully consider your health needs. If you're looking for a watch with health tracking and safety alerts, consider one that offers professional monitoring so that any alerts or accidents don't go unnoticed.

Follow this step-by-step guide to sync your devices

Many smartwatches can work just fine on their own. But if you want to take advantage of all that your device has to offer, you'll need to sync it with your smartphone. Here's how to pair a new Apple Watch with an iPhone.

1. Make sure that your iPhone is updated to the latest version of iOS. To see if an update is available, go to the Settings app, select *General*, then tap *Software Update*.

2. Swipe down from the top, right-hand corner of the screen to open the Control Center. Make sure the *Bluetooth* and either the *Wi-Fi* or *Cellular Data* buttons are enabled.

3. Place the Apple Watch on your wrist and press and hold the power button until the Apple logo appears on the screen.

4. Hold your iPhone near your Apple Watch, wait for the Apple Watch pairing screen to appear on your iPhone, then tap *Continue*. You can also go to the Apple Watch app on your iPhone, then tap *Pair New Watch*. If your smartphone's camera isn't working, tap *Pair Apple Watch Manually* at the bottom of the iPhone screen and follow the instructions.

5. When prompted, position your iPhone so that your Apple Watch appears in the viewfinder in the Apple Watch app.

This will pair the two devices. Keep your devices close to each other while they sync.

The steps for pairing an Android watch with an Android smartphone will vary depending on which manufacturer and version of Android you're using. Here's how to sync your phone with a watch that uses Google's Wear OS.

1. Make sure that Bluetooth is enabled on your phone.

2. Turn on your watch.

3. Open the Wear OS app. If you don't already have it installed, you can download the app from the Google Play Store or your device's approved app store.

4. Tap *Set it up*.

5. On your watch, follow the on-screen instructions to choose a language and accept the terms of service.

6. On your smartphone, follow the on-screen instructions until you find the name of your watch.

7. Tap the name of your watch. If you don't see it, check that your watch is powered on. If the screen of your watch says *Tap to begin*, do so. Then choose a language, accept the terms of service, and tap *Refresh* when the screen says *On your phone, download & open: Wear OS*.

8. A code will appear on your phone and watch screens. If the codes are the same, tap *Pair* on your phone. If the codes are different, restart your watch and try again.

9. Follow the on-screen instructions to finish setting up.

Stay on top of apps with these tips

To make the most of your smartwatch, you'll need to manage all of its apps. This user guide can help you find new ones and delete the ones you no longer use.

Apple Watches. Follow these steps to add new apps to your Apple Watch.

1. Press the digital crown on the side of your watch to go to the home screen.

2. Open the App Store.

3. Tap *Search*. Either use your finger to write out your search, or use the voice dictation feature to find apps.

4. Tap an app to see its description, ratings and reviews, and screenshots.

5. If the app is free, tap *Get*. If you have to pay for the app, tap the price and confirm your purchase.

6. When prompted, double-click the side button under the digital crown to download and install the app.

You can also add apps to an Apple Watch using your iPhone. First, download the app from the App Store onto your phone. Then go to the Watch app, tap the *My Watch* tab, and scroll down to the Available Apps section. Tap on an app to install it on your watch.

To view all of the apps on your watch, press the digital crown on the side of your watch to view the home screen. You can change the layout of the apps by pressing and holding an app and dragging it to a new location. If you'd rather see all of the apps in a list view instead of the default grid view, turn the digital crown to scroll to the bottom of the page. Tap *List View*. If you want to delete an app from your watch, try the following steps.

- In grid view, press an app icon until an X appears. Tap the X and then press the digital crown when you're finished.

- In list view, swipe left on an app and then tap the trash icon.

Android smartwatches. Follow these steps to add apps to a smartwatch using an Android smartphone.

1. On your phone, open the Google Play Store.

2. To find new categories, select the *Categories* tab.

3. Tap *Watch apps* or *Watch faces* and choose the item you want to install.

4. To download an app or a watch face onto your smartwatch, tap *Install*. Your watch must be synced with your phone when you do so.

Here's how to add apps right from your smartwatch.

1. Press the power button to go to your list of apps.

2. Open the Google Play Store. You'll be signed in automatically with the Google Account you used to set up your watch.

3. To search for an app, tap *Search*. Tap the keyboard to type out a search, or tap the microphone to do a voice search.

4. Select the app you wish to download and tap *Install*.

To delete an app from your watch, do the following.

1. Press the power button to view all of your apps

2. Open the Google Play Store.

3. Swipe down from the top of the screen.

4. Tap *My Apps*.

5. Tap the app you wish to remove, then scroll to the bottom and select *Uninstall*.

The preceding steps work for most smartwatches that run on Android's Wear OS 2. However, directions may vary depending on your device's manufacturer.

Track workouts with your device's built-in fitness app

Smartwatches have built-in apps that let you track your daily activities and measure your fitness over time. Some also feature recommended training routines and exercises. Here's how to start your workout.

1. Open the Workout app on your smartwatch's home screen.

2. Select the type of exercise you want to do. Most watches offer a variety of activities, including walking, swimming, and even pickleball. If you don't see the workout you want, swipe to the bottom of the screen and check if there's an option to add more activities.

3. Once you begin your workout, your watch will display relevant information. For example, if you're walking, the watch screen may display the distance you've traveled, how fast you're going, and your heart rate.

4. To end or pause a workout, swipe on the screen and tap either the *End* or *Pause* buttons.

Some watches have features that automatically detect when you're exercising. They can record information about an activity even if you forget to start a workout on your watch. To check if your watch has this feature, go to the Settings or Health app on your smartwatch and look for an *automatic workout detection* option.

From REM to restless — how smartwatches can track your sleep

Many smartwatches can help you measure the quality and duration of your sleep. The idea is simple. Wear your watch to bed and the device will measure your heart rate, respiration rate, and movement. In the morning, you'll see a summary that tells you whether you've had a great night's sleep or not.

But before you rush out and buy a smartwatch to monitor your sleep habits, you should know that these devices aren't a substitute for a medical sleep study. If you think you may have a condition, like sleep apnea, consult a doctor.

It's best to use your watch's sleep-tracking features to gain insight into your sleep patterns. For example, you may notice that your sleep scores are higher and you feel better rested on days when you don't have caffeine after noon.

Never miss a dose: Apps help you stay on track

Managing your prescription medications can be a handful. But it doesn't have to be — your smartwatch can remind you to take your pills.

Apple Watches. If you own an iPhone or iPad as well as an Apple Watch, you can use the Health app to keep track of your medications and log when you've taken them.

1. On your iPhone or iPad, open the Health app. On an iPhone, tap *Browse* and then select *Medications*. On an iPad, tap the sidebar and select *Medications*.

2. Tap *Add a Medication* to start a new list of drugs and supplements. If you want to add a new item to an existing list, tap *Add Medication*.

3. Type the name of the medication or supplement into the search field, then tap *Add*. Some phones also let you use the camera to scan and identify your medications. To use this feature, tap the camera icon next to the search box and follow the on-screen instructions.

4. After selecting your medication, follow the prompts to choose the type of medication you're adding, the dosage, and the color and shape of the pill. You can also create a schedule for when the medication should be taken.

5. Tap *Done*.

If you set a medication schedule, you'll receive notifications on your Apple Watch reminding you to take your medication at the scheduled time. Here's how to log that you've taken your pills.

1. When you receive a notification to log your medications on your watch, tap the notification.

2. Tap the current medications schedule. For example, this may be all the medications you take in the evening.

3. Tap *Log All as Taken*. Your watch will record the dosage, the number of units taken, and the time you took the medication.

4. To log individual medications, scroll down, tap *Taken* below a medication, then select *Done*.

5. To change the status of a logged medication, tap it, select *Taken* or *Skipped*, then tap *Done*.

Android Watches. Certain Android smartwatches, like the Samsung Galaxy, have built-in features that you can use to track your medications. However, most Android smartwatches don't come with this capability. But you can download an app from your device's approved app store to manage your medications.

4 key health-tracking features

Smartwatches can sync with your phone to send text messages, answer calls, and stream music — all from your wrist. Plus they can track vital health data. That's important because keeping yourself in shape greatly increases the odds that you'll remain independent.

So consider these features when shopping for a smartwatch.

- Heart rate monitoring. A small sensor detects your heart rate to let you know how hard your ticker is working. Some watches have the capability to perform an electrocardiogram to warn you about potential heart problems before you even realize something is wrong. This feature could save your life.

- Blood oxygen sensor. This keeps an eye on your body's blood oxygen level and alerts you if it's getting dangerously low.

- Blood pressure monitoring. Some watches use electrical sensors to give you this health info, but it's not always as accurate as the device used in your doctor's office.

- Stress monitoring. This feature uses heart rate data and skin sensors to gauge your stress levels. It suggests breathing exercises and relaxation techniques if your stress is too high.

Of course, you shouldn't rely exclusively on your smartwatch. If you think you may be suffering from a significant medical incident, get in touch with your doctor right away.

The ABCs of apps

A beginner's guide to mobile and desktop apps

You need apps to do just about anything on a smartphone, tablet, or computer. Without these software programs, you wouldn't be able to surf the web or text your family and friends. There are two main types of apps you need to know about.

Mobile apps deliver easy, go-everywhere computing. Mobile apps are called native apps because they run only on the operating system they were designed for.

Apple iPhones and iPads include apps made for the iOS operating system. Android smartphones and tablets use apps for the Android operating system. An Android app can't run on iPhones or iPads, and an iOS app won't run on Android devices. Fortunately, though, many apps come in both iOS and Android versions.

Mobile apps work differently than desktop software. That's because app designers simplify and repackage desktop websites, software, and other products so that they're easier to navigate with swipes and taps on a small screen.

Sometimes that means mobile apps have fewer features. But don't worry — you'll also find mobile apps loaded with all kinds of special powers. For example, the Waze smartphone app can speak the directions to your destination while you drive and even adjust those directions en route to avoid traffic jams.

"Go native" with desktop apps. These applications run on desktop and laptop personal computers (PCs). They include apps created for Windows or for macOS.

Like mobile apps, desktop applications are native apps, so they can run only on the operating systems they were made for — either Windows or Macs. Some apps are available for just one operating system, while others maintain one version for Windows and another for macOS.

Must-know tips for finding the very best

If you can think of something to do on your computer, phone, or tablet, there's probably an app for it. These software programs can help with grocery shopping, give you step-by-step advice for work-outs, and even find discount codes for online shopping. While it's tempting to search the web for new apps, you shouldn't download them from anywhere but your device's primary app store.

That's because the ones listed on app stores have been tested to make sure they're safe and secure. But that's not always the case for third-party apps you find on the web. If you download them, there's a good chance you could accidentally infect your device with a virus or other malware. Here are a few other ways to make sure you choose the best apps for your device.

- Read reviews and top app lists at technology sites like *pcmag.com*, *lifehacker.com*, and *cnet.com*.

- Visit the app store for your device, and look for lists with titles like *Top Free Apps*, *Top-Rated* or *Most Popular*. You may even find lists for individual categories such as *Health & Fitness* or *Productivity*.

- Sometimes several apps have the same name. To ensure that you have the right one, check the app's name, icon, and other information in its details or product page at the app store or the app maker's website.

- On a mobile app's details or product page, see how many downloads or installations the app has. The more downloads, the better. If it has thousands of downloads, read some of the reviews, and check the app's ratings.

- Look for key features. Read the description and reviews carefully to see if you get all your must-have attributes. For example, do you want an app you can use on both your smartphone and computer? You may need a mobile app that also has a web or desktop version.

- Check for tutorials, lists of frequently asked questions, and troubleshooting tips on the app's detail or product page.

The big 3: Get to know your app stores

Ready to add new apps to your device? Here's how to navigate the main app stores.

Microsoft Store. If you want to add apps to your Windows computer, you should use the Microsoft Store. Open it by clicking this icon on the Taskbar or by going to the Start menu.

1. The Microsoft Store will open to a home page that displays recommended apps. Scroll up and down to view additional items. The recommended apps will change on a regular basis.

2. Use the sidebar on the left-hand side of the screen to navigate to different app categories in the Microsoft Store.

3. Click the *Apps* option in the sidebar to view more apps. Scroll up and down to view different categories.

4. To see a collection of the most popular free apps, click on the *Top free apps* heading.

5. To view additional app categories, click the buttons below the top panel of the home page.

6. Click on an app to view more details, such as its developer information, reviews, and features.

7. Select the *Get* button to download a free app. If it isn't free, click the price and confirm the purchase to download the app.

8. Any apps that you download from the Microsoft Store can be found in the Start menu. These apps will be labeled as *New* until you use them.

Apple App Store. This online store is the default option for all Apple devices. However, the App Store version your device has will be slightly different if you have a computer with macOS or a mobile device, such as an iPad or an iPhone. Here's how to use the App Store on a computer.

1. Open the App Store by clicking this icon in the Dock. If you don't see it, click the Apple icon in the top menu bar and select *App Store*.

2. Use the sidebar to select different categories of apps or to search for a specific app.

3. Click the app you want to download to view reviews, developer information, and other details.

4. Select the *Get* button to download a free app, or select the price to purchase a paid app. If an app shows an *Open* button instead of *Get* or the price, it's already on your computer.

Here's how to use the App store on iPads and iPhones.

1. Open the App Store by tapping on its icon. It will open to a page that shows recommended apps.

2. Use the top toolbar to view different app categories. Tap on a category to view the full range of apps.

3. Tap an app to view more details about it. To download an app, tap the *Get* button or the price.

Google Play Store. This is one of the most popular app stores for Android smartphones and tablets. Here's how to use it.

1. Tap this icon to open the Google Play Store.

2. Tap on the *Apps* option in the bottom toolbar and swipe up and down to view recommended apps on the Play Store's home page.

3. Tap the buttons at the top of the screen to view different categories of apps, such as games or weather apps. Swipe from right to left on the buttons to view different options. Tap the *Categories* button to view every app category in the Play Store.

4. Tap an app to view details, such as reviews, developer information, and screenshots of the app.

5. Tap *Install* to download a free app. If the app isn't free, tap the price to purchase and download it.

Free app? Watch out for hidden costs

Found a great app that doesn't cost anything? Be careful. You may wind up paying in one way or another. Watch out for these categories of "free" apps.

- Ad supported. This kind of app works like a radio station. Instead of charging you, app makers charge advertisers for placing an ad in the app. Sure, you can download and use the app for free. But if the ads drive you crazy, some apps let you pay a one-time fee to permanently remove them.

- Free trial version. This type of app is free to download and use for a limited time. When the trial period ends, you must either pay for the app or uninstall it.

- Freemium. A combination of "free" and "premium," this app is free to use, but you'll need to pay to get the premium version with more features.

- Free of charge. Some apps are genuinely free, while others demand personal information. For example, you may be required to register with your email address.

Hidden costs aren't always difficult to catch. Here's how to find them.

- Check the details or product page in the app store. Read all the information on these pages, including reviews and links.

- Look for information next to the *Get* or *Install* button.

- Read the licensing agreement. Check for a link to that information on the app's product or details page, or find it on the app maker's website. Otherwise, read the licensing agreement during installation, or as soon as the app makes it available.

- A warning box about possible fees or purchase requirements may appear when you begin using the app or when a trial period ends.

Don't miss out — act fast to get a refund

If you accidentally bought an app or just have buyer's remorse, don't panic. You may be able to get your money back if you request a refund right away.

Android apps. The Google Play Store issues refunds for paid apps if you start the request shortly after you purchased the software. However, you can only request a refund for the same app once. If you buy it again, you won't be eligible for a refund. Here's how to ask for your money back.

1. Go to *play.google.com*.

2. Click your profile picture at the top, right-hand side of the screen.

3. Click *Payments & subscriptions* and go to *Budget & order history*.

4. Find the entry for the app you wish to return and click *Report a problem*.

5. Select the option that describes your situation.

6. Complete the form and note that you'd like a refund.

7. Click *Submit*.

8. You should receive an update on your requested refund within four days.

If your return isn't accepted by the Google Play Store, you may be able to get a refund from the app developer. Here's how to find the contact information you need.

1. Go to *play.google.com* or open the Google Play Store app on your device.

2. Browse or search for the app.

3. Select the app to open its details page.

4. Scroll down to the *Developer contact* section.

Apple apps. The Apple App Store offers refunds for apps, subscriptions, and in-app purchases. Here's how to request your money back.

1. On an iPhone or iPad, open the App Store, tap the *Apps* option in the bottom toolbar, and select *Request a Refund*. On a computer, open the App Store, scroll to the bottom of the app window, and click *Report a Problem*.

2. Sign in with your Apple ID when prompted.

3. Select *What can we help you with?* and choose *Request a refund*.

4. Select the reason you want a refund. Apple will warn you that you'll lose access to the app or service if the refund is accepted.

5. Hit the *Submit* button.

6. Once the request is submitted, it can take up to 48 hours before it is accepted or denied.

How to set up automatic updates

Developers constantly update their apps to fix performance issues, patch security holes, and add features. While you can go to the app store to find new updates, it's much easier to set up your device to automatically find and install the latest version of an app.

Windows computers. Follow these steps to enable automatic updates in the Microsoft Store.

1. Open the Microsoft Store and click the Microsoft account icon in the top, right-hand corner of the window.

2. Select the *Settings* option.

3. Toggle the *App updates* button to *On*.

Apple computers, smartphones, and tablets. Here's how to enable automatic updates for a computer that uses macOS.

1. Open the App Store.

2. Click the *App Store* option in the menu bar.

3. Select *Settings*.

4. Toggle *Automatic Updates* to *On*.

Apple's iPhones and iPads both use the Settings app to enable automatic updates.

1. Open the Settings app.

2. Select *App Store*.

3. Go to the *Automatic Downloads* heading and toggle the *App Updates* button to *On*.

Android smartphones and tablets. If you get your apps from the Google Play Store, follow these steps to enable automatic updates.

1. Open the Google Play Store.

2. Select your Google account icon in the top, right-hand corner of the screen.

3. Choose the *Settings* option.

4. Tap on *Network Preferences* and then select *Auto-update apps*. Select *Update all apps over Wi-Fi or data*, *Update with a limited amount of mobile data*, or *Update over Wi-Fi only*.

Phone plans may cap the amount of data you can use each month before charging you a fee. If you're worried about running out of data, make sure that your mobile devices update their apps only when they're connected to Wi-Fi.

To do this on Apple iPhones and iPads, go to the Settings app, select *App Store*, and go to the *Cellular Data* heading. Make sure the *Automatic Downloads* button is toggled to *Off*.

On Android phones and tablets, go to the Google Play Store and select *Settings*. Tap *Network Preferences* and go to *Auto-Update apps*. Choose *Update over Wi-Fi only* to prevent these devices from downloading app updates over mobile data.

Settings made simple: An easy guide to navigating any app

Want to get the most out of your apps? You'll need to know how to access all of the options tucked away in their settings menus and toolbars.

With computer apps, you can usually find their options by clicking on the menu bar at the top or bottom of the screen. Select a menu option to view more information. Mobile apps, however, may require you to tap an icon to access the menu.

You'll also need to find the main settings menu so you can change the app's features to best suit your needs. Here's how to find this menu.

- On computers, click either the app's name or the *File* option in the top menu bar, then select *Settings or Preferences*.

- For tablets and smartphones, tap the menu icon in the app and select *Settings* or *Preferences*. If you don't see this option, open your mobile device's Settings app and go to *Apps*. Tap the name of an app to view its settings menu.

Clear out the clutter — delete unwanted apps in seconds

Is your phone, tablet, or computer loaded with apps that you don't need? Not only is it annoying to have dozens of apps cluttering your screen, these unused programs could slow down your device. Here's how to delete these apps for good.

Windows 11.

1. Open the Start menu and click the *All* button.

2. Right-click on the app you wish to delete.

3. Select *Uninstall* to delete the app.

You can also remove programs from a windows computer using the Control Panel. Here's how.

1. Click the search box in the Taskbar and type in the words "Control Panel."

2. Open the Control Panel.

3. Select *Programs* and go to *Programs and Features*.

4. Press and hold on the app you want to remove and select *Uninstall* or *Uninstall/Change*. Then follow the directions on the screen.

MacOS.

1. If the app you wish to uninstall is currently open, close it before trying to remove it.

2. Open the Launchpad app.

3. If you don't see the app you wish to delete, type its name in the search box at the top of the screen.

4. Click and hold on any app until the app icons on the screen begin to jiggle.

5. Press the X button next to the app icon you wish to delete, then select *Delete* to confirm.

This method will only work for apps that you have installed from the Apple App Store. If you are unable to delete an app using Launchpad, try using Finder instead.

1. Open Finder on your Mac.

2. Find the app that you want to delete, then select it. Most apps are in the Applications folder, which you can open by clicking *Applications* in the sidebar of any Finder window.

3. Drag the app you wish to delete into the Trash. Or select the app, click on *File* in the menu bar, and choose *Move to Trash*. You may have to enter your computer's password to confirm the deletion.

4. To finalize the deletion, you will need to empty the Trash. Right click on the Trash app and select *Empty Trash*.

iPads and iPhones.

1. Press and hold on any home screen until the apps begin to jiggle.

2. Tap the — on the app you wish to delete.

3. A box will appear asking if you want to remove the app. Select *Delete App* to uninstall it from your device. If you want to keep the app on your tablet or phone but remove the icon from your home screen, select *Remove from Home Screen*.

Android tablets and smartphones.

1. Press and hold the app you wish to delete and drag it to the top of the screen.

2. Tap the *Uninstall* button and select *OK* to delete it. If you wish to keep the app on your phone or tablet, but want to remove the icon from your home screen, select *Remove*. This process may be slightly different depending on the version of Android your device uses. Certain phones and tablets may use the *Remove* option to delete apps.

While these steps can be used to delete almost any app, some computers, tablets, and smartphones have pre-installed apps that cannot be removed from the device.

Capture stunning photos with your smartphone

Get ready to snap: How to take lots of picture-perfect shots

You don't have to be a photographer to take high-quality photos. Smartphone cameras are getting so sophisticated that it's easy to get professional-looking snapshots with just the click of a button. Here's how.

- Keep your phone's camera clean. Smudges and dust will ruin any photo. Gently wipe the lens with a microfiber cloth.

- Don't be afraid to take several shots of the same scene. Your phone can store hundreds, if not thousands, of photos. That means you can take dozens of pictures and pick the best ones later. You can easily delete any that don't turn out well.

- Don't rely on digital zoom. When you zoom in on a subject with your smartphone's camera, your phone simply enlarges the image at the center of the frame and crops out the edges. That's the same thing that would happen if you snapped the picture and edited later. And if you zoom in too far, the photo may turn out blurry or grainy.

- Turn on your camera's grid to help frame your photos. Most smartphones can superimpose a 3x3 grid over an image. Use it to make sure that your subject is framed properly. Professional photographers often use the rule of thirds to make their pictures more interesting. That means the subject of your photo should take up one-third of the image while the background takes up the other two-thirds.

- Get creative with lighting. If it's too dark, you may want to use the flash mode. Or check to see if your phone has a long exposure mode. The shutter will close more slowly, giving the photo sensor more time to gather light in dark environments. The result? A stunning picture. However, you may need to use a tripod or rest your phone on something to hold it steady. Otherwise your photo may turn out blurry.

- Try using the High Dynamic Range (HDR) function. When this feature is enabled, your phone captures several versions of a photo at different exposures. It then uses software to combine the images into a single picture with more vibrant colors and details.

- Use portrait mode to get professional results. Some phones have a portrait mode feature, which can be used to blur the background behind a subject. This makes the photo look like it was taken with a high-end camera instead of a smartphone.

6 surefire ways to take the perfect selfie

Why ask someone to take your picture when you can do it yourself? These days you can easily snap a selfie with your smartphone's front-facing camera. To do so, open the Camera app on your phone and tap the circle with arrows at the bottom of the screen. Once you're done, use these tips to take great photos.

- Experiment with angles. Holding your phone straight in front of you can cause your selfie to be unflattering. Instead, raise your device slightly above your head and use your eyes to look up into the lens. The idea is to keep the camera up and your chin down.

- Pay attention to light. If your face is covered in shadows or if there's a bright light behind you, your selfies may turn out dark and dull. Try to face towards a light source so that your face is clear and well lit.

- Frame the background carefully. When you're on vacation, you may want to snap a selfie near a famous landmark. After all, who wouldn't love to have a photo in front of the Eiffel Tower? Position your camera until you can see both yourself and the landmark. Try zooming out or using your phone's wide lens.

- Use the auto timer so that you have more time to focus. When you press the button to take a selfie, you also have to focus on holding the camera steady. But if you use your smartphone's timer, you can get the perfect shot after you've started the countdown.

- Try a selfie stick. These telescopic sticks attach to your smartphone and have a button on the handle you can use to take a photo. A selfie stick lets you get different angles and capture more of the background in a photo.

- Create more depth of field. Some smartphone cameras let you adjust the aperture — the opening that lets in light — before you snap a photo. Wider apertures create blurred backgrounds that help the subject stand out. Look to see if there's an f button at the bottom of your screen. If there is, tap it and drag the slider to adjust the aperture.

Make your photos pop with these tips

The best photographers in the world edit their pictures, so why shouldn't you? Smartphones cameras take high-quality shots that you can later turn into works of art. And editing photos on your phone is quick and simple. To get started, select a picture form the Photos app on your phone and select the *Edit* button.

- Use automatic edit to spruce up your snapshots in a flash. This feature automatically enhances the colors, saturation, and exposure on photos so that you don't have to manually make adjustments. Tap the button that looks like this to use this feature. Even if you don't like the results, you can use automatic edit as a starting point for further adjustments.

- Try tweaking the colors. Swipe between the different color settings, such as exposure, saturation, and warmth, and use the sliders or a dial to adjust the image. Experiment with different settings to see how they change your photo.

- Crop the image. Doing so lets you remove parts of a picture or straighten an image if it's crooked. Press the *Crop* button to start. Drag the border around to crop out the background. You can also use sliders or a dial to adjust the angle of the photo.

- Add a filter. This is a quick way to enhance a photo or just add some fun flair. You can make a photo's colors warmer or cooler, black and white, or even sepia. Once you're done with your edits, tap *Done* on an iPhone or *Save* on an Android.

- Don't be afraid to experiment. If you hate the way an edited photo turned out, don't worry. You can still recover the original. On an iPhone, tap the three dots at the top, right-hand corner of the screen and select *Revert to Original* to erase your edits. On an Android, tap *Edit* and select *Revert*.

Picture this — AI can transform your shots

Artificial intelligence (AI) may sound like something from a sci-fi movie, but it's being used more and more. Tech companies have even introduced powerful AI tools that you can use to transform you photos with ease.

Android smartphones. The Google Photos app has a powerful feature, called Magic Editor, that uses AI to enhance and modify your pictures. Here's how to start using Magic Editor.

1. Open the Google Photos app.

2. Select the photo you want to edit.

3. Tap the *Edit* button.

4. At the bottom left-hand side of the screen, tap *Magic Editor*.

There are certain preset options you can apply to photos. Follow these steps to use them.

1. When you're in Magic Editor mode, tap *Preset*.

2. Select a preset. To scroll through your options, swipe left.

3. Tap the check mark in the bottom, right-hand corner of the screen.

4. If you want to continue to edit your photo, repeat steps one through three.

5. When you're finished with your edit, select *Save copy*.

You can also use Magic Editor to move, resize, and erase elements of a photo. Here's how.

1. When you're in Magic Editor mode, tap or draw a circle around the part of the photo you want to edit. For example, you can tap on someone in the background of a photo if you want to delete them or move them to another spot in your picture.

2. The object you chose in the previous step will be high-lighted. If you want to change what you have highlighted, tap

Refine selection. To select more objects to edit, tap *Add selected.* To remove an object from your highlighted selection, tap *Subtract.*

3. To move your selection, touch, hold, and drag it to another area.

4. To change the size of your selection, touch, hold, and pinch it with two fingers to make it smaller. Conversely, you can distance your fingers to make your selection bigger.

5. To remove your selection, tap *Erase.*

6. To apply the edit, tap the check mark in the bottom, right-hand corner of the screen.

7. When you're finished with your edit, select *Save copy.*

Magic Editor also has a feature, called Reimagine, that lets you change the appearance of parts of your photo. So if you highlight the sky of a landscape photo, for example, you can change it from a bright day to a starry night. Here's how to use it.

1. Tap *Reimagine* at the bottom of the screen.

2. Enter a prompt to change the content or the elements of your selection in the text field. Be as specific and descriptive as possible.

3. Swipe to view other options. When you find one you like, tap the check mark to finalize the edit.

Magic Editor isn't available on every Android device. Check the Google Photos app to see if you have access to it.

iPhones. Certain iPhone models have a feature called Clean Up. It uses AI to remove objects from a photo and then fill in the background. It's currently available only on iPhones with Apple Intelligence. If your phone has this feature, follow these steps.

1. Open the Photos app and select the photo you wish to edit.

2. Tap the *Edit* button and select *Clean Up*. Some items may be highlighted automatically so that you can quickly remove them.

3. Tap or circle what you want to remove. Just know that selecting a person's face can make it blurry or pixelated.

4. Tap *Done*.

Turn pixels into prints with online printing services

You don't need to keep all of your photos stuck on your smartphone forever. Instead, you can get them printed. All you have to do is go to a photo printing website and upload your favorite snapshots. Then, for a small fee, you can get your pictures printed and delivered to your doorstep. Here are a few to consider.

• Nations Photo Lab, at *nationsphotolab.com*.

• Shutterfly, at *shutterfly.com*.

• Snapfish, at *snapfish.com*.

• Walgreens Photo, at *photo.walgreens.com*.

• Walmart Photo, at *photos3.walmart.com*.

Have a box of old photos? Scanning apps, such as PhotoScan or Genius Scan, let you use your smartphone's camera to create clear, crisp digital copies of your favorite pictures. Then you can upload them to one of these photo printing websites and have them placed into a beautiful album complete with labels showing exactly who and what you're looking at.

From amateur to expert — smartphone video tips for everyone

Smartphone cameras aren't limited to just capturing photos. You can also shoot video with them. In fact, these devices are so good at making films that they've been used to record some major motion pictures. Follow these steps to create home movies that rival anything you'll see on the big screen.

1. Open the Camera app and swipe along the bottom bar until you reach the *ideo* option. Tap the round button to begin filming.

2. Try to move your phone slowly and steadily to capture action.

3. Place your finger and thumb together on the screen and slowly distance them to zoom in. Place your finger and thumb on the screen and pinch them together to zoom out. Try to do this slowly, otherwise the resulting video may look jerky and unnatural.

4. Tap this button to pause a video recording.

5. Tap this button to stop recording and save your video.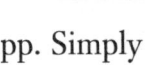

All of your phone's videos will be stored in the Photos app. Simply tap on one of your recordings to watch the footage.

Master the art of seamless video editing

Have a great home movie that runs too long? Or maybe you want to brighten up the footage of your Caribbean cruise before showing the video to your friends. Either way, you can use your Photos app to edit your films in a snap. Here's how to do this on an iPhone.

1. Open the Photos app and select the video you want to edit. Videos are identified by the time stamp on their thumbnail.

2. Tap the *Edit* button.

3. Move the sliders on both sides of the video timeline to change where the video starts and stops. To preview your trimmed video, tap the play icon.

4. To change the exposure, color balance, and other image settings, tap the *Adjust* button. Select the *Auto* option, or manually change settings by swiping between options and adjusting the sliders.

5. To apply a filter to your video, tap the *Filters* button. Select the filter you wish to use, and adjust the slider beneath the video to change the intensity.

6. To crop or rotate a video, tap the *Crop* button. Drag the thick borders on the screen to crop the video. Use the slider beneath the video to rotate it.

7. Tap *Done* to save your edits.

8. If you want to undo your changes, select the video and tap the three dots in the top, right-hand corner of the screen and choose *Revert to Original*.

Here's how to edit your photos on an Android smartphone using the Google Photos app. If your phone doesn't have this app, you can download it from your device's app store.

1. Open Google Photos and select the video you wish to edit.

2. Tap *Edit*.

3. To trim the video to a different length, tap and drag the handles to select the portion of your video that you want to keep.

4. To fix a shaky video, tap *Stabilize*.

5. To change the exposure, color balance, and other image settings, select *Adjust*. Choose the type of effect you want to apply to your video, move the dial to make changes, and select *Done*.

6. To add a filter to your video, select *Filter*. Choose the one you want and use the dial to change the intensity of the filter. If you wish to remove a filter, tap *None*.

7. To crop a video, select *Crop*. To crop the video to a different aspect ratio, tap *Aspect ratio*. Use the dial above *Rotate* to straighten the video. You can also tap *Rotate* to turn the video 90 degrees.

8. To add words or drawings to a video, select *Markup*. Tap *Pen* to draw, select *Highlighter* to add highlights, or tap *Text* to add text. When you're finished, tap *Done*.

Smart ways to save your data

Backup basics — ensure your files are never lost

You'll never have to worry about losing priceless photos or important documents on your computer, smartphone, or tablet if you create regular backups. This way, if your computer is ever damaged or your smartphone gets stolen, you'll be able to retrieve all your data. Here are two ways to create a backup.

- Physical backups. This involves saving your device's data to an external storage device, such as a thumb drive. All you have to do is plug the drive into the USB port and copy any files or photos that you want to save. This method is simple and fast. However, you must take care of the external storage device. If it gets damaged or lost, you'll lose access to all the copied data.

- Cloud backups. Cloud storage and backup companies store data remotely on secure servers. This lets you upload and recover data from any device that has an internet connection. So you won't have to worry about a lost or damaged external hard drive that contains your backup. However, some cloud services may charge a monthly fee if you have large storage needs.

Microsoft OneDrive: A simple way to back up Windows computers

OneDrive is the default cloud backup service for Windows computers. You get 5 gigabytes of free cloud storage space with this service, but you can add more for a monthly fee. Here's how to set up OneDrive.

1. Open the Settings app and click on the *Accounts* option in the left-hand sidebar.

2. Go to the *Account settings* heading and select *Windows backup*.

3. Click the *Set up syncing* button next to *OneDrive folder syncing*.

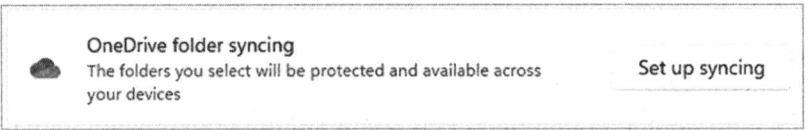

4. If prompted, sign in with your Microsoft account.

5. The folders on your device's hard drive will be displayed. Toggle the button next to any folder that you want backed up to *On*.

6. Your OneDrive files will appear in File Explorer in the OneDrive folder. To view them, click this icon in the Taskbar to open File Explorer. Select the *OneDrive* folder from the left-hand sidebar.

Your files will be regularly backed up to the cloud as long as your computer is connected to the internet and there is enough storage space available in your OneDrive account. If you don't have an internet connection, your computer will create a copy of the data and sync it to your cloud account when your computer is able to connect to the internet again.

If you want to change or manage your folders that are synced to OneDrive, follow these steps.

1. Right-click the cloud icon in your taskbar.

2. Select *Settings* and go to *Account*.

3. Click *Choose folders*.

4. Toggle folders to *On* to back them up to OneDrive, or toggle them to *Off* to remove them from the storage service.

You can use a tablet or smartphone to access files that have been stored in your OneDrive service. All you have to do is download the Microsoft OneDrive app from your device's approved app store and log in with the same email you use for your Microsoft account. If you want to find your OneDrive files while you're using another computer, you can go online to *onedrive.live.com* and log in using your Microsoft account.

Learn how to set up iCloud on your Mac, iPhone, or iPad

Apple's cloud backup service, iCloud, is the default option for iPhones, iPads, and computers that use macOS. If you use this service, you'll get access to 5 gigabytes of free storage. You can also upgrade to iCloud+, which lets you pay a monthly fee for up to 12 terabytes of storage space. Here's how to set up iCloud on a Mac.

1. Click the Apple icon in the menu bar at the top of the screen.

2. Go to *System Settings* and click your name at the top of the sidebar. If you don't see your name, click *Sign In*, enter the email address or phone number you used to set up your Apple account, and enter your password.

3. Click *iCloud* and then select the apps or folders you want backed up to the cloud.

Here's how to set up iCloud backups on an iPhone or iPad.

1. Open the Settings app and tap your name at the top of the screen. If you don't see your name, tap *Apple Account*, then sign in with the phone number or email address you used to set up your Apple account. Enter your password.

2. Tap *iCloud*, select an app or feature, and then toggle *Sync this [device]* or *Use on this [device]* to *On*.

3. Tap *See All* or *Show All* to see more apps. Toggle the button next to any app you want backed up to *On*.

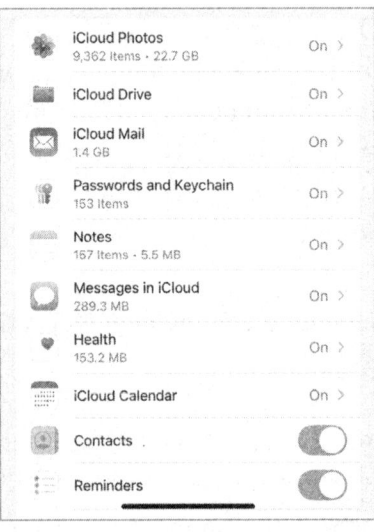

You can also access anything saved in your iCloud account by going online to *icloud.com*. Log in using the email address or phone number you used to set up iCloud. Enter your password.

Use Time Machine to keep your Mac files safe

Macs have a feature called Time Machine that lets you back up all the data on your computer to an external hard drive. All you have to do is plug your drive into a USB port and set up Time Machine. Your device will then automatically back up your files, photos, emails, and documents for you. Here's how to set it up.

1. Insert a compatible, external hard drive into your computer's USB port. Make sure that you don't use this external drive to store any other data.

2. Click the Apple icon in the top menu bar and select *System Settings*.

3. Click *General* in the sidebar and choose *Time Machine*.

4. Click *Add Backup Disk* or click the + button.

5. Select your connected storage device and click *Set Up Disk*. Your Mac might ask if you want to wipe the storage device so that it can be used for Time Machine. Select a different backup drive if you don't want to erase any data.

After Time Machine is set up, it will automatically create hourly backups for the past 24 hours, daily backups for the past month, and weekly backups for all previous months. The oldest backups will be deleted when your backup drive is full.

You can use Time Machine backups to restore files if you accidentally delete them from your computer. Here's how.

1. On your Mac, open a window for the item you want to restore. For example, to recover a file you accidentally deleted from your Documents folder, open the Documents folder.

2. Open the Launchpad app and open Time Machine.

3. Use the arrows and timeline to browse local snapshots and backups.

4. Select one or more of the items you want to restore, then click *Restore*. These items will return to their original location. For example, if an item was in the Documents folder, it will be returned to the Documents folder.

Set up Google One to back up your Android data

Most Android devices use Google One to create cloud backups. This service provides 15 gigabytes of free storage space, but that amount will be reduced by data from other Google apps such as Gmail, Google Drive, and Google Photos.

Here's how to set up Google One on an Android smartphone or tablet.

1. Open the Settings app.

2. Tap *Google* and select *Backup*.

3. Follow the on-screen instructions to turn on automatic backups and select the files that you want to save to the cloud.

4. To review your backup settings, tap *Manage backup*.

5. To view and manage the data that your phone or tablet will automatically back up, return to the previous screen and go to *Backup details*.

If you run out of storage space, you won't be able to save files, photos, or other data from your phone to the cloud. Additionally, you'll no longer be able to send or receive emails on your Gmail account. But you can either purchase more storage or clean out your existing backups to create more space. Here's how to do so.

1. Install the Google One app on your smartphone or tablet if you don't already have it. You can find it on your device's approved app store.

2. Open the Google One app and select either *Buy more storage* or *Clear storage space*.

3. If you select *Clear storage space*, the app will identify photos, files, and emails that take up large amounts of storage. Select items you wish to remove and delete them until you have enough space. You won't be able to recover anything you deleted.

You can also free up Google One storage space using your computer. Here's how.

1. Go online to *one.google.com* and select *Storage* in the left-hand sidebar.

2. Click *Clean up space*.

3. The app will recommend certain categories of items to delete, such as old emails or files that take up large amounts of storage space. Select *Review* to view every item in that category.

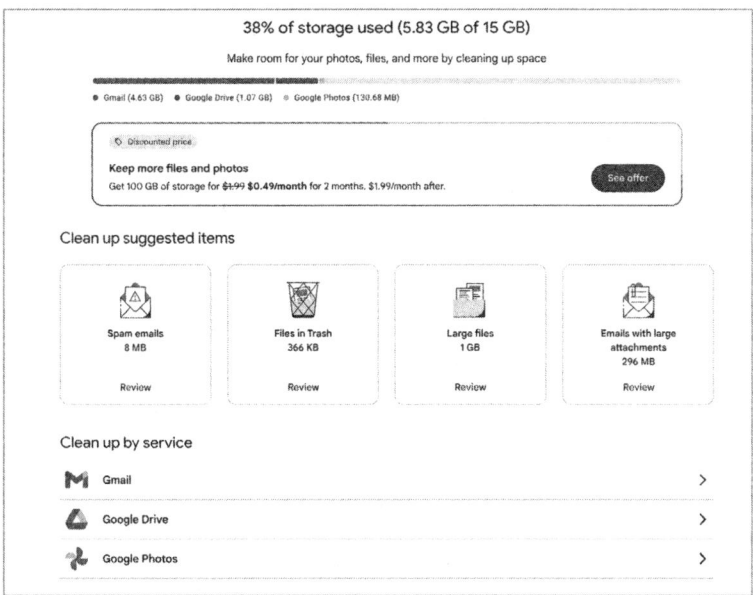

4. Click individual items to select them, then click *Delete*. Or if you wish to delete everything in the category, select *Delete All*.

5. If you'd rather clean up data from a specific app, select one of the options below *Clean up by service*. For example, click *Gmail* if you want to delete old emails.

6. The items will be displayed in a list or grid, with the largest files at the top. Select one, then click *Delete* to remove it from the drive. You won't be able to recover anything you deleted.

Lost your files? Here's how to get them back

Yikes! You accidentally deleted the photos from your grandson's birthday party. No worries — it's possible to recapture lost data, even if you've trashed it. Here's what every computer user needs to know.

Check your recently deleted files. When you delete something from your device, it usually isn't erased automatically. Here's how to check and see if you can recover items.

- Windows computers. Open the Recycle Bin to view recently deleted files. If you see the one you wish to recover, right-click on it and select *Restore*.

- Mac computers. Open the Trash to view your recently deleted files. Right-click the one you wish to restore and select *Put Back*.

Restore from a backup. Already cleared out your recently deleted files? You may still be able to recover your data if you backed it up. Here's how to do so using Window's OneDrive service.

1. On your computer, go to *onedrive.live.com/login*.

2. Sign in with your Microsoft account.

3. Click on *Settings*, go to *Options*, and select *Restore your OneDrive*.

4. On the Restore your OneDrive page, select a date from the drop-down list, such as *Yesterday*, or select *Custom date and time*.

5. Use the activity chart and activity feed to review the recent activities that you want to undo. Any activities you select will be restored.

6. To undo all the activities you selected, click *Restore*.

If you use a Mac, follow these steps to recover files from the iCloud storage service.

1. On your computer, go to *icloud.com/recovery*.

2. Sign in to your Apple account.

3. Click *Restore Files*.

4. Select each file you want to restore, or choose *Select All*.

5. Click *Restore*. Look for your recovered files in the folders they were in when you deleted them. For example, if a file was in the Pages folder when you deleted it, look for the recovered file in that folder.

Try these super strategies to find free cloud storage

In the real world, clouds can come together and create a large, continuous blanket across the sky. In the digital world, it's not so simple.

Sure, it would be great if you could combine your free 15-gigabyte storage from Google with your free storage from OneDrive, Dropbox, Amazon, and iCloud. But cloud service companies don't want to make it that easy. After all, they make money when you run out of free space and have to buy more.

Fear not, penny-pinchers. There are ways to spread your information across several different free services. You just have to be willing to do a little extra work.

Use different backups for your phone and computer. Each device has a "native" backup service. For example, you can use iCloud or Google One to save everything on your smartphone. You can use a different cloud storage service to store the files on your computer.

Choose separate providers for your media. Back up your photos to a specialized photo cloud service like Shutterfly. Everything else can be saved to a general cloud backup like iCloud or Google One.

Don't back up all folders to the same place. When you install cloud backup software to your computer, you can specify the folders that you want backed up.

If you install more than one backup service, you can specify which folders you want backed up to each one. You might have different project folders, or folders for different parts of your life, such as work, personal, and school.

Open several email accounts to get more service. You probably have a few email addresses. Even if you don't, it's easy and free to create them. Most cloud providers let you sign up for a separate account with each email address. Combine this tactic with the others, and you'll boost your cloud coverage in no time.

You don't want to start from scratch whenever you buy a brand-new piece of technology. Most likely you've spent hours tweaking your settings and organizing your files.

The good news? If you regularly backed up your old device, you can use the data from your previous computer, smartphone, or tablet to set up your new one. While you're getting your new piece of tech set up, look for an option that says *Complete Setup from Backup* or something similar. Follow along with the steps on the screen, and soon you'll have all your files, apps, and settings in order.

Essential tools for internet safety

Get the plan you want at a price you can afford

Paying for the internet on a fixed income can put a huge dent in your budget. But with a few savvy shopping tips, you can find plans that won't break the bank. Here's how.

- Consider buying your own modem and router to save money over time. Companies often rent this equipment as part of their internet service. They usually charge around $20 a month, and that can add up over time. A top-tier modem costs around $200, so you'd start saving within a year.

- Watch out for optional add-ons. Internet companies may offer additional products for free when you contract starts, only to charge you for them after the promotional period expires. You may find that you're paying for equipment, like Wi-Fi extenders, that you don't need. Or you might have services, like access to streaming channels that you don't want, included in the cost of your bill.

- Negotiate the price. If you call your provider's customer service line, you may be able to work out a better deal. If that doesn't work, you might switch to a cheaper plan or find other cost-saving measures.

- Lower your internet speeds. You don't need a Lamborghini to drive to the corner market. Likewise, you don't need top-tier internet speeds to stream movies at home. Internet companies pitch these lightning fast internet hookups because they're also the most expensive option. But you may be able to get away with a slower connection. If your house has five devices or fewer connected to the internet at any given time, you probably don't need anything faster than 100 megabits per second.

- Check to see if you qualify for help. Certain providers have free or low-cost internet plans for low-income households. For example, eligible households pay just $15 a month for Comcast's Internet Essentials program. Details vary depending on your location and carrier. Reach out to your internet company and research other local providers to see what options you have.

Wi-Fi speed problems? Here's how to fix them

If your internet connection is laggy and websites feel like they take forever to load, you're not alone. A slow Wi-Fi signal is the number one complaint of home computer users. Here are four reasons why your internet is sluggish, and some simple ways you can speed up your connection.

- Your tech is too far away from your Wi-Fi router. The farther your devices are from your router, the weaker their signal is. Try moving your device closer to see if your internet speed improves. If you can't move the device, you may try repositioning the router. Just make sure that the router isn't tucked away in a corner or cabinet. Another way to improve a weak signal is to use a Wi-Fi extender or repeater. This device can boost the Wi-Fi signal throughout your entire house.

- You're using the wrong frequency. Most routers give you the option to connect to either a 2.4 gigahertz (GHz) or a 5

GHz Wi-Fi signal. A 2.4 GHz connection is slower, but is better at traveling through doors, walls, and other obstacles. A 5 GHz connection offers much faster speeds, but the signal drops off if your devices are too far away.

- You have too many devices using the router at the same time. Think of your Wi-Fi a bit like your home's water heater. If everyone tries to use hot water at once, there won't be enough to go around. Try to limit the number of devices that are using the internet if you notice it seems slow. You might also consider upgrading to a faster connection from your internet service provider if the problem continues.

- Your router has been infected with malware. Hackers and thieves target more than just computers and smartphones. They may infect your router, too, which can cause the speed to slow down. If you suspect this is the case, reset your router to factory settings. Make sure to update it with the latest firmware. Then set a new, strong password for your Wi-Fi.

Safe surfing 101: How to set up your Wi-Fi router

Your Wi-Fi router is your gateway to the internet. If it's not secure, any online device that you use at home could quickly be exposed to hackers and other scammers. So follow these steps to protect your router from digital intruders.

First, start by accessing your router's security settings. To do so, enter your router's internet protocol (IP) address into a web browser's address bar. Most routers use 192.168.1.1 as their IP address, but yours may be different depending on the brand and model. Check to see if yours has its IP address printed on it.

Once you access the settings menu, you'll need to log in. If you haven't created a new password, the default one should be printed somewhere on the router. If this default password doesn't work and you can't remember your login information, try resetting your browser to its factory settings. Check for a small reset button.

Here are a few things you should do from the settings menu.

- Change the name of your Wi-Fi network. The default network name set by the manufacture tells hackers what kind of router you have. That means they may know just how to exploit the device's default security settings. Click on the box titled *Network Name* or *Wireless SDD* to change this info.

- Use a strong password. You don't want to stick with the password printed on the side of your router forever. Instead, you should use one that has a mix of special characters, letters, and numbers. Make sure it is at least 10 characters long.

- Turn on network encryption. This process encodes any data that is transmitted over your network. That means if someone is spying on your network traffic, it will be much more difficult for them to decipher what they see. Look for the *WPA 2* or *WPA 3* options in the settings menu.

- Enable the built-in firewall. A firewall screens any incoming and outgoing traffic and filters out suspicious activity or unauthorized connections.

- Check for updates. Companies regularly update their software to fix security flaws. If your browser's firmware or software is out-of-date, hackers may be able to access your home network.

Turn on your computer's firewall to double your defenses

You may want to set up a firewall on your computer. In the event that a hacker or virus manages to slip through your router's security, it's a good idea to have extra safety features in place. Follow these steps to turn on your computer's built-in firewall on Windows 11.

1. Open the Settings app and go to *Privacy & security*.

2. Click on *Windows Security* and select *Firewall & network protection*.

3. Select *Private network* if you're on your home Wi-Fi. Select *Public Network* if you're using a public internet connection, say at the airport or in a coffee shop.

4. Toggle *Microsoft Defender Firewall* to *On*.

Here's how to enable the Firewall on a Mac.

1. Open the System Settings app and select *Network*.

2. Go to *Firewall*.

3. Toggle the *Firewall* button to *On*.

Steer clear of sketchy websites

Scammers are at it again — this time they're creating fake websites to gain access to your identity. With their fraudulent but legitimate looking online stores, flight booking sites, and bank login pages, the con artists hope you'll feel safe enough to enter your personal information. And once you've typed in your username and password or your credit card information, they've got all they need to spend your money.

Fortunately, following these tips can help you steer clear of these scam websites.

Heed the warnings. Many standard antivirus programs flag dangerous websites. Plus, some search engines and web browsers have built-in tools to detect problem pages or hide them from view altogether. Although these tools may occasionally flag legitimate sites in error, it's generally wise to heed these warnings.

Don't guess the address. Unless you're certain of a site's address, don't type it right into your web browser's address bar. Whole scam empires are built on sites whose URLs are one letter off from the address of a more popular page or end in .com instead of .gov.

Instead, type the name of the website you seek into a search engine, and then click the site's link in the search results. That way, you can guarantee you land on the right site. Even better — bookmark your favorite sites for easier access.

Check the link. Suppose you're on a web page, and you see a link to a site that looks interesting. Before you click the link, it pays to verify where it will take you.

To do so, simply hover your mouse pointer over the link. The associated URL should appear in the bottom-left corner of your browser window. If the URL looks shady — for example, it contains a suspicious domain — don't click the link.

Do some research. If you want to be absolutely, positively certain a site is safe, run its address through a website safety checker. These tools troll servers looking for dangerous sites and can tell you if the URL you entered is one of them.

For example, you can use Google Safe Browsing at *transparency report.google.com/safe-browsing/search*. Type a web address into the search box under the *Check site status* heading to find out more information about a website.

Use an ad blocker. Pop-up ads aren't only annoying, they're dangerous. The FBI warns that scammers create ads that impersonate popular brands and websites. When you click on one of these ads, you'll be directed to a page that can infect your computer with malware.

Fortunately, it's easy to stop these ads for free with a pop-up blocker. You can download these browser extensions from your browser's approved app store.

Important security settings stop cybercriminals in their tracks

Web browsers offer different security tools and settings to head off cyberattacks. Here's what you need to do to stay safe while you surf the web.

Clear your cookies. When you visit some websites, they deposit a small file called a "cookie" on your computer. The site might then use this cookie to verify your identity the next time you visit, or even track your other activities online.

Cookies are potentially dangerous for two reasons — they may violate your privacy, and they can be intercepted by hackers, who can then use them to assume your identity online. To prevent this, change your browser's settings to delete and disable cookies.

You may have to search your settings to figure out where to do it. On Google Chrome, for example, you would go to Settings >

Advanced > Privacy and security > Content settings > Cookies. Look for a similar path on other browsers.

Undo auto-fill. Some browsers automatically fill in your personal info on sites that request it. While this auto-fill feature is super convenient, it may also be super dangerous.

That's because some sketchy sites hide info boxes on their web pages. When your browser detects these boxes, it fills them with your information automatically — without your knowledge. To prevent this, simply deactivate your browser's auto-fill feature.

Hide location information. Most browsers track geolocation information and share it with third-party websites. On the pro side, this makes it easier for these sites to find location-specific information, like restaurant recommendations and local movie times.

On the con side, this data may contain sensitive information — like your home address — that could fall into the wrong hands. To protect your privacy, disable your browser's geolocation settings to prevent websites from tracking your device's location.

Don't let your passwords fall into the wrong hands

One click, no stress: Never forget a login again

It seems like every app and website requires an account. Subsequently, you need to create a username and password for each one. But you don't have to keep track of all those words, numbers, and phrases in your head.

Not if you use a password manager. These apps securely store all the information you need to easily log in to your accounts.

Your device may already have a password manager. For example, Apple devices use the Passwords app to store your details. Android device use the Google Password Manager. You can also download third-party apps. Here are a few to consider.

- 1Password, at *1password.com*.

- Dashlane, at *dashlane.com*.

- Keeper Secrets, at *keepersecurity.com*.

After setting up a passsword manager, you can use these apps to conduct a security audit on the passwords that protect your bank accounts, email, and other online accounts. Here's what these apps will look for.

- Weak passwords. Your password manager should flag any that are considered too short or easy to guess. Replace them with more complex passwords.

- Recycled passwords. If hackers manage to find your login information for one account, they may use those details to attempt to break into your other accounts. After all, you don't want someone to access your bank account just because they have your Facebook password.

- Data leaks. Some password managers may send you an alert if your account information has been potentially compromised in a data breach. With that information, you can change your passwords before hackers get a chance to use them.

It's a good idea to perform a security audit at least once every year to help keep your passwords — and the bank accounts, email, and more that they're linked to — safe.

The ins and outs of creating a strong password

If you don't have strong passwords on all your accounts, it doesn't take much for a cybercriminal to wreak havoc on your life. For example, if a hacker manages to get into your email account, it only takes a few short steps to lock you out. Then they can follow the links to your bank accounts, credit cards, health records, and more.

So if you want to stop this from happening, you need to create strong passwords. Here are a few ways to make hackers move on to someone else's account.

Use your password manager's built-in features. If you have a password manager app on your

You've probably been told that you should change your passwords regularly to keep your online accounts safe, but cybersecurity experts warn against this. If your passwords are complex and secure, you don't need to change them. Experts warn that changing your login details frequently may cause you to use weaker, easier-to-guess passwords.

tablet, smartphone, or computer, you can use it to create and store long, complex, and difficult to crack passwords.

Whenever you first log in to a new web account or app, simply click or tap in the password box. Your password manager will offer to create a new password and automatically store it so you don't have to remember it.

Make your own passwords. If you want to create a password without the help of an app, follow these tips. Doing so ensures that hackers would need centuries to guess your password.

- Make your passwords as long as possible. They should be at least 10 characters.

- Use a mix of capital and lowercase letters, numbers, and symbols.

- Avoid using obvious passwords — like "123456," "qwerty," and "password1."

- Don't include your personal details, such as birthdays or pet names.

Passkeys — the next step in safe and secure digital authentication

Passkeys are a new way to sign in to websites. Although not every website offers them yet, they're safe, easy to use, and more secure than passwords.

So how exactly do passkeys work? Think of them a bit like spy codes. When you first set up a passkey for a website using your smartphone, tablet, or computer, a pair of unique digital keys will be created. One of them will be stored on the website. The other will be stashed on your device. After that, when you want to log in to that website, you'll first need to verify your identity by entering a PIN or scanning your face or fingerprint.

The website will then send a code that only your device's unique key can decrypt. Your device will instantly crack the code and send it back to the website. Once the website's key verifies that the code was decrypted, you'll be logged in.

This means that you won't have to remember passwords. And it makes it more difficult for scammers to steal your account info from a fake website. Even if they intercept your device's codes, they won't be able to use this data to log in to your accounts.

Here's how to create a passkey on a website that offers this service.

1. Go to the website you wish to create a passkey for. Some websites may require you to already have a user account.

2. Select the *Create Passkey* option. This may be called something different depending on the device or website you're using.

   CREATE A PASSKEY

3. Select whether you want to use face recognition, fingerprint scans, or a PIN to verify your identity when logging on. These options may be different depending on your device.

4. When you sign in to the website, select the *Use Passkey* option.

How to recover from a hacked password

It can be scary to find out that your password has been compromised in a data breach. Here are the three things you can do to make sure your personal information isn't at risk.

- Change your compromised password right away. If you use the same password or similar ones on any other accounts, you should change those as well.

- Keep an eye on your accounts. Regularly check your bank accounts for suspicious transactions. You'll also want to monitor your other online accounts, including investment, social media, and credit card accounts. If you get notified that an unrecognized device is trying to log in to one of them, it may be a sign that a different account has been hacked.

- Set up alerts with the major credit bureaus. Hackers often try to break into people's online accounts so that they can learn enough information to steal their identity. You can set up alerts with Equifax, TransUnion, and Experian so that you're notified any time an account in your name is opened. If you don't recognize the account, you can report the fraud before a criminal goes on a spending spree with your money.

Locked out of Windows? Try these super quick solutions

It finally happened — you forgot your password and now you're totally locked out of your Windows computer. Thankfully, you may still be able to get back in without having to reset your device to its factory settings. Try these three tips to log back in.

First, do this.

1. Select the account you use to sign in to your computer.

2. Click *I forgot my password* on the lock screen.

3. Confirm your email address and choose if you wish to receive your verification code via email or text.

4. Click *Get Code*, then enter the code you receive. Select *Next*.

5. Create a new password and click *Next*.

If this step doesn't work, you may be able to reset your Windows password online using another computer or mobile device. Here's what to do.

1. Go online to *account.microsoft.com* and select *Sign in*.

2. Choose the *Forgot password?* button.

3. On the next screen, enter an email address that you have access to and select *Get Code*.

4. Enter the code and reset your password.

5. If you don't have access to an email address, click *I don't have any of these* and follow the on-screen instructions to create a new password.

If none of those options work you may be able to change your password using a password reset disk. All you need to do is plug it into your computer's USB port and follow the on-screen prompts. You'll need to do this well before you get locked out, though.

Follow these steps to set up of these discs.

1. Sign in to your computer and insert a USB drive.

2. Open the Control Panel app and select *User Accounts*.

3. Click *Create a password reset disk* to open the Forgotten Password Wizard panel. Click *Next*.

4. Select the USB drive from the drop-down menu and click *Next*.

5. Enter the password you use to log in to your computer. Click *Next*.

6. You will receive a message when the password reset disk has finished setting up. Click *Next* and then *Finish*.

Unlock the secrets of effective web searches

Google more effectively with this expert advice

You don't need to scroll through hundreds of search results to find what you're looking for on the internet. Follow these tips instead.

Use operators to narrow down your search. These symbols and phrases can help refine your search.

- Use quotation marks for exact phrases. Say you're trying to track down an old friend from high school. Search for the name "Jane Mary Smith" and you'll get results for people named "Jane Mary," "Jane Smith," "Mary Smith," and so on. But if you put the name in quotes, you'll only get results for "Jane Mary Smith" in that order.

- Use the minus sign (-) to exclude a word. For example, if you want to learn about pumas, or cougars, a search for the word "puma" will result in lots of information on Pumas, the shoes. But try "puma -shoes," and many of the footwear results will disappear. You can also search for "puma cat."

- Use an asterisk (*) for an unknown or variable word. This is useful if you're trying to remember a song lyric, such as the opening line of "Summertime." Type "the * is easy" and you'll see the lyric, "the living is easy," as well as other examples, such as "the first step is easy," and "predicting the future is easy."

- Use "site" to search within a website. You hear from a friend that flaxseed helps fight cholesterol and is a tasty ingredient in many foods. So you go to your favorite recipe website and search within it — "site:allrecipes.com flax." The results will include web pages, videos, and images from the website.

Make sure that you don't add any spaces between these search operators and your keywords. For example, a simple search for "site:allrecipes.com" will bring up all the information you're looking for. But your results won't be narrowed down if you type "site: allrecipes.com."

Try out Google's built-in tools. Google also offers an advanced search, which lets you enter in different phrases, keywords, and number and date ranges to help you further pare down your results.

To use it, go online to *google.com* and enter a search in the text box. Hit enter, then at the top of the search results page, click *Tools*. Select *Advanced Search*. You can narrow down your search results by language, the last time a web page was updated, where the text appears on a website, and more.

Step-by-step advice for setting up your search engine

Your web browser has a default search engine. So if you go to its address bar and search for something instead of typing in a URL, you'll be taken to a page of results. For example, if you do a search for, say, "caterpillar" in the Microsoft Edge browser, you'll be taken to Bing. But do the same in Apple's Safari, and you'll get results from Google.

Most web browsers let you change the default search engine. Here's how to do so while using Microsoft Edge.

1. Open the Microsoft Edge app on your computer.

2. Click on the three dots at the top, right-hand corner of the screen and select *Settings*.

3. Select *Privacy, search, and services* in the left-hand sidebar.

4. Click on *Address bar and search*.

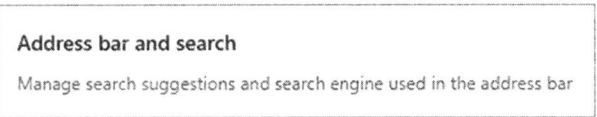

5. Click the box next to *Search engine used in the address bar* and select a new option from the drop-down menu.

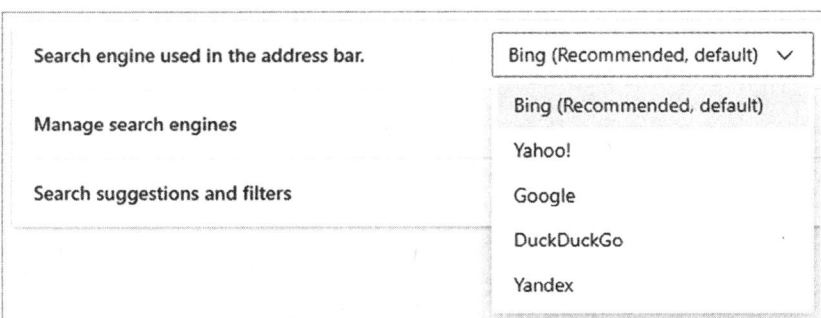

6. To be able to search from the address bar of a new tab, click on the box next to *Search on new tabs uses search box or address bar* and select *Address bar* from the drop-down menu.

Follow these steps to change the default search engine on a computer that uses Apple's Safari.

1. Open the Safari app on your computer.

2. Select *Safari* in the top menu bar and click *Settings*.

3. Click on the *Search* option and select the box next to *Search engine*.

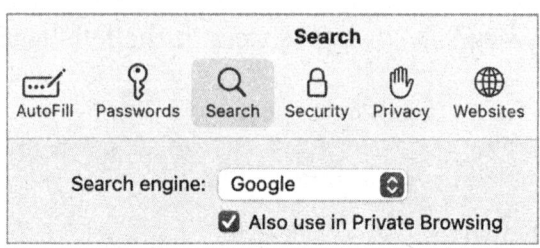

4. Choose a new search engine from the drop-down menu.

The magic of Google Images — when a picture is worth 1,000 words

Have you ever searched online for a hotel and been impressed by pictures of a huge room and amazing swimming pool? Then you arrive and discover that the accommodations aren't nearly as beautiful. You can avoid this and spare yourself the disappointment with a quick image search on Google.

But don't stop there. Along with checking out a hotel before booking, you can use Google Images for shopping and research. Here's how to get the most out of this handy feature.

Use suggestions from Google Images. When you do an image search, the results come with related or suggested searches. For example, an images search on "New York" will pull up suggestions that include Times Square, Manhattan, Central Park, and Christmas.

Take advantage of Images search tools. Search for images by size, color, usage rights, type, and time. These options appear above results once you do an initial search.

You can choose sizes ranging from icons to huge. The Color tool lets you pick a predominant color. Usage rights labels show you images you can reuse for free and even edit. And with Type, you can search for Face, Photo, Clip art, Line drawing, and Animated.

Easily save pictures to your computer. Click on images that interest you. When a larger version appears, right-click, then select *Save image as* to make a copy on your computer. But first, check out the related images to see if you like any of those better.

Find diagrams and more. You can find a lot more than just photos and clip art in image searches. Let's say you're buying new living room furniture. A search for "living room furniture" will show all kinds, but not different ways to arrange it. But add the word "diagram" and you'll get a ton of ideas on how to set up your new furniture.

Remember — maps are images too. If you're traveling to Boston on vacation, you'll probably want a sightseeing map. Instead of searching scores of tourist websites to find a good one, do an image search. A search for "Boston tourist sights" will give you mostly photos, but add the word "map" and you'll get hundreds of Boston maps.

Master Google's reverse image search

Ever needed to search for something that's just too hard to sum up in words? Maybe you're trying to find paintings similar to one you saw in a museum. Or perhaps you're trying to identify a plant blight that's ruining your garden.

That's where reverse image search comes in. This lets you use an image instead of text to find results in a search engine. Here's how to conduct this type of search in Google.

1. Go to *google.com* on your computer or use the Google app on your smartphone or tablet.

2. Select the camera icon in the search bar.

3. If you're using a smartphone, your camera will open. Tap the magnifying glass button in the center of the screen to take a photo and search for results based on it. Or tap the photo icon in the lower, left-hand corner of the screen to add a photo from your device.

4. On a computer, tap the *Upload a file link* button to add an image. If you've found an image online that you want to use, right-click on it and select *Copy image link*. Paste that link into the text box.

5. The results will be displayed. Select the link or image to view more information.

9 things you never knew Google could do

Google isn't just for searching the web. It wants to be your go-to tool for everything. Here are some fun things you can do with Google that you never expected.

Make math easy. Need a calculator? Google can help out. Click Ctrl+n or Cmd+n to open a new window and search for an equation, for example, 9 * 9 (with spaces). That returns an answer and a calculator to go with it.

Decipher the metric system. Running a 5K and trying to figure out how far that is? Do a search on "5 kilometers to miles." You'll find out that you're running 3.1 miles. And if you want to check out the 10K, the handy conversion calculator is right there.

Convert currencies. If you're going to be traveling abroad — Japan, for example — and need to understand prices, simply search for dollars to yen. You can also enter an amount, like 500 yen to dollars. You'll get exchange rates and a currency-conversion calculator.

Check the market. Get stock prices and charts by searching for a stock ticker. For instance, search for AAPL and get market prices and charts for Apple. You can also type just a company name with "stock price."

Calculate tips like a pro. Tired of figuring out tips in your head? Just type the bill amount like this: "tip $34.80." Don't forget the dollar sign. This is especially helpful when you're splitting the tip. A calculator gives you the tip amount and allows you to customize according to the amount of the bill, tip percentage, and number of people paying.

Watch the weather. When you travel, you have to know what to pack. Type "weather" and a place name and you'll get detailed information on how hot or cold it is and whether you need to bring an umbrella.

Keep up with flights. Search for a flight number such as UA100 to get instant flight status. You'll also get links to websites where you can watch the flight's progress via radar. You'll be amazed at just how many planes are in the air at any one time.

Set a timer. Just tell Google how much time you need. Your search will look something like "10 minute timer." If it doesn't kick off automatically, select *Start* to begin a visual countdown. An alarm will sound when time runs out. You can stop, reset, and even make the timer full screen.

Track your packages. Never lose a package again. Enter your tracking number, click *Search*, and see exactly where that store item is. Whether it's en route or hanging out at the post office, you'll know when to expect it.

AI joins the search party

Artificial intelligence (AI) is becoming more and more common in the digital world. And search engines are embracing this technology to help users sift through dozens of web pages.

How? Developers have implemented AI tools that can remember and understand your previous searches. For example, if you frequently search Google for information about computers, searching for the word "Apple" will give you more results about the tech company than the fruit. Other search engines have AI tools that can sum up the results for you, so you don't even have to click a link to find the answer to a question.

AI tools already exist on certain computers and web browsers. Google's Gemini, for example, powers that company's search results. Windows uses AI Copilot to help users search the web and find items on their computers.

Here are a few other AI-powered tools that can help you search the web.

- Perplexity at *perplexity.ai*. When you enter a search into Perplexity, this website will sum up the results from several websites and provide links to the web sources it used. You are limited to only a few searches a day, however, unless you sign up for a paid account.

- You at *you.com*. This AI search engine will sum up the answers to your searches in a conversational tone. It will also include footnotes to the websites where it got the information from. It's free to use, but offers a premium subscription with more advanced features.

- Brave Search at *search.brave.com*. This search engine offers increased privacy and security. It blocks trackers and ads on websites, and has an "Answer with AI" feature that uses AI to sum up your search results. You can also download the Brave browser to your computer for more features.

Keep your devices infection-free

The menacing world of malware explained

Malware is just what it sounds like — malicious software. It has just one purpose — to damage or exploit a computer, server, or network. Maybe the cybercriminal behind the malware wants to have some fun — the digital equivalent of vandalism. More often, malware is the product of a criminal enterprise whose aim is to steal your identity or other valuable information.

Here are a few ways this dangerous software can wreak havoc on your life.

- Spyware monitors all your digital activities and sends sensitive information — like passwords and financial data — back to the spyware's creator.

- Ransomware encrypts data on your computer, so you can't access your files or even use your device. Hackers will then demand payment to restore your data and computer.

- A backdoor attack creates a way for a hacker to secretly access and take over your machine. The fraudster can then do everything from accessing your personal files to using your computer to send spam emails.

Malware is categorized by how it spreads from device to device. If you get to know these threats and how they work, you'll be more alert to the dangers they pose.

Viruses. These rogue bits of code attach themselves to programs or files on your computer. When you open the infected file, the virus makes a copy of itself, or "self-replicates," and then infects another program or file. When you run that one, the virus spreads again, and so on, until your computer is crippled.

If an infected computer is connected to a network, like the internet, the virus can spread to other computers by exploiting security holes in the target computer's operating system, programs, or plug-ins.

Worms. Much like viruses, these also self-replicate to spread through a computer or network. However, worms don't require the user to open a program or file. Instead, they can multiply all on their own.

Trojan horses. Named after the Greek legend, these pose as useful apps or files. When you download a Trojan horse, it will infect your device with damaging malware. Hackers typically spread Trojan horses by tricking users into installing them, either by sending phishing emails with malicious links or attachments or by embedding these links in pop-up windows in your web browser.

Stay a step ahead — antivirus apps keep hackers at bay

It's important to protect your computer from viruses and other malware. Fortunately, these devices come with built-in software that can help keep your data safe from these online threats. Here's how to access the antivirus tools on a Windows computer.

1. Open the Settings app and select *Update & Security*.

2. Select *Windows Security*.

3. Use these tools to scan for viruses and malware, update your computer's firewall, and set up other security measures.

Computers that use macOS have software, called XProtect, that works automatically in the background to find and eliminate viruses.

These built-in tools are a good first step towards protecting yourself from malware. But don't stop there. Third-party antivirus apps provide an extra layer of security. Here are a few options.

Free antivirus apps. If you want to protect your computer from everyday hacks and other threats, a free app may be the way to go. You'll want to download one that detects and prevents malware from infecting your computer, monitors your home network for signs of hackers, and keeps fraudsters from locking you out of files. Check out these free apps.

- Avira at *avira.com*.

- Malwarebytes at *malwarebytes.com*.

- SpywareBlaster at *brightfort.com*.

Paid antivirus apps. While there are many free antivirus apps available, paid apps offer the strongest security features. In addition to stopping everyday threats, these apps can also block hackers from taking over your computer and spying on you through your webcam. They also automatically update other apps with known security flaws and can permanently delete files with sensitive information. These apps may require a fee, however you may be able to cover multiple computers, smartphones, and tablets with a single subscription. Consider one of these options.

- AVG at *avg.com*.

- Bitdefender Antivirus Plus at *bitdefender.com*.

- McAfee Antivirus at *mcafee.com*.

- Norton Antivirus Plus at *norton.com*.

- Sophos Home Premium at *sophos.com*.

Hackers and scammers work around the clock to come up with new ways to break into your devices. Fortunately, the developers who make antivirus tools create software updates designed to block the latest digital threats.

But these security fixes won't do your computer any good if you don't download them. That's why it's important to regularly check your antivirus app for updates. Go to the settings menu in the app to make sure your software is running the latest version.

Even better, check to see if you can turn on automatic updates. This feature allows your computer to automatically download and install the newest version of an antivirus app whenever an update is available.

Computer running slow? It could be a virus in disguise

The sooner you realize that your computer is infected with malware, the sooner you can prevent fraudsters from stealing your information. Here are seven red flags that suggest your device may have been hacked.

- You notice strange pop-up ads on your screen, even when you aren't using an internet browser.

- Files are changed, moved, or deleted without you doing anything to them.

- Your computer runs slowly or crashes and freezes for no reason.

- Important files or apps are locked and you're unable to access them.

- Your computer's battery performance starts to decline.

- Your antivirus software stops working or can't be turned on.

- Your computer runs out of storage space even though you haven't saved any new files.

While none of these signs offer absolute proof that your system is under attack, they might indicate a problem — especially if you notice more than one.

Vaccinate your PC against nasty viruses

The internet is riddled with spyware and other dangerous malware. But protecting your computer, identity, and information is fast, easy, and free if you follow these tips.

- Beware of suspicious attachments. If you receive a message from an email address or phone number you don't recognize, don't open any attachments or click any links in the body of the message. Scammers hide dangerous malware in these messages. Make sure to read the address and phone number carefully, too. Some cybercriminals may use contact details that look similar to people you know.

- Avoid unsafe downloads. Only access apps and files from your device's approved app store and trusted websites. If you're not 100 percent sure if an app — or anything else — is safe to download, follow former first lady Nancy Reagan's advice and "just say no."

- Use a pop-up blocker. Lots of pop-ups are just ads. They're annoying, but basically harmless. But some pop-ups are more than merely annoying — they're dangerous. Clicking their links can install hazardous malware on your machine. To protect your computer from these dangers, install a pop-up blocker from your web brower's app store. Some web browsers may have built in pop-up blockers. To check, go to the browser's settings menu and look for a block pop-ups or safe browsing option.

- Install a firewall. A firewall acts as a security system for your computer. It monitors network traffic to and from your device, and permits or blocks the transfer of data based on a set of security rules. For example, a firewall might block traffic from a site that distributes malware.

- Back up your system. In case your efforts to prevent a malware attack fall short, you should set up your system to back up your files on a regular basis. Don't forget to store the backup on an external hard drive or on the cloud. That way, if you fall victim to a virus or other type of malware, you can use the backup to restore your system to its pre-infected state.

5 fixes for a computer infected by ransomware

If a hacker manages to slip some ransomware onto your system — usually by way of a Trojan horse — you'll know it. You'll be unable to use your computer and access your files, and you'll likely get a menacing message, too. The question is, what should you do?

First off, don't pay the ransom. Doing so just encourages hackers to launch more ransomware attacks. Besides, there's no guarantee your system will be restored. Remember, these are criminals you're dealing with.

Next, follow these steps to rid your computer of malware and reclaim your data.

1. Disconnect your computer from the internet. Hackers can't take over your computer if they have no way to connect to it. Turn off your device's Wi-Fi connection or unplug its ethernet cable. If you can't disconnect from the internet, turn off your device until you can safely do so.

2. Quickly remove any external storage devices. Many malware attacks specifically target external hard drives or USB drives so that you can't recover any of the data that the hackers encrypted.

   > If your computer is infected with malware, hackers may be able to turn on your webcam remotely and spy on you. To prevent anyone from peeping on you without your knowledge, cover your webcam with a small piece of tape when you're not using it. Just be sure to keep the sticky part off the lens.

3. Wipe your system clean. You may be able to use an antivirus app to remove any malware. Failing that, you might need to restore your device from a previous backup. Reset your computer to factory settings, then reinstall all your files and apps that you stored in the cloud or on an external drive. If you're not sure how to do so, reach out to an IT professional for assistance.

4. Try using a decryption tool. Your antivirus app may have tools to help you identify and remove ransomware. If not, you can find free tools that can unlock files that have been encrypted. Go to sites like *avg.com/en-us/ransomware-decryption-tools* or *avast.com/en-us/ransomware-decryption-tools* to identify the type of ransomware and download the fix you need.

5. Reset all your passwords. If hackers gained access to your system, there's a chance they were able to compromise your passwords too.

Surfing safely — avoid dangerous websites

Unfortunate, but true. You could visit any website — even one that's 100 percent legit — and find yourself at risk of downloading malware. For example, hackers once distributed malware by advertising on major websites, including The New York Times and The Atlantic.

Still, some websites are markedly more dangerous than others. To limit your chances of encountering this dangerous software, steer clear of these particular types of websites.

Torrent sites. These websites, like The Pirate Bay and others, enable you to quickly download large files. They work by chopping the file into a gazillion little pieces and harnessing dozens — maybe even hundreds — of computers to send small scraps of the file at once.

Are there legitimate uses for torrent sites? Maybe. But mostly they're used to distribute pirated movies, music, and other copyrighted files. No surprise — they're also a haven for malware.

To avoid getting hacked — not to mention prosecution for violating copyright laws — stay away from torrent sites.

The "dark web." Sounds like the name of a scary movie. It's actually a shady corner of the internet where online communications are completely anonymous.

The dark web does have some legitimate uses. It's often home to journalists and freedom fighters who operate in repressive countries. But it mostly traffics in illegal drugs, weapons, stolen data, fake IDs, malicious software, and so on. This is not a part of the internet where you want to hang out.

Fortunately, you can't really stumble onto the dark web by accident. It takes special software, like a Tor browser, to get there.

Whenever you surf to a new website, think carefully about the type of material it deals with and whether it's a likely place for hackers to do their dirty work. The more aware you are, the less likely you'll fall victim to cybercriminals.

AI revolutionizes everyday life

The future is now: Decoding the basic fundamentals of AI

Artificial intelligence (AI) can seem confusing. But it doesn't have to be if you learn the essentials of this amazing technology.

Firstly, you'll want to know what AI is. In simple terms, AI is a technology that allows a computer to perform tasks that would normally require human intelligence — things like problem solving and decision making. This type of high tech analyzes a ton of data, processes it, and learns from past mistakes to improve in the future. Once considered a topic for a sci-fi movie, AI has certainly changed the way we live.

For example, let's say you don't know what to stream on TV. Netflix can recommend a movie based on your past viewing preferences. Need directions to a meeting? Digital assistants can get you there by tracking your phone's GPS. Or perhaps you need to say, "thank you very much," in Portuguese. Google Translate's algorithm will instantly tell you it's "muito obrigado."

AI has also changed the way we connect with others. Suppose, for instance, you want to buy flowers. No need to drive to the florist. Just go online and browse — a customer service chatbot will even give you suggestions. How? It uses AI and other language processing technology to understand and interpret your conversation with it.

Transform your AI experience with these 5 essential tips

Perhaps you're looking to improve your game of chess or need a pattern for knitting a winter scarf. Or maybe you require assistance with an acceptance speech or want to better understand quantum mechanics.

None of these tasks should pose a problem. That's because AI chatbots like Claude, ChatGPT, Copilot, and Google Gemini can help. Here's how to pose your questions — called prompts — so that you find exactly what you need.

Talk like you would to a person. Don't use stilted or technical language when typing a question to an AI chatbot. Its software is designed to generate text responses in a conversational way. So use everyday language. There's no need to ask "Can you explain the thermodynamic and molecular processes involved in the transition of water from liquid to solid?" when "How does water turn to ice?" works just fine.

Be specific. It's a good idea to narrow down your questions. This will help limit irrelevant responses. Let's say you're running low on groceries. Don't ask, "What can I make with just a few ingredients in my kitchen?" It's better to request recipes for what you have on hand. You'll get responses that you can use if you ask, "What I can make with eggs, bread, spinach, and feta cheese?"

Ask open-ended questions. You'll get a much more detailed response from an AI chatbot if you avoid asking "yes or no" questions. For example, a response to "Was George Washington tall?" will tell you that he was 6 feet, 2 inches tall. You'll get a greater picture of the man — including height, build, facial features, skin tone, posture, hair color, and dental health — if you ask, "Can you tell me about George Washington's physical features?"

Provide context. Your prompt could be a simple question like "What are some good exercises?" You'll most likely get an answer like "squats, deadlifts, rowing, jogging, and broad jumps." But you'll get better tips if you include relevant background information. With the prompt, "What are good exercises for a 75-year-old woman who wants to avoid falling?" you'll get a list of balance, strength, and mobility exercises, along with tips on how long and how often to do them.

Consider tone. Suppose you needed to create invitations to a professional fundraiser and your grandson's seventh birthday party. You'd probably ask a chatbot to write the invitations very differently. So in your prompts, give clues like "formal and professional," "persuasive," "friendly and conversational," and "funny," along with information on your target audience — in this case, adults carrying checkbooks and second graders looking for fun — to get the best results.

Properly phrasing your questions will certainly help in your quest for information. However, it's important to know that AI sometimes gives factually incorrect responses, or ones that are a mixture of truth and fiction.

That's because AI doesn't assess whether the particulars it provides you are correct. Instead, it generates the most likely string of words to answer your prompt. Moreover, this technology can't distinguish between biased and unbiased data. So if you're using an AI chatbot to help you with something important — like academic research — it's always a good idea to fact check and verify the content.

Protect yourself from voice cloning scams

Madeline panicked when she got the phone call. Her granddaughter was in desperate need of money after wrecking her car and getting locked up in jail. So Madeline didn't think twice about sending her money. After all, the caller sounded exactly like her granddaughter.

But it was a scam. Now, instead of leaving a nest egg behind for her children and grandchildren, Madeline was out thousands of dollars.

That's because fraudsters had used artificial intelligence (AI) to create a fake — but very convincing — audio of her granddaughter's voice. That's right, con artists calling you can sound just like a family member or friend. It makes it easy to trick unsuspecting victims into forking over cash.

So how can you protect yourself from these scams? Create a private password that you share with family members. This way, if you get a distressing call requesting money, you can ask the person on the other end of the line to prove their identity by telling you the word.

If you haven't managed to do this ahead of time, ask the caller a personal question that only your loved one would know how to answer. For example, you could say, "I just want to make sure this is really you. Remember when I told you who my favorite singer is? What's her name?"

You can also verify the identity of a caller with these tips.

- Crooks can spoof phone numbers to make them appear legitimate. So never trust caller ID. Instead, hang up and call the person at a number you know is theirs.

- Call another family member who could verify — or contradict — the story you're being told.

Finally, be careful about what you share online. Fraudsters can use this information to learn about your friends and family — making it easier to impersonate a loved one.

Chatbots — get more done with less effort

There's so much hype about artificial intelligence (AI) these days. But what can it do for older adults? A lot, actually. Here are four activities that AI chatbots can help you with now — and one thing you should always avoid.

Plant a garden. ChatGPT and other AI chatbots are more than just tech tools. They're your personal gardeners, too. Just type in your location and ask for help planting a garden. You'll instantly get advice on your area's climate, what to plant in summer and fall, how to deal with pests, and composting. You can also inquire about maintenance tips, irrigation, and the materials needed for your project.

Plan a holiday meal. Let's say your family is coming to visit over the Thanksgiving holiday. No need to get into a tizzy over meal planning. Just tell an AI chatbot that you need recipes. You can narrow down your options by letting it know your level of cooking experience, the number of guests, your budget, and how many meals you'll need to cook. Don't have a deep fryer? Include that info and the chatbot will tell you how to roast, braise, grill, or smoke a tasty turkey.

Brush up on your language skills. Retirement is a great time to travel. And speaking even a few words of your host country's mother tongue goes a long way. So ask a chatbot to help you out with vocabulary lists on specific topics — whether it's food, sports, hobbies, or basic greetings and introductions. It can also assist with grammar, conversation skills, local expressions, and more.

Works great for, say, ordering in a restaurant, asking for directions, or buying tickets for a show.

Improve your memory. Research suggests that playing brain games can help delay age-related cognitive decline. AI chatbots can certainly help you with this. Simply ask what kind of memory-boosting puzzles and games it has. You'll likely get a host of suggestions — from riddles and brain teasers to spelling bees and word recall. Or ask it to play a trivia game with you. You can even pick the topic, whether it's sports, general knowledge, science, music, or literature.

Of course, it's fine to ask a chatbot for suggestions on things like resume writing, travel, and budgeting. You can even ask it to give you advice on your taxes. But never include any personal information — like your social security number or home address — in your queries.

Why? Every entry you make is collected and stored. That makes the companies that run these AI chatboxes a key target for hackers. And you definitely don't want your personal data to be compromised in a security breach or fall into the hands of an online fraudster.

Stay in touch with digital communication

Catch up anytime: Remain close across distances with Skype

Lots of seniors live alone and find it hard to get out at times. It's a situation that can lead to feelings of isolation. But technology can help fight loneliness. That's because your computer makes it easy to talk to your loved ones — without costing a dime.

All you need is Skype. It's a popular video calling service that lets you connect with other Skype users for free. Interested? Here's how to get started.

Set up Skype on your computer. To use Skype on your Windows or Mac computer, you need to download and install the software. You'll be able to find Skype for Windows or Skype for Mac at *skype.com/en/get-skype*. After you create an account and log in, you're ready to find contacts and make calls.

Note that your Skype username doesn't need to be your full name. But it will be visible to all Skype users, so choose wisely.

Find and save Skype contacts. To find other Skype users, type their name or Skype username in the search box. When you find the person you want to add, click their name under the *Skype Directory* heading.

Schedule calls in advance. Ready for a long chat with Aunt Becky in Sarasota? Before you jump on Skype, give her a heads up.

Skype needs to be open on both your computers to make or receive calls, so it helps to schedule your call in advance. Plus Aunt Becky might like the chance to fix her hair and makeup before making her video debut!

Click the correct icon for a video or audio chat. When you're ready to call, select Aunt Becky's name from your contacts list. On the right, you'll see a panel that shows your call and chat history. In the upper right, click the video camera icon to make a video call, or click the telephone handset icon to make an audio-only call.

If your aunt has Skype open, she'll hear your call and see your name on the screen. To answer your call, she'll click a green button. If you're the one receiving a call, simply click the green button that appears on your screen. Voila — you're connected.

> To use Skype on your computer, it needs a microphone. To have video chats with your family or friends, you'll also need a webcam. Most computers today have a built-in mic and webcam, which work great for Skype calls.

The ultimate guide to solving common video call problems

Video calls are a great way to chat with your grandchildren or see friends and family who live far away. However, because this type of communication requires a lot of data, you may have trouble with the quality of the video or sound. If you're having an issue, these tips can help.

Use your Wi-Fi connection instead of cellular data. The better the quality of your internet connection, the better your video call.

If you make a video call from your smartphone while you're on the road, you'll use your cellular data. A wireless internet connection transfers data faster and offers better video quality than a cellular data connection.

Also, the closer you are to your wireless router, the more easily it can handle all that video data. When you're at home, you might find that sitting closer to your router improves the quality of your video chats.

Boost your internet connection speed. You can improve your internet connection's ability to handle video in several ways.

- First, close all the programs on your computer except for Skype or the video-chatting application you use. Most programs connect to the internet and will use space on your internet connection. By closing these programs, you free up that space for Skype video calls.

- If you're still having issues, consider upgrading your internet speed. When you signed up for internet service, you likely chose a connection speed. In most cases, slower connections are cheaper. If you enjoy frequent video chats, paying a little extra each month for a faster connection may be worth it.

Wear headphones for improved audio. During a video call, your smartphone or computer's built-in microphone is often far from your face. Plus your microphone can pick up the conversation from your speaker, causing more audio problems. When you use headphones with a built-in microphone, the mic is closer to your face and doesn't pick up the sound coming through your headphones, so it's easier for you to hear.

Enhance your lighting for a better picture. You can improve the picture in your video chats by adding an extra lamp behind your computer monitor. Or, if you have a laptop, sit near a window and face the natural light.

How to use your smartphone for video calls

With a camera, microphone, and internet, your smartphone has everything you need to make a video call. The one part that varies is the software that helps you make the video connection.

If you and your contact both have iPhones. You can use FaceTime, which is Apple's video-chat feature. Simply open the contact on your phone and tap either the video or FaceTime icon to make a video call.

If you have an iPhone and your friend has an Android phone. Open their contact details, and you'll see a video icon. If you and your contact both have the Skype mobile app or another compatible video-calling app, you can make a video call via that app by tapping the video icon. Or you can open your video-calling app and make the call directly from the app.

If you don't have a compatible app and you tap the video icon, you'll see a screen with information about adding Skype credits, which you need to make a Skype call to a mobile phone or landline. If you use a different video-call app, you may see a help screen from that app instead.

If you have an Android phone. The steps for making a video call depend on your phone model and service provider. Some Android models display a video-calling option when you open a contact. For this option to work, you and your contact might need to have the Google Meet app, which is Google's video-calling app. You can also make video calls to another Android or an iPhone via the Skype mobile app.

232

Instead of hunting through your inbox or folders to find a message, use your email's search feature. The trick is to choose a search term that's specific enough to narrow down your messages to the one you're looking for. Here are some tips for choosing a search term.

- Combine a contact's email address with a term. If you're looking for your sister's Christmas list, you might enter her email address and the word "Christmas" or "list" in the search box.

- Use quotes to find an exact phrase. If you want to tell your search tool to look for two words right next to each other in a message, add quotes around the two words.

- Use a minus sign to exclude a word. For example, if you're on a committee for a local organization but you're not looking for the meeting minutes, type the organization's name and "-minutes" to exclude those messages.

10 terrific tips for getting rid of annoying junk emails

Email spam comes in many forms — from unwanted marketing messages and fake antivirus warnings to money scams and fraudulent shipping notifications. But you don't have to keep getting these unwanted communications. Here's how to avoid them.

Change your marketing email settings. After you make an online purchase or sign up for a newsletter, you might receive too much email from that organization. You can avoid this by clicking a link labeled *Manage Settings* or something similar at the bottom of an email from that organization. Then choose an option to receive fewer messages, such as weekly or monthly messages instead of daily emails.

To tell the organization to stop sending you messages, click an *Unsubscribe* link. Remember — you should only click email links if you're certain the email is legitimate. Real businesses typically send emails from addresses containing the company's domain after the "@" symbol. For example, abc@amazon.com.

Spammers, on the other hand, often use public email domains such as abc@gmail.com or abc@yahoo.com. Looking for another telltale sign of a spam email? You'll know it's fake if you receive a verification notice for an application, account, or email list that you didn't sign up for.

Mark as spam. If you find an unwanted email in your inbox, don't delete it. Instead, mark it as spam so that your spam filter will know not to let any more emails from this address into your inbox. Conversely, if a message you want ends up in your spam folder, you need to tell your filter that the message wasn't spam. To mark messages as spam or not spam, look for a button in the toolbar above your list of email messages. The button may be labeled *spam* or *junk*.

Block an email address. Most email services let you block an email address so that future messages go to your spam folder. To block an address, you can usually select the message in your inbox

Did you know that hackers can intercept your emails during transmission? That's why you should never email anything containing sensitive or confidential data. Instead, use secure file transfer tools that encrypt your files during upload, transit, and download. It's a good way to safeguard your info.

and then click a *Block* button in the toolbar at the top of your email window.

Create an approved list of contacts. Want an easy way to slash the number of junk emails you receive? Create a whitelist. This is a list of email contacts from which you always want to receive messages. With some email services, you can set up your inbox so you see only messages from whitelisted addresses, such as friends and family. To add an email address to a whitelist, create a filter in your email so that messages from that sender never go to spam.

Use a third-party tool to manage spam. If your email service's built-in spam tools don't work well for you, a third-party tool designed to manage spam can help. Most third-party tools work with specific email services, so look for one that works with yours. You can find free and paid options.

For example, BoxBe works with AOL, Yahoo!, Outlook, and Gmail. It can help you create whitelists, block senders, and flag and remove spam messages. If you use the Chrome web browser and Gmail, you can add a plug-in to your browser that can help you remove spam email messages.

Check out these other ways to say "no" to email spam.

- Create one email account for personal messages and a different account for online shopping and any other websites that ask for your email address. That way, most of your spam will end up in your secondary account.

- Don't open an email if you know it's spam. Some of these messages contain software that tells the sender you've opened the mail, which could lead to more spam messages. Simply block the email address.

- Don't display your email address in online membership directories and social media pages. Spammers use these sites to collect email addresses.

- Don't open a message from a suspicious or unfamiliar address. Because if you do, and you click any links in it, your email address could end up being sold to other spammers.

- Be careful about sharing your email address with online businesses. Some may sell this information. You can also check a company's online privacy policy to learn how it will handle your email address.

Uncomplicate your life: Let Gmail handle all your email

So you changed your email address once or twice, and maybe set an account for work. Then your internet provider gave you an address that might have important messages. Pretty soon, checking your email means logging on to AOL, Yahoo Mail, Xfinity, and Outlook.

One solution is to use a complicated email "client" that can bring mail from different accounts to one place. But you may have to take a college course to learn how. A far easier fix is to use Gmail. It lets you receive all your emails together and check them on any device. And you don't have to pass Computer Science 101 with a C or better first.

Keep using your old addresses right in Gmail. Google doesn't have a "me only" mentality. Gmail can serve as an email program for multiple email accounts. The messages come in right alongside your Gmail.

To add email addresses, start by opening Gmail's settings. Click the gear icon on the right above your emails, and choose *Settings*.

Now the first thing many people do when they first see Gmail's settings is panic. Don't do that. There's a lot of information, because it's a powerful program, but the settings menu has a friendly *Learn more* link that pulls up easy instructions.

How to pull in email from other addresses. Along the top of the Settings page is a line of tabs such as *General*, *Labels*, and *Inbox*.

1. Choose *Accounts and Import*.

2. Halfway down the page, find *Check mail from other accounts*.

3. Click *Add a mail account*.

4. Type in the email address and click *Next*.

5. Choose *Link accounts with Gmailify* to get the most features.

6. Type in the email account's username and password.

7. Select the setting you want and click *Add Account*.

That's all there is to it. Now you can manage your other email account(s) from Gmail.

Send email as another address. When you send messages from Gmail, they can be labeled as coming from your Gmail address or other addresses.

1. Choose *Accounts and Import* from the Settings menu.

2. Find *Send mail as*.

3. Click *Add another email address*.

4. Enter your name and the address you want to send from.

5. Here, Gmail wants to send a verification email to the address you're adding. Click Next Step > Send verification.

6. Click *Add Account*.

7. Sign into the account you added.

8. Open the confirmation message you got from Gmail and click the link.

9. In the message, click the *From* line. If you don't see this, click the space next to the recipient's email.

10. Select the address to send from.

If you want to always send from your other address, you'll need to change both your default "From" and "reply-to" address. If you only change the "From" address, replies will go to your original Gmail address by default.

You'll get the best mobile Gmail experience by downloading the free Gmail app on your phone or tablet. And if you want to check your email on someone else's device, you can do it without the app. Just open a browser and go to *mail.google.com* to log in.

Social media fosters personal connections

The power of politeness — keep a respectful social media presence

You know how to mind your manners in person, but do you know how to do it online? Here are three etiquette rules that everyone should follow.

Just the facts, ma'am. It's all too easy to spread misinformation on social media. That's unfortunate because your followers trust that the particulars you're providing are correct. So before you repost a story or share a link or photo, double-check that it's accurate. The same goes for any details that you might include in a blog post. You can ensure the accuracy of your information by going to websites like *mediabiasfactcheck.com*, *snopes.com*, *factcheck.org*, and *truthorfiction.com*.

Don't engage in online arguments. Some people — called trolls — post inflammatory messages on the internet just to get a rise out of others. Others may simply publicize opinions that you don't agree with. But don't get drawn in and respond with anger. Such online conflicts rarely lead to meaningful discussions. Instead, they often turn into a war of words that creates a hostile online environment. Even worse, you could damage a relationship with family or friends.

Get permission before certain posts. You wouldn't want someone to secretly tape conversations with you and then play the recording for others. So why share a screenshot of private emails, texts, and direct messages with a third party? Doing so is an invasion of privacy. The same goes for photos. Maybe the people in the picture don't want their faces posted online for all to see. So always ask for permission before sharing conversations and photos on social media.

So you've finally decided to create a Facebook account to stay in touch with family and friends. No problem — you'll be happy to know it's easy to do. Just go to your computer and follow these steps.

1. Go to *facebook.com* and click *Create New Account*.

2. Enter your name, email or mobile phone number, password, date of birth, and gender.

3. Click *Sign Up*.

4. To finish creating your account, you need to confirm your email or mobile phone number.

You can also create a Facebook account with an app on your smartphone.

Dive into Facebook's hidden gems

Your Facebook news feed is set up for endless scrolling. But you don't have to limit yourself to just that. This social networking site offers other features to help you stay in touch with others.

Connect with people who share your interests. Facebook has groups for just about any interest. Whether you're a movie buff, sports aficionado, or technology nerd, you can find Facebook groups that let you connect, learn, and share with people who have similar interests. It's easy to find a group. On the desktop version of Facebook, in the *Explore* section of the left-hand sidebar, click *Groups*.

You'll find a similar option in the Facebook app. Go to the Groups page and click the *Discover* tab in the upper left. You'll see categories of groups at the top. Click a category to see related groups. To join a group, select the *Join* button next to the group name. Just know that there are two types of groups. Anybody can join a public group. Private groups require an approval process.

Stay informed about local activities. Looking for something fun to do this weekend? You can discover, plan, and respond to happenings in your community with Facebook Events. To find out more, click *Events* in the left-hand sidebar or under the main menu in the Facebook mobile app. On the Events page that appears, select *Discover*. You can then see events in your area and filter them by time and location.

To keep track of events that interest you, click the *Interested* button. You can find details about the event any time by selecting *Events* in the left-hand sidebar and checking the *Upcoming events* list that appears on the Events page.

Enjoy videos handpicked for you. Facebook Watch is a selection of video channels with shows that are popular with Facebook users. When you select *Watch* in the left-hand sidebar, you can browse videos that Facebook thinks you'll like.

The Watch video channels include cooking and baking shows, original comedy, drama, news programming, and live feeds. You'll also find content on many other things, including pets and art projects. And you can see videos from groups you follow. Keep checking back for new things to watch.

Stay safe on Facebook with these helpful hints

Of course, you'll want to protect your Facebook account from cybercriminals. The following tips and tricks will help keep your information secure.

Keep personal information private. Be sure that your home address isn't included in your Facebook profile. After all, you don't want the whole world knowing where you live. To delete your address, go to your computer and log into your Facebook account. Below your profile picture, click *About*. On the left side, select *Contact and Basic Info*. Next to your address, click *Edit*, then delete your address.

The same goes for your phone number. To delete it, click your profile picture in the top right, then select *Settings & privacy*. Go to *Settings*, then *Accounts Center*, followed by *Personal details*. Click *Contact info*, and then select the mobile phone number you'd like to remove. Click *Delete number*, then *Delete*.

Protect your credit card data. Sure it's convenient to buy items with your credit card on Facebook Marketplace. But it could be dangerous to have that information on file. What if Facebook had a data breach? In addition, someone could gain access to your personal data if your smartphone or computer were lost or stolen.

To delete you credit card information, go to your computer and click your profile picture in the top right. Select *Settings & privacy*, then tap *Settings*. Click *See more* in *Accounts Center* on the left side, and tap *Meta Pay*. Click next to a card or account below Payment Methods, and select *Remove card*.

Adjust your privacy settings. By doing so, you can control who has access to your posts, personal information, friends list, and more. Simply click your profile picture in the top right corner of your toolbar. Select *Settings & privacy*, then click *Settings*. Under *Audience and visibility*, choose the option you want to change for privacy. You can also select the audience right before you post something on Facebook. Go to *facebook.com/privacy/center* to learn more about controlling your privacy.

Unlock the fun: Creative ways to get the most from Instagram

Instagram is a free photo and video sharing app. It lets you upload photos or videos and share them with your followers or a select group of friends. You can also view, comment, and like posts shared by your friends on Instagram.

If you like scrolling through photos and videos in your Instagram feed, you may enjoy these other Instagram features, too.

> How you set up an Instagram account depends on whether or not you already have a Facebook page. For more information on your options, go to *help.instagram.com*, click *Manage Your Account*, and then select *Signing Up and Getting Started*.

- Stories. Instagram Stories is the place to share what you're into or what you're up to on the fly — whether you're posting candid moments from a walk around your neighborhood or a video showing how you improved your golf swing. You watch Instagram Stories by clicking the circles that appear above your main feed. In the Instagram app, Stories appear at the top. The posts last only 24 hours and then disappear.

- Highlights. Instagram Highlights allows you to save and categorize the Stories on your profile so followers can still view them after 24 hours have passed. Typically, Instagram users save their most interesting stories to their Highlights. Not every Instagram enthusiast uses Highlights, but public figures often use this feature to showcase their best work and to let you know what you can expect from their profile. To find an Instagram user's Highlights, click their profile name to visit their page. The Highlights are little circles above the square images posted to the main Instagram feed.

- Explore. Instagram Explore lets you browse and view photos, videos, and other content posted by an array of Instagram users. The app chooses what you see based on the Instagram profiles you follow. To find the Explore page on Instagram's website, click the compass icon in the upper right. In the mobile app, look for the magnifying glass icon at the bottom. If you see an image you like, click to see the full post. You can also see the profile that posted the image and a link to follow it.

Want to create your own story on Instagram? Here's how.

1. Tap the camera icon in the top left of your screen.

2. Select the large circle at the bottom of the screen to take a photo, or tap and hold to record a video. If you'd like to pick a photo from your phone's library or gallery, swipe up from anywhere on the screen.

3. Click the letter or pencil icons at the top to write or draw something, or the smiley face icons to add a sticker or filter to your photo.

4. If you'd like to make sure a particular person sees your story, you can tag them. Tap the letter icon, then type @ followed by their username, and select the person from the names that appear. They'll get a notification that you've mentioned them in your story.

5. When you're ready to share, tap *Your Story* in the bottom left.

Safeguard your accounts from hackers and thieves

Swindles carried out over social media cost Americans some $1.4 billion a year. Fortunately, you don't have to fall victim to these cons. Simply follow these policies to avoid them.

Pick strong passwords. If you aren't careful with your passwords, someone could sign into your social media accounts and impersonate you or find sensitive information that they can use to steal your identity. A good password will be at least 10 characters long, have both uppercase and lowercase letters, and a number and symbol. It's important to use unique passwords for each of your online accounts so that all of them aren't at risk if one is compromised.

Don't take the bait. Never click links on pop-up messages or posts that promise to be amazing, shocking, or sensational. Doing so could take you to a site that lets con artists hijack your account or steal your personal information. The same goes for direct messages from online "friends" pressuring you to click a link or download an attachment. These accounts may have been hacked.

Know who you're dealing with. Never give out any information online unless you know the website you're using is legitimate and not a replica created by a cybercriminal. Look for "https" (the "s" stands for secure) before the web address. You should also see a padlock to the left of the address. Another option? Use a website safety checker like Google Safe Browsing.

Be guarded with money. Some scammers may pose as a love interest in dire need of emergency funds. Others might promise a good job in return for a small "advance fee" to secure a position. Either way, never allow anyone to rush you into sending them money. Nor should you ever send funds via wire transfer or reloadable cards unless you're 100% sure that the recipient is a trusted family member or friend.

Think twice before taking online quizzes that promise to offer insights into your personality or intelligence. At best, your answers can be shared with advertisers looking to identify and target a new audience. At worst, cybercriminals can use the information to steal your identity.

How is that possible? These tests often contain questions on things like your favorite color, your first pet's name, or the name of the city you were born in. If scammers gain access to your responses, they can use them to create phishing emails — the kind used to gain sensitive information — that are tailored to your interests.

In addition, many of the inquiries in these quizzes are common security questions needed to reset the passwords for online accounts, including the one with your bank. You don't want this information to fall into the wrong hands as it can lead to unauthorized access and fraud. Your best bet? Steer clear of these quizzes.

Manage your finances with online banking

Make the most of your money: Easy steps to save big

Tired of high bank fees and low interest rates? It may be time to switch to an online bank. They usually give you the best interest rates, especially for savings accounts. You'll find rates regularly at 4% or more. And without the overhead costs of maintaining a physical location, online banks usually have lower fees. You can easily find current savings account rates with comparison tools like the ones at *bankrate.com/banking/savings/rates* or *nerdwallet.com/rates/savings-account*.

Once you've found your preferred online bank, you'll want to verify that it's FDIC-insured. This designation guarantees that, in the unlikely event of the bank's failure, your deposits are insured up to at least $250,000. Luckily, verifying an online bank is simple — you just need to check the FDIC BankFind page on the web at *banks.data.fdic.gov/bankfind-suite/bankfind*. You can feel protected when you know your institution is insured by the government.

Ready to open an account? You'll have to offer up some personal details. But you shouldn't worry about security. These banks have robust security systems set up, so all you have to think about is how to get the ball rolling.

- Apply online. You'll have to turn over your Social Security number and digital copies of your ID to most online banks. Be prepared to give out contact information, like your phone number, email, and street address, too.

- Make your first deposit. You'll need to put money into your new account to get it set up. Luckily, most online banks give you several ways to do this. Often the easiest option is to transfer money from your old account.

But don't hand over your info if you have concerns about security on your end of the internet. Check the address bar at the top of the bank's web pages to make sure the URL starts with "https." That means the site is secure.

And never do your online banking in public places. Coffee shops, bookstores, or anywhere else with free Wi-Fi might not have a safe connection. Scammers could monitor your transactions and swipe your account info without your knowledge. Use password-protected Wi-Fi, and try to do your banking on your own network.

Empower your banking with these 4 tips

Digital banking can be a huge timesaver. You can monitor your accounts, track your transactions, transfer funds, and pay bills — without setting foot in your local branch. Unfortunately, though, there's a troubling downside. As with shopping over the internet, online banking can open you up to theft and fraud.

Following are four easy measures you can take to keep your experience free of cybercrimes.

Go incognito and keep your sessions private. By default, when you go online, your web browser keeps track of sites you visit and other information. If your internet session involves a visit to your bank's website, this information could include sensitive data like your account number, balance, statement, and so on. Even after you close your browser, this data could remain on your device — which means if a hacker or thief compromises your computer, they may be able to capture it.

Fortunately, most web browsers have a special feature that lets you browse anonymously, usually called Private Browsing or Incognito Mode. When you use this feature, the browser still tracks your browsing activity but wipes it from your system when you end your browsing session.

Do a two-step for double the protection. Most financial institutions support the use of two-step authentication for online banking. This means that rather than simply entering your username and password to log into your account, you must enter this information plus something else — usually a code sent to your mobile device. If your bank allows for two-step authentication, you should use it.

View your statements online. Financial statements can contain all sorts of personal info, including your home address, account number, balance, and transaction

> Make sure you use a strong password when setting up your online bank account. You can prevent hackers from guessing your password by creating one that contains a combination of symbols, numbers, and uppercase and lowercase letters. It should be at least 10 characters in length.

history. This makes them particularly attractive to thieves who want to steal your identity. That's why robbers raid mailboxes and even trash cans and dumpsters for paper statements. To foil these fraudsters, you can cancel mail delivery of paper statements and view them online instead.

Sign up for banking alerts. These notifications — via text alerts or email — alert you to any potentially fraudulent activities. They'll let you know, for example, of new credit or debit card transactions, unusual account activity, password changes, or a large purchase or withdrawal. If you suspect foul play, immediately contact your financial institution and change your passwords.

Banking on the go with your smartphone sure is convenient. But you still have to keep your information secure. So create a complex passcode for your phone, and enable the auto-lock feature. You'll also want to make sure the passwords you use for mobile banking are not automatically saved on your phone. And you should set up your phone with remote tracking. If your phone is lost or stolen, you can use this feature to erase your personal data.

When banking from your phone, use your bank's app and not the website. Download it from an official app store. Don't save your username on your phone, and don't use the same password you have for other apps. If you lose your phone, notify your bank immediately. Thankfully, if your phone and bank app are hacked, your liability limit is only $50. And most banks waive this charge.

Secure your accounts: Top strategies for dodging scams

It seems like fraudsters will do just about anything to gain access to your bank account. So keep an eye out for this common trick.

With this online scam, you might receive a text or email that seems to be from your bank. It may urge you to take immediate action — like confirming your personal information to keep the account from closing — in an effort to get you to act quickly without thinking. These messages might include a link that looks like it leads to your bank's website, but it actually takes you to a fake page. If you enter your password and username, the fraudsters will be able to log in to your actual account.

Clicking these links may also install malicious software on your device. This malware may steal your banking information, such as your credit or debit card numbers. And sometimes you might get a message that asks you to call a fake customer service number. If you call it, you could find yourself talking to someone fishing for personal information.

It's important to know that banks will never ask for personal information — including PIN numbers, account passwords, one-time passcodes, credit card numbers, or Social Security numbers — via text, email, or phone calls. And if you receive a call from someone who says they're from your bank, take down their name and hang up. Then call your bank using the number on the back of your credit or debit card.

Embrace the safety of electronic bill payments

You might want to reconsider if you're still paying your bills by check. That's because fraudsters can gain a wealth of personal information — your name, address, account and routing numbers — from a lost or stolen check. Then, with a fake ID, they could walk into your bank and start making withdrawals. Some swindlers use chemicals to wash off all the information on a check other than the signature. Then they make the check out to themselves, fill in any amount, and cash it.

Don't let this happen to you. Set up online bill pay with your bank. It's easy to do. First, you'll want to log in to your bank account, find the online Bill Pay tab, and select the company you'd like to pay. If it isn't there, you'll have to type in the name. You'll also need to add your account number and other relevant information. For payments that are the same each month, like your mortgage or car payment, you can set up automatic recurring payments.

For other bills, you can make one-time payments. Just be sure you ask your bank how many days it will take them to process your transactions. This way you'll know when you should log in to your account and pay your bills.

Crafty crooks often look for pre-approved credit card offers in the mail. If thieves intercept one of these offers addressed to you, they could easily apply for the card and have it sent to themselves.

Assuming the application goes through, these criminals might well rack up thousands in charges — ruining your credit in the process — as quick as you can lick a stamp. But you can put an end to these mailed credit card offers, as well as the risk of identity theft that comes with each one.

You can choose not to get these invitations — as well as tons of junk mail from insurance companies — by calling 888-5-OPT-OUT or visiting *optoutprescreen.com*. Just know that your ability to opt out lasts only five years. For a more permanent solution, fill out the "Permanent Opt-Out Election" form on the website, print it out, and mail it in.

Amazing tips for preventing ID theft and fraud

9 smart ways to stop ID thieves dead in their tracks

Americans lose billions upon billions of dollars each year to online fraud. No wonder roughly half of all baby boomers worry about their privacy when they're logged on to their devices. But you don't have to be scared. Just follow these tips.

Update your software. Software updates often fix bugs that hackers use to access your data and infect your computer with malware. Be sure to regularly update your computer, phone, tablet, and other devices regularly to keep cybercriminals from exploiting any known security weak spots.

Never share passwords. You might be surprised to learn that a poll of 1,500 consumers found that nearly 80% of them admitted to sharing a password with someone outside the home. It's a dangerous thing to do, even if the other person is trustworthy. Why? If you share this information on an unencrypted platform — think text, emails, and chats — hackers can gain access to it. Moreover, you don't know if the network the other person is using is secure.

Be wary of public Wi-Fi. When you're out in public, try to steer clear of free Wi-Fi. You don't want to fall victim to hackers who take advantage of a network's poor security to steal your passwords and take over your online accounts. Your best bet? Turn off the auto connect option that automatically links your device to nearby networks. You can disable it through the Settings app on your phone, laptop or tablet.

Protect your online presence. For extra protection, use two-factor authentication when logging in to your online accounts. Along with your username and password, you'll need an additional code — which is sent to your cellphone or email address — to complete the login. This helps keep hackers out of your bank, email, and social media accounts, even if they've stolen your password.

Use different passwords. Never use the same password for different online accounts. Doing so is dangerous for one simple reason — if a fraudster gains access to one of your accounts, he'd be able to hack into all of them if you used the same password. Stay safe by using unique passwords for all your accounts.

Here are four more of the easiest steps you can take to stay safe online.

- Beware of "shoulder surfing," a process in which someone looks over your shoulder when you're logging in with your password or paying a bill with your credit card. Turn your body or use your hand or a piece of paper to shield your info.

- Be sure all your mobile devices have a remote wipe capability. This way if your smartphone or laptop is lost or stolen, your data won't be compromised if it falls into the wrong hands.

- Don't click the "Save password?" prompt when logging into a website. If you do, anyone who uses your device can easily access all your saved passwords. Instead, use a password manager.

- Install antivirus software to block malware from infecting your device.

Uh-oh — you're surfing the internet when a pop-up notification appears on your screen. It says your computer is infected with a virus or is at risk of crashing. The message prompts you to call a "tech support" number or click a link.

Don't do it. Fraudsters may be trying to infect your computer with malware, sell you a worthless repair service, or gain remote access to your device.

It's important to know that security pop-up warnings from real tech companies will never ask you to call a phone number or click a link. If you're worried about a virus or other security threat, go to the software developer's website to find its phone number. Call the company and explain what happened. Or consult a trusted tech security expert.

Been a victim of ID theft? Here's what to do

Maybe someone has gotten hold of your credit card number. Or perhaps you've received a notice that your Social Security number was exposed in a data breach. Either way, you'll want to take action right away. Here's how.

- Lock down compromised accounts. For each affected account, call the company's fraud department, tell them your identity has been stolen, and ask them to freeze the account or shut it down.

- Place a fraud alert on your credit report. This informs lenders that they should contact you before extending new credit in your name.

- File a report with the Federal Trade Commission. Visit *identitytheft.gov* to report the theft. This site also offers resources for formulating a recovery plan to fix your credit.

- Check other accounts. Review your credit report to see if anyone opened any new accounts in your name. If so, contact each company's fraud department, tell them you're a victim of ID theft, and ask them to close the account.

- Report the theft to your local police. Filing a police report offers you protection from companies that attempt to collect debts resulting from your identity theft.

5 foolproof ways to foil phishing attacks

One of the most common forms of scams aimed at computer users is known as phishing. This is a relatively simple form of cybercrime as it doesn't require a complicated virus or spyware.

Instead, phishing involves asking people for their sensitive financial information, such as bank account details and logins for online accounts. Why on earth would anyone willingly hand that information over? The phishing request is usually made through an official looking, albeit fake, email. Phishing emails can pretend to come from some of the following organizations:

- banks, with a message saying your account has been suspended

- courier services, with a memo saying there's a problem with a delivery they have for you

- a cloud service, such as iCloud or Dropbox, with a warning that your account has been locked

- any organization where users have online accounts, with a notice that claims they have noticed suspicious activity or need you to confirm some personal information

Included in the phishing email are details of what the problem is and how it can be remedied. Unfortunately, the "remedy" usually involves clicking a link, which takes you to a page where you have to enter financial details to resolve the issue. Needless to say, this doesn't fix anything — since there never was a problem — but instead provides the phishers with your crucial financial details.

Phishing emails can seem intimidating, and it may be tempting to perform the requested action. However, the golden rule is that you should not click on any links in an email that you have doubts about. Instead, take a few minutes to try and discover if the email is legitimate. Here's how to determine if an email link to an internet site is safe.

Check whether you have an account with the organization. Millions of phishing emails are sent every day, in the hope that users will have the service or account named in the email. Whenever you get a such an email, take some time to check whether it is relevant to you or not. If it is, examine the email further to find out if it is genuine.

Inspect the address of the email. Phishing emails are usually disguised to show the name of the company they are claiming to be from. However, the email address at the top may be very different and bear little resemblance to the actual company. It takes less than a second to click, right-click, or tap on the name of the email sender to view the full email address.

Note the language, spelling, and grammar. If there are numerous spelling or grammar errors, this could be a sign the email is not genuine.

Search the web for alerts. The online community is excellent at keeping on top of scams. Other people will undoubtedly have received the same phishing email as you and posted warnings about it.

In addition, stay tuned into government watchdog sites that post consumer alerts about current exploits. The Federal Trade Commission, for example, keeps its website updated on the latest scams. Go to *consumer.ftc.gov* and click *Scams*.

Look up the company's actual website online. Check on the internet to see if the named company has reported any problems.

Freeze your credit to keep ID thieves at bay

Identity theft comes in many forms. Someone pretending to be you might wipe out your bank account, get a loan, or claim your tax refund. So it's no surprise that having your identity stolen can destroy your quality of life.

The Federal Trade Commission says credit card fraud is the No. 1 source of identity theft. Fortunately, you have a way to put the kibosh on ID thieves before they open a card in your name.

Simply freeze your credit by going to the websites of the three major credit bureaus. You'll find them at *equifax.com*, *transunion.com*, and *experian.com*. This shuts off access to your report from anyone but you, preventing fraudsters from opening accounts or borrowing money in your name. You can also call the credit bureaus and tell them to freeze your credit. There's no charge for the service, but be prepared to answer some questions to verify your identity.

You'll need to temporarily lift the freeze if you apply for a loan or credit card.

- Equifax — 888-298-0045

- TransUnion — 800-916-8800

- Experian — 888-397-3742

> When Joe checked his monthly bank statement, he was horrified to see an unauthorized transaction. Someone had managed to steal $30 from his checking account. After some further digging, Joe saw that the same thing had occurred in each of the previous six months.
>
> So how did it happen? Some fraudster had copied the bank account and routing numbers on one of Joe's checks. With that information, the con artist had all the information he needed to set up automated payments from Joe's checking account. Once that was done, the funds were automatically transferred each month into an account controlled by the scammer.
>
> Because Joe didn't regularly review his mail from the bank, he didn't notice the money was missing until $210 had been stolen. You can avoid this happening to you by consistently reviewing your bank statements. And instead of writing checks for recurring expenses like rent and utilities, set up auto pay or settle your bills online.

Online privacy — tips for avoiding data collection

Ever go online and search for something — a bedspread, say, or a crock pot — only to get bombarded with ads later on for that very same item? If so, you're not alone. Advertisers often place tracking cookies on websites in order to send targeted advertisements to your electronic devices.

But your lack of online privacy doesn't stop there. Companies collect information about you that you might share online, including your name, birth date, gender, and phone number. This data, and other details about your life — your age, hobbies, favorite web sites, and online purchases, for example — is valuable because it helps businesses to personalize marketing efforts and increase profits.

While companies typically don't make such data public, security breaches do occur. And when that happens, your personal information can get sold to identity thieves.

Fortunately, you can minimize your digital footprint with the following tips.

- Review a company's privacy statement to determine what information is collected and how it may be secured, stored, and shared. You can find helpful links to the privacy policies of dozens of popular businesses online at *staysafeonline.org/ resources/manage-your-privacy-settings*.

- Delete any accounts and apps you no longer use.

- Opt out of people search websites that collect personal information, including someone's age, date of birth, marital status, and address. The companies that gather this data either provide it for free on the internet or compile it into a report for sale.

- Enter only required information — often marked with an asterisk — when filling out online forms.

- Clear your browsing and search history, and delete cookies. If you visit a website that offers the option to "Reject all cookies," take it.

- Limit the personal information you post on social media platforms.

Tired of getting all those targeted ads based off of your online shopping activity or search history? If so, you can turn off advertisement tracking on your devices web browser. You can also download an ad blocker.

Theft after death — smart moves to protect your loved one's estate

It's sad to say, but death isn't the end of identity theft. Scammers steal the personal information of the dead to open credit card accounts, collect government benefits, and take out loans. And they'll often commit this crime right after someone passes away, hoping that relatives are too busy grieving to notice the fraud.

While surviving family members aren't responsible for the bogus charges and claims, this lawbreaking can add months — even years — to the estate settlement process.

So where do thieves collect details about the deceased? Sometimes at hospitals and funeral homes. More often, they find information in obituaries. So it's best to exclude things that make it easier to steal your loved one's identity, including his birth date, middle name, birthplace, home address, and mother's maiden name.

In addition, the executor of the estate or next of kin should contact the Social Security Administration (SSA) at 800-772-1213 to report the death. The SSA can lock the deceased's Social Security number so that thieves can't steal benefits.

Not sure how reputable a charity is? Before you write a check, get the real scoop so you don't get taken. You can easily look into the organization's credentials at *charitywatch.org*, *charitynavigator.org*, or the Better Business Bureau's Wise Giving Alliance at *give.org*. You'll find information on the charity's finances, accountability, and transparency.

You'll also want to send copies of the death certificate to the financial firms that the departed did business with. Shutting down an account? Ask that it be marked "Closed: Account holder is deceased." And don't forget to cancel your loved one's driver's license to prevent a con artist from getting a duplicate.

Finally, mail a copy of the death certificate to the three major credit bureaus — Equifax, TransUnion, and Experian — and ask that a "deceased alert" be placed on the person's credit report. A few weeks later, check the report to ensure that no suspicious activity has taken place.

Ward off tax ID theft with this easy step

You've probably heard about tax-related identity theft. It's when someone steals your Social Security number and other personal information to file a fake tax return and steal whatever refund may result. You may not even know you're a victim until the IRS rejects your legitimate return because it's been flagged as a duplicate.

To battle such crimes, the agency is offering an Identity Protection Personal Identification Number (IP PIN) to all taxpayers who want one. It will give you a six-digit number — known only to you and the IRS — that will be used to verify your identity when filing a return.

To join the IP PIN program, go to *irs.gov/identity-theft-fraud-scams/get-an-identity-protection-pin* and click *Get an IP PIN*. You'll need to set up an online account. The PIN is generally available in your account from mid-January through mid-November.

Keep the number in a safe place until it's time to do your taxes. Remember, this is a single-use PIN. You must get a new one each year. Without the correct PIN, the agency will either reject or delay the processing of your return.

Save time, shop smart with e-commerce

Get the best deals with these hacks

It's easier than you think to pay rock bottom prices on everything you buy online. Just follow these tips to keep more money in your wallet.

Compare prices virtually. Remember when you had to run from one store to the next, checking to see who had the lowest price on an item? Fortunately, those days are long gone. You can now comparison shop online — just go to a website that performs the comparisons for you. You can review the prices on a wide range of products, and go straight to the site with the best offer. No easier way to save. So have some frugal fun on these price comparison websites.

> You can find all kinds of free stuff. Just surf to the website *freestufffinder.com* to get freebies and coupons for just about everything. You'll find similar offerings at *freebies4mom.com*, *freeflys.com*, and *freebie shark.com*.

- Pricepirates, at *pricepirates.com*.

- Google Shopping, at *shopping.google.com*.

- PriceGrabber, at *pricegrabber.com*.

- Yahoo! Shopping, at *shopping.yahoo.com*.

Take advantage of rewards. It's easy to save money with browser extensions — plug-ins that you can download on web browsers like Chrome or Safari. They'll alert you to special deals and rebates while you shop on the internet. The browser extension Honey, for example, will automatically pull up coupons and discount codes. Rakuten's plug-in lets you activate cash back rewards and apply coupons at checkout. Other big names in browser extensions include BeFrugal and CouponCabin.

Abandon your shopping cart. If you're not in a rush to buy, just add the items you like to your online cart and step away from the site. Many retailers keep an eye on these unfinished purchases and often try to tempt you back with a discount code in your email. Some may even alert you if the price drops on something you wanted. Just make sure you start the checkout process and enter your email. Then sit back and wait for those deals to roll in.

Like most people, you're probably looking for new ways to save on clothing. No worries — you'll never have to pay full price again. Try these hacks to get the best deals.

For starters, you can shop at thrift and consignment shops for preowned apparel at discounted prices. Don't have any in your area? Then simply go online to websites like *goodwillfinds.com*, *thredup.com*, and *swap.com*. Buying secondhand clothes not only saves you money — you're doing your part to help the environment by keeping such items out of landfills.

But what happens if a special occasion is coming up — a wedding, say — and you need a formal outfit that you'll probably wear only once. Look no further than online clothing rental shops like *renttherunway.com*, *armoire.style*, and *nuuly.com*. Depending on the site, you can pay to rent an item once or purchase a monthly subscription that comes with multiple rentals at no extra charge.

Worth the splurge? Here's how to decide

Yippee! The package you ordered online has finally arrived. But then you open it and disappointment sets in. The blouse you bought seems poorly made. And the bath mat is way too small. Unfortunately, situations like this happen far too often. But they don't have to. Simply follow these tricks to determine if an online product is worth buying.

You'll first want to read the online reviews of customers who have already bought the product that you're interested in. These evaluations might also include photos and the pros and cons of the item. Then do an online search for the merchandise along with the words "complaint" or "scam." All of this information will come in handy when you're deciding if you want to make a purchase.

Next, you can ensure the quality of an item by reading the product details section. You'll learn the material an item is made of, along with features like the product's size and weight. This way you won't be in for any surprises after making a purchase. Finally, you should avoid shopping on bargain clothing and furniture websites where quality may be an afterthought. After all, cheaply made goods are more likely to rip or break easily. It's better to wait for a sale at a higher-quality, trusted website.

These websites can unlock major savings

You can find loads of coupons and other deals on the following websites. Or you could download their mobile apps through the Apple App Store or Google Play Store. This way you can save no matter where you are.

- RebatesMe (*rebatesme.com*) offers discounts and cash-back rewards through its partnership with more than 7,500 stores worldwide.

- TopCashback (*topcashback.com*) is a cash-back website that also offers promo codes to save even more at checkout.

- Groupon (*groupon.com*) provides coupons for local restaurants, entertainment, events, and for online and brick-and-mortar stores. You can find discounts on vacation packages and hotels as well. This website also has a growing inventory of affordable items at its marketplace Groupon Goods.

- Coupons.com (*coupons.com*) compiles the latest deals and offers online and printable coupons.

- The Krazy Coupon Lady (*thekrazycouponlady.com*) has digital, printable, and manufacturer coupons and rebates. The site also tells you which combination of coupons you can use on sale items at a particular store.

But don't stop there. You'll also want to visit the best online shopping sites that will save you the most money. Of course you'll want to check out *ebay.com* and *amazon.com*. But you'll also find great deals on things like home goods — from rugs and chairs to towels and sofas — at *overstock.com*. You'll find similarly discounted items at *wayfair.com*.

In the market for all things electronic? Then check out the sales at *newegg.com*, *microcenter.com*, and *techbargains.com*.

Protect your payment info when you shop online

Online shopping has steadily increased over the years. In fact, more than 75 percent of Americans purchase items this way. And why not? It's convenient to buy things from the comfort of your own home.

Just know one thing — you should never pay with your debit card when ordering things over the internet. Doing so makes you vulnerable to financial fraud and could potentially cost you your life savings. That's because your debit card is directly linked to your bank account, which makes it easy for cybercriminals to spend all the money in your checking account if they intercept your card's information.

> Looking to get a good deal on a microwave? Perhaps you're in the market for a cheap snowblower. No worries — you can now buy government surplus online at auction websites like *govdeals.com* and *gsaauctions.gov*. You'll find that they sell everything from furniture and electronics to vehicles and building supplies.

Banks offer some level of protection for debit card fraud, but it's generally not as much as you'd get for credit card fraud. If a criminal wipes out the funds in your checking account, you won't have access to that money until the unauthorized charge is resolved. That could be problematic if you rely on those funds for bills and daily expenses. On the other hand, you won't lose any money if a scammer goes on a spending spree with your credit card information. Your best bet? Use your credit card when shopping online.

Here are some other ways to protect your payment information when purchasing items over the internet.

- Avoid using public Wi-Fi. Hackers using the same connection could steal your credit card data and other personal information. If you absolutely must use public Wi-Fi, protect yourself with a virtual private network (VPN) so that cybercriminals won't be able to see what you're doing.

- Use two-factor authentication. Getting a passcode by text message is a simple method to verify that you are the legitimate owner of the credit card. The passcode is good for only one use and expires shortly after it is sent.

- Make sure your computer has updated security software in place. After purchasing something online, completely log out of the website before exiting. And don't let your computer remember your credit card information.

Here's a surprising secret that one of the most famous online stores hopes you never learn. You can save a fortune by purchasing Amazon's used, pre-owned, or open-box items. Just go to *amazon.com* and type "resale" into the search bar near the top of the page.

But the discounts don't stop there. You can save up to 70% on Amazon's overstock items. To find them, go to Amazon's home page and type "Amazon outlet" into the search bar. You can refine your search by categories such as "beauty," "kitchen," or "books." And don't forget about Amazon's lightning deals. They're short-time offers on items that may be deeply discounted. Find them by typing "lightning deals" into the search bar.

Lastly, you can go to *amazon.com/coupons* for more savings on your purchases. Virtually clip each coupon and add your selection to your cart. The company will apply the discount at checkout.

Don't miss these proven tips for avoiding product delivery fraud

Ordered something online? Most likely the retailer or delivery company sent you a text message or email with shipment and delivery information in it. It's a good way to keep track of your purchase. But unfortunately, fraudsters are now sending out similar notifications in an effort to steal your identity or financial information.

These scam messages — which look like they're from a legitimate carrier — often say that a package is on its way or that there's a problem with its arrival. They contain links to update your delivery or payment preferences. You might also get a voicemail message or a "missed delivery" notice on your door with a number to call.

At first, you may think you should follow the directions. But don't. Clicking the link may bring you to a website that prompts you to enter personal information. That simple action could install malware on your device. The next thing you know, a criminal has access to the usernames and passwords for your bank and social media accounts. And if you decide to call the phone number, it may be answered by a scam "operator" asking you to verify the credit card number you used to make a purchase. Either scenario could end in disaster.

You can avoid falling for these cons by knowing that package delivery services won't ask for personal information. In addition, be wary of any emails or texts saying that your package will be returned to the sender if you don't act immediately. If you haven't bought anything online recently, a notification of this type is most likely a scam. Also misspelled website addresses, like *fed-ex.com* or *ups1.com*, are another indication of potential fraud.

4 essential ways to steer clear of shady shopping sites

It's safest to shop on sites you know are on the up-and-up. Look for the online arm of a reputable brick-and-mortar store or an established internet-only outlet like Amazon.

But what if you find the exact thing you've been looking for on a site you've never heard of? In that case, it's best to do a bit of investigating beforehand. Here are four tips to test a site's trustworthiness.

Check the security indicators. Before entering your credit card number online, make sure the website is secure. Look for a padlock icon in the address bar at the top of the web page. This indicates the connection is encrypted, so all the information that travels between you and the website is protected. And make sure that the page's URL starts with "https" instead of "http." The added "s" indicates that the site is secure.

Look at the site's design. You should know that the websites of fraudulent online stores may have spelling and grammar errors. Their design may also be shoddy. Then there's the matter of pricing. If the site advertises bargain-basement discounts — say 55% off the going rate — think twice.

Confirm that you can get hold of them. Most reputable shopping sites want you to be able to get in touch with them. That's why they include contact info, like a physical address, phone number, and email link. If a site is missing this information, it might be an indication that it's more shifty than safe. In addition to contact info, a reputable shopping site should also spell out various policies, such as its privacy policy and its return policy. Having these available is another thumbs-up.

Read the reviews. Before buying an item from a website, take a minute to read reviews about it. Simply enter the site's name and the string "+ review" in a search engine like Google or Bing and see what pops up. Or try searching review sites like the Better Business Bureau (*bbb.org*), Trustpilot (*trustpilot.com*), and SiteJabber (*sitejabber.com*). If reviews of the site are sub-stellar, it's best to steer clear.

You need to save your online receipts, just like you would paper receipts. That way, if you run into a problem — like your package is mysteriously delayed or disappears en route — you'll have all the info you need to follow up.

One easy way to do this is to create a special "Receipts" folder in your email program to store them. Or if you want to get fancy, try using mobile apps like Zoho Expense, Veryfi, or Expensify.

These apps, available for download on iPhone and Android devices, allow you to scan and store receipts and other documents on your smartphone.

Tired of being on hold? Try these simple ways to get help fast

Oh no! You still haven't received that winter coat you ordered online. So you call the retailer's customer service department and find yourself endlessly pushing button after button. Wouldn't it be great to speak to a real person and be able to easily bypass those recorded menus?

Fortunately, you can still get the human touch with almost every customer service call. Just follow these shortcuts.

Consider the time. High call volume impacts how long you have to wait. So be strategic when you pick up the phone. Mondays and Fridays are usually a company's busiest days. Generally, it's better to call on Wednesdays and Thursdays. The best time to get in touch? Between 7 a.m. and noon.

Use the phone. You might get someone on the line if you repeatedly press the 0 button on your phone. If that doesn't work, you can say the word "operator" a few times when the voice activated phone system asks you to state the reason of your call.

Go to the web. You can get your problem solved quickly by going to *gethuman.com* and typing in the name of the company you want to contact.

The service will provide you with the best number to call, the average wait time, and an option to skip waiting on hold. You can also download the GetHuman mobile app.

Request a callback. Many customer service departments will ask you if you want to request a callback. When that happens, you'll be able to confirm your phone number. The call will then end, while the company's phone system retains your contact information. It will automatically return your call when an agent becomes available.

Savvy solutions for easy health care management

Tips for a successful telehealth visit

Technology makes medical appointments easier than ever. In fact, all you need to talk to your doctor is internet access and a computer, tablet, or smartphone. These online appointments are convenient and — most importantly — a great way to save money.

If you're new to telehealth, you'll want to use these five handy tips for making the most out of your virtual visit to your doctor's office.

Know what to expect. Check the details of the visit that your doctor's office sends you by text, email, or message in your patient portal for information on starting your visit. It's also important to check with your doctor's billing department and your insurance company for details on cost and coverage. If you can't afford a virtual meeting or don't have insurance, let your health care provider know. There may be an alternative to this type of visit.

Consider looping in a friendly face. You may normally want to bring a friend or family member to your doctor's office so they can help you remember certain concerns or interpret information from the doctor. With virtual visits, you may be able to loop these people in, no matter where they are in the world. Before your appointment, ask if you can add a third person to your video call.

Gather relevant information. In the day or so leading up to your scheduled meeting, jot down any symptoms or problems you've had. You'll also want to make a list of questions for your doctor. If your appointment is with a new caregiver, have your medical history available. And don't forget to collect any materials you might need for the visit, such as a blood pressure log or a list of your medications.

Set up for the visit. Find a quiet, comfortable place where you can sit and talk to your health care provider without worrying about being overheard. In addition, test your tech out ahead of time. You don't want to miss the meeting because your computer needs an update or your camera isn't working. Practice logging on to the video conferencing app your doctor uses. You'll also want to make sure that your internet connection is working ahead of time. If you need help troubleshooting, consult a tech-savvy friend or family member a few hours before the appointment.

Keep needed devices nearby. During your virtual meeting, keep any medical device you might need within reach — whether it's a scale to weigh yourself or a thermometer to take your temperature. You'll also want to have a pen and paper by your side to take notes.

Visit the Eldercare Locator at *eldercare.acl.gov* or call 800-677-1116 to find local resources that can give you information about the different Medicare plans available. This government website also connects older Americans and their caregivers with information on available senior services.

4 ways to save a bundle on medications

Older adults spend, on average, more than $600 a year on prescription drugs. That's a lot of money. Fortunately these tips may help you pay for your medicine.

Patient Assistant Programs. These initiatives are run by pharmaceutical companies who voluntarily provide free or low cost prescription drugs to people who can't afford them. You can go to *rxassist.org* to search for your medications and eligibility requirements.

If you have Medicare Part D drug coverage, you can also find these programs at *medicare.gov/pharmaceutical-assistance-program*.

Free samples. Your doctor might have just the thing you need to slash drug prices. Simply ask her for a few free samples next time she writes a prescription. If you're lucky, you might go home with medicine without having to pay a penny for it.

The Extra Help Program. This Medicare program helps people with limited income and resources pay for Medicare (Part D) drug coverage premiums, deductibles, coinsurance, and other costs. It also offers reduced-price drugs, which in 2025, were capped at $4.90 for each generic drug and $12.15 for each brand-name drug. To apply, go to *ssa.gov/medicare/part-d-extra-help*.

State Pharmaceutical Assistant Programs. Many states provide financial assistance for prescriptions and drug plan premiums. Coverage varies widely by state. For example, some programs help cover the cost of prescriptions that Medicare Part D doesn't pay for. Others may provide access to medications for certain diseases. To see if your state has one of these programs, go to *medicare.gov/plan-compare/#/pharmaceutical-assistance-program/states*.

Here's an easy way to find out how well your area hospitals compare with each other.

The Centers for Medicare & Medicaid Services rates more than 4,000 hospitals nationwide on issues like surgery complication rates, mortality rates, and effectiveness of care. Go to *medicare.gov/hospitalcompare* and type in your ZIP code to see how well the facilities in your area measure up.

You'll also want to see if the hospital is accredited by The Joint Commission, a nonprofit with a mission to improve the quality of U.S. health care. Find out by searching online at *qualitycheck.org*.

Try these hacks to prevent tech stress

Whether you use your electronic devices for doing the crossword or sending out text messages, technology keeps you entertained and connected. But what happens when the negatives outweigh the positives? You may feel like throwing in the towel if arthritis hampers your ability to use your gadgets. But don't give up — adapt.

Research suggests that the neck is particularly vulnerable to tech stress. That's because people are using handheld devices — think cellphones and tablets — more than ever, leading to a condition called text neck.

It's a painful stress injury caused by jutting your head forward when using mobile devices. To make matters worse, text neck could lead to inflammation and permanent arthritic damage.

How can you avoid it? Keep your head upright, with your ears aligned with the center of your shoulders. And take time away from your gadget every 20 minutes or so to relieve stress in your neck and shoulders. Hold small devices like smartphones up high so they align with your eyes.

Tech use can also impact your hands and wrists. Try these tips to avoid triggering arthritis pain.

- Use a tablet holder to hang on to your device without needing to grip it tightly.

- Enable virtual assistants like Siri or Google Assistant on your phone. Then instead of navigating the phone with your fingers, you can ask it to calculate a tip, make a call, or conduct an internet search.

- If your thumbs hurt from texting on your phone, try using a thick stylus to tap out the letters.

- Use a split keyboard design for your desktop computer. Both halves of the keyboard are placed on a curve that provides a more comfortable typing position.

- Try an ergonomic mouse. The vertical mouse looks like a standard mouse turned on its side, so you're holding it in a more natural "handshake" position.

- Keep your mouse close to your keyboard and in front of you — rather than off to the side — to avoid straining your arm and shoulder.

- Gel rests that lie along the edge of your keyboard can provide wrist support when typing on your computer.

Americans spend billions on supplements each year. But is it wise to trust the health benefits the companies in this industry are trying to sell you? Not necessarily. That's because the U.S. Food and Drug Administration doesn't approve dietary supplements before they go to market.

That gives manufacturers a lot of leeway in advertising. So be wary of bogus claims that the product can cure or treat a disease. Some labels may even contain meaningless phrases like "clinically tested ingredients" or "pharmaceutical grade" in the hopes that they will increase the supplement's appeal. But just because the product is tested doesn't mean it works.

Make sure your supplement's packaging displays the "USP Verified" mark. This indicates that the product meets formula requirements set by the U.S. Pharmacopeial Convention. It guarantees a supplement's purity, as well as accurate labeling. You can visit *quality-supplements.org* to find all the supplements that have passed this testing.

Medical ID theft — it's not what your doctor ordered

It sounds like a nightmare. Someone pretending to be you has been admitted and released from the hospital. Next thing you know, the billing department is hounding you for payment. Bad dream? Nah. Just the tip of the iceberg when it comes to the trials faced by victims of medical identity theft.

That's right — scammers don't just want your credit card information anymore. They're going after your health benefits, too. This crime occurs when a fraudster hijacks your personal information — name, health insurance details, and Social Security number, say — and uses it to get medical care. That includes anything from doctor visits and surgeries to prescriptions and medical equipment.

The effects can be devastating, both financially and medically. The con artist's unpaid bills can wind up on your credit report, for example. And if he falsifies insurance claims, your premiums can go way up. Not only that, the identity thief's medical information — his blood type, allergies, and test results, for example — can get added to your health records and jeopardize your future care.

Are you getting overcharged for your health care services? You can find out in an instant by going to *fairhealthconsumer.org* to learn how much a medical procedure typically costs when seeking care in your area.

Of course, you'll want to avoid this mess. Be sure to follow these precautions.

- Carefully guard your Medicare and other insurance cards.

- Destroy prescription labels before throwing them in the trash. They may contain sensitive personal details.

- Ask your doctor's office if you can identify yourself without having to provide your Social Security number.

- Watch out for offers of free medical equipment in exchange for your Medicare number.

- Never give health care information to anyone who calls, emails, or texts you unexpectedly.

Surprisingly, strangers aren't the only crooks who commit this type of fraud. You'd never suspect it, but roughly one-third of medical identity thieves are family members of the injured party. But no matter who's responsible, the warning signs are the same.

- You get calls from debt collectors for medical services you didn't receive.

- You receive mail from health care providers you don't know.

- Your health insurer says you've reached your benefit limit when you haven't.

- You find errors in your Explanation of Benefits statement.

- You see unfamiliar medical debt collection notices in your credit report.

So what should you do if you find out you've been victimized? Immediately file a police report and contact your insurance company. Ask your health care providers for a copy of your records and alert them to any errors.

Virtual helpers: Top resources for your health questions

If you're looking for free health information and advice, you've come to the right place. That's because it's easy to gain access to the world's top health experts 24 hours a day. All you have to do is go online to immediately contact 10 of the best ones.

- The U.S. National Library of Medicine (*nlm.nih.gov*) is the place to go to get all your questions answered from the world's largest collection of medical information. This website provides information on topics like aging, genetic diseases, clinical trials, and diseases and conditions — including preventive measures, diagnostic tests, and therapeutic regimens.

- The Cleveland Clinic (*clevelandclinic.org*) has thousands of videos, articles, podcasts, and infographics to help you take control of your health. You can also download free mobile apps to make your life healthier. To see all this, simply visit *my.clevelandclinic.org/health*.

- The Centers for Disease Control and Prevention (*cdc.gov*) provides a wealth of information on diseases and conditions, infectious outbreaks, environmental health, and more.

- MedicineNet (*medicinenet.com*) has easy-to-read and authoritative medical information for consumers. Topics include common diseases and conditions, medical procedures and tests, diet and weight management, and medications.

- The University of Michigan (*umich.edu*) has created a glossary to help you understand the meaning behind confusing medical terms. You can find it by going to *medicaldictionary.lib.umich.edu*.

- The U.S. Food & Drug Administration (*fda.gov*) publishes the latest on the safety of drugs, biological products, medical devices, and the U.S. food supply.

- Drugs.com (*drugs.com*) delivers a searchable list of drugs, an interaction checker, pill identifier, symptom checker, a drug comparison tool, and more.

- OpenMD (*openmd.com*) lets you search billions of medical documents from organizations, journals, and databases. It also has a health directory and a medical dictionary.

- The Merck Manuals (*merckmanuals.com*) cover thousands of topics in all fields of medicine. You'll find easily understandable information on medical topics, symptoms, drugs, and emergencies by clicking the *Consumer Version* icon.

- Medscape (*medscape.com*) is an online destination for physicians and health care professionals, offering the latest medical news, and drug and disease information.

More than a third of Americans say they get less than seven hours of sleep each night. That's bad news. A lack of rest can cause daytime drowsiness, memory problems, and a poor attention span.

If you're not getting enough shut-eye, you might consider downloading a sleep app or two. Some provide tutorials for relaxing pre-bedtime activities like yoga. Others help you fall asleep with the help of stories, guided breathing exercises, or relaxing music.

Some even monitor your sleep habits. Just download a sleep tracker app and place your smartphone face down next to you when you go to bed. These apps often rely on the sensors embedded in your phone to track your body movements and breathing rates throughout the night.

They then use this data to give you an accurate record of your nightly sleep patterns. Tracker apps also help you identify trends and make informed decisions to improve your sleep.

Protect yourself from Medicare scams

When is high season for Medicare fraud? During the open enroll-ment period, from Oct. 15 to Dec. 7. Still, you need to keep an eye out for scams all year long.

That's because tricksters may call you and pretend they want to verify your identity to update your Medicare card. Or they may offer free medical supplies or claim you qualify for a refund. Be wary. They're after your Medicare number or other sensitive details.

Calls from Medicare are rare, so be on guard if you get a ring from a supposed representative. In fact, you'll usually get a written statement in the mail before you get a phone call from a govern-ment agency.

Here's how to spot potential scams.

- Don't trust the name displayed on your phone. Scammers can fake a caller ID.

- Hang up if anyone calls and asks for your Medicare informa-tion. Legitimate Medicare employees have your Medicare number on file.

- Don't be pressured into making a hasty decision. You have until December 7 to enroll, and Medicare doesn't offer extra benefits if you sign up early.

- Don't talk to anyone who suggests their plan is preferred by Medicare. The truth is that Medicare doesn't endorse a spe-cific plan.

You can go to *smpresource.org* for help prevent, detect, and report health care fraud, errors, and abuse. To report someone pretend-ing to be affiliated with Medicare and other Medicare scams, call 800-633-4227.

Monitor your expenses with cutting-edge tools

These tech hacks will help keep your spending in check

Ah, the joys of budgeting. Don't you just love keeping track of every single penny you spend? Of course you don't! That's why you should let technology do it for you.

Budgeting apps like Honeydue, PocketGuard, and Rocket Money — along with websites such as *monarchmoney.com*, *everydollar.com*, and *creditkarma.com* — are easy to use. They track your spending, and make custom budgeting and savings goals. Some of them can be linked to your financial accounts. Others may move a little money from your checking account and stash it for you in a savings account before you can spend it.

Worried about sharing your bank information with one of these apps or websites? Don't be. Most of them securely encrypt your financial information. In the unlikely event that a hacker does get hold of your money, federal laws will protect you — the same laws that shield you if an identity thief steals from your bank account or goes on a spending spree with your credit card.

But be vigilant about checking your accounts for suspicious activity. The sooner you report any fraud to your bank, the less money you're on the hook for losing. And if you access these services from your smartphone, be sure to lock it with a secure code in case it gets stolen.

You can also check out apps like YNAB (You Need a Budget) and its sister website *ynab.com*. After you set up your account, you can either connect it to your bank and automatically import transactions or enter all your bills and receipts manually. YNAB is free for the first 34 days. After that, you'll have to pay a fee to download the software.

It's easy to lose track of how much you spend each month on streaming. But you can say on top of these expenses by downloading a free subscription tracker from your app store. With it, you can monitor all your recurring payments. Some trackers even send alerts when your next bill is due.

Social Security and Medicare: Where to go to stay in the know

Feeling baffled and bewildered at the thought of applying for Social Security? Join the club. A report by the U.S. Government Accountability Office says many Americans don't fully understand how Social Security rules will affect their retirement benefits. To make matters worse, claims specialists often fail to provide adequate information to the public.

That's what happened to Anne and Peter, a couple who applied for Social Security at age 68. An agent reviewing their applications advised them to file for retroactive payments, which they did. What didn't she tell them? They'd take a huge tax hit on the lump sum payment and see their monthly benefits reduced over their lifetimes. So how can you avoid making similar mistakes?

- If you're looking to unravel the secrets of Social Security, go to the official government website at *ssa.gov*. You'll find loads of key information to guide you through the ins and outs of different claiming strategies and more.

- Need help navigating the Medicare maze? Use *medicare.gov* to create or log in to an account, find health and drug plans, and locate and compare care providers — including doctors, hospitals, home health services, and medical equipment suppliers — near you.

You know how important your Social Security number is. So do scammers. And they will go to considerable lengths to obtain it. Here are three scams that can have hackers running to the bank with your Social Security money.

- Phone scams, where the crooks claim to be from the Social Security Administration and say your benefits will stop unless you provide certain information, including your Social Security number.

- Email or text cons — called phishing scams — that ask for the same details as a phone scam.

- Mail scams, where you receive a flyer offering additional Social Security services if you fill in and return the attached form, which includes a request for your Social Security number.

Want to make sure your Social Security number is safe? Never provide your Social Security number to a caller, never click the link to a suspicious email, and never assume that a mail offer asking for personal information is legitimate.

Learn how to stop scammers from stealing your Social Security benefits

Harry wanted to max out on his Social Security benefits. So he held off applying for them until a few months before his 70th birthday. But when the retired car mechanic went to file his claim, he was horrified to learn that someone was already receiving payments in his name.

Harry was one of roughly 110 million Americans who fall victim to data breaches each year. In his case, hackers used his stolen Social Security number and other readily available information to open an online account with the Social Security Administration (SSA).

> Never put usernames and passwords in your will. It could create a security nightmare for your heirs. That's because wills become public documents, available for all to see. It's better to write up a list of your usernames and passwords and let a trusted family member know how to access it.

Don't let this happen to you. You can beat these identity thieves to the punch by signing up for an online My Social Security account. Doing so will prevent no-good scammers from creating a bogus account in your name. Simply go to *ssa.gov/myaccount* and select *Create an Account*. Once you've done that, log in every few weeks to check for suspicious activity. While you're at it, you can also estimate future retirement benefits, or manage the ones you already receive.

Speaking of benefits, the SSA bases the amount you get each month on how much money you earned over the course of your career. But employers can make mistakes when filing annual wage reports with the SSA. For example, they might report your earnings with an incorrect name or Social Security number. Sometimes companies even provide inaccurate salary amounts.

If that happens and you don't catch the problem in time, you could wind up getting much less than you deserve. You don't want to file for Social Security benefits only to find there's a decade-old mistake on your earnings record.

That's why the SSA recommends checking your earnings history each August to catch any errors from the previous year. To do that, go to your online My Social Security account.

No one likes paying taxes. But when you do, it's nice to think you'll get something back. The good news is you can. The taxes you paid get you free info and assistance with prescriptions, rent, food, utilities, Social Security, veterans benefits, and more — even help with your taxes.

Simply pay a visit to the website *benefitscheckup.org*. It's run by the National Council on Aging and is a treasure trove of information just for seniors about benefits programs throughout the United States.

To find out what specific benefits are available in your area, enter your ZIP code into the box on the homepage, and click or tap on the *Get Started* button. There's also an online live chat option you can use for queries and information.

After looking through all the great information on this site, you may start to think your taxes have been a good investment for retirement after all.

Save a bundle with these free tax prep tools

Here's some good news. The IRS runs two programs that are dedicated to tax return preparation and counseling. Tax Counseling for the Elderly (TCE) offers free tax help to people who are 60 and older. The program specializes in questions about pensions and retirement-related issues unique to seniors. And Volunteer Income Tax Assistance (VITA) helps people who speak limited

English, have a disability, or have an income of $67,000 or less.

Both of them are free thanks to trustworthy volunteers. And no need for quality concerns about working with them. All VITA and TCE volunteers must take and pass IRS-approved tax law training.

> The fastest and safest way to get a refund is to file your taxes electronically and receive the money as a direct deposit. You eliminate the risk of a check getting lost, stolen, or destroyed.

To find out where to go locally for TCE or VITA, go online to *irs.treasury.gov/freetaxprep* or call the IRS toll-free at 800-906-9887.

Remember that signing your tax return means you agree with everything on it. Before you sign, review the return, and ask questions until you understand its contents.

Watch out for emails or text messages about a tax refund. It's a scam. The con artist contacting you is hoping you'll click a link to check on your "tax refund e-statement" or to "fill out a form to get your refund." Don't do it — the fraudster might steal your identity or infect your phone or computer with malware.

Know that the IRS won't send you an email or text without your permission. And you can easily check the status of any pending refund by going to *irs.gov/wheres-my-refund*. You'll need your Social Security or individual taxpayer ID number, your filing status, and the exact refund amount on your return.

Think you've been a victim of identity theft? Report it to the Federal Trade Commission at *identitytheft.gov*. You can also create a free, customized recovery plan by going to this website.

Assistive tech redefines aging in place

Don't miss these essential apps for independent living

More than three quarters of U.S. adults over the age of 50 prefer to remain in their homes as they get older. If you count yourself among them, you'll want to learn about the following apps that make aging in place easier to do.

Nutrition apps. Like most seniors, your appetite and thirst may have diminished as you've aged. But poor nutrition puts you at risk for diseases like osteoporosis and heart disease. So a healthy diet is still important. The Water Balance and Waterlogged apps, for example, can remind you when to drink water. And the EatWise app can help you keep track of your meals.

Check-in apps. Every older adult who lives alone needs one. With these apps, it only takes a moment to let your loved ones know you're OK. So how do they work? Apps like Snug and CheckinBee will ask you to check in at a scheduled time each day. If you don't do so within a certain period of time, the app will notify your designated contacts so that they can come to your assistance.

Magnification apps. These software programs make reading small text — like the kind on receipts and prescription bottles — much easier. Using the device's camera, the app displays what it sees on the screen and lets you zoom in and out. Some magnification apps will also activate your phone's flashlight.

The Magnifying Glass + Flashlight app can be used on both Apple and Android smartphones.

Medication apps. You'll want to take advantage of apps like Care4Today and Dosecast that schedule medication reminders. The best ones give you information about possible side effects, and help you reschedule missed doses. Some, including the Medisafe app, even let your caregiver or family members know that you've taken your pills. That's important for their peace of mind.

Keep forgetting where you left your keys? No worries — simply attach a Bluetooth tracker to your key ring. Then pair the device and its app with your smartphone. Next time you can't find your keys, tap a button in the app. If you're within a certain distance of your keys, the tracker will emit a loud sound.

Ridesharing apps. You may have stopped driving, but that doesn't mean you can't still live independently. Going to the supermarket or meeting friends is easy to do when you use rideshare apps — Uber and Lyft are popular — to get where you're going.

As a bonus, you can also order food through the Uber Eats app. And Lyft offers one year of free Grubhub restaurant delivery to its Lyft Pink customers.

Diagnosis apps. These apps that assess your symptoms and identify related conditions aim for accuracy, but their biggest draw is convenience. Freely available 24/7, you can input your symptoms and allay your fears at 11 p.m.

But don't rely on them for the final word because doctors still diagnose conditions more accurately. Instead, use diagnosis apps, including Symptomate and Ada, to inspire questions for your doctor.

If you or someone you love has low vision, arthritis, or other physical limitations, using a computer doesn't have to be difficult. Visit *microsoft.com*, scroll to the bottom of the page, and click the *Accessibility* link. You'll find great tips on how to make the computer easier to use.

For example, you can change the screen colors to improve the contrast between items or use *Magnifier* to enlarge text. You can use *Narrator* to read what's on your screen or announce notifications. Windows even offers settings to help you avoid using the keyboard or the mouse. Check for similar settings and tools on your Mac.

Tech to the rescue: 3 smart devices to help boost your memory

Our memories aren't the best as we age. That's why technology is such a blessing. Check out all the ways it can help you recall things.

Smart speakers. Say you have trouble remembering tasks. Your home assistant has your back. For example, Google Home lets you automate a sequence of events with a simple command. You can program your device to turn on your smart lights, tell you about the weather, and remind you to call your friend when you say, "Hey Google, good morning."

Medication reminders. Not sure if you took your medicine today? Sometimes keeping track of your pills seems harder than juggling a dozen balls. So why not invest in a smart pillbox that sounds alarms and automatically dispenses your pills when it's time for a dose. You'll pay about $25 and up for dispensers you fill and program yourself.

Smartphones. These devices can help you keep on top of a busy schedule. Use your smartphone's calendar app to keep track of upcoming events and its alarm app to remind you of appointments. Keep forgetting your passwords? Store them in your phone's notes app, protected by a single security code. You can also use this app to record addresses, lists of errands, and important reminders.

> There's no need to panic if you can't recall where you parked your car at the mall or supermarket. Apps like Parkify and Find My Car can save your car's location, show you where it's at, and guide you back to its location.

Tune into a whole new world with these high-tech hearing devices

About one-third of older adults have hearing loss, and the chance of developing this problem increases with age. That can make it difficult to have a conversation with friends or follow the dialogue in a movie. But the following products can help. You can buy them at a variety of retail outlets or online.

Personal sound amplifiers. These little devices are not hearing aids. But they're perfect for seniors and just about anyone who wants to increase the volume of the sounds around them — like bird watchers seeking to locate a golden-crowned sparrow by its singing. Or let's say you're sitting in the back row of a lecture hall. Can't hear the speaker? Just pull out your sound amplifier ear buds.

Wireless TV headphones. Maybe your family and friends are always asking you to turn down the volume on your television. Or perhaps you just want to watch a movie while your grandchild naps nearby. Either way, these headphones guarantee that you can watch your favorite shows without disturbing anyone. And because they're wireless, you won't have to plug them into the TV. That means you can watch from anywhere in the room.

Hearables. These earbuds are similar to personal sound amplifiers because they raise the volume of the sounds around you. Some even allow you to customize elements like frequency ranges.

However, hearables can also connect via Bluetooth to other electronics like smart TVs. You can adjust the television's volume in your earbuds without affecting the loudness that others hear. Not only that — some hearables can monitor your heart rate and temperature, track your activities, stream music, and even translate languages.

Want to connect with other people who live with hearing loss? Get plugged into a support group at *hearingloss.org*, powered by the Hearing Loss Association of America. Poke around the site to find tools on living with hearing loss and news about the latest technological and medical advances.

Age comfortably in your home with these tech tools

Aging in place has never been easier or safer thanks to user-friendly tech devices. Read on to learn how they can help you live independently for years to come.

Emergency alerts let you call for help. Falls can be deadly, especially if hours pass before you can call 911. And you can't ask someone to keep an eye on you every single second, right? Turns out, you can, with Personal Emergency Response Systems (PERS).

These devices — which you can wear as necklaces, bracelets, or belts — allow you to call for help.

An unmonitored device that calls a friend or family member at the press of a button will cost you a one-time payment of around $30 and up. Need a more advanced device that detects falls automatically, alerts an ambulance, and calls a dispatch center? They're a bit pricier, with fees that clock in around $35 to $50 a month.

Remote monitors show your loved ones how you're doing. Are your children always worrying about your well-being? Do they want to hire someone to come over every day? Maybe you don't want a stranger in the house, but you don't want your family to fret, either. So what can you do?

Remote monitoring systems are a good compromise. You get to stay home alone, and your loved ones don't have to worry. Monitors range from sensors that alert your family when you're up and about to cameras that let them drop in remotely to check on you.

Wearable gadgets keep track of your vital signs. You could spend thousands every year on a nurse who comes over each day to check your blood pressure and heart rate. Or you could make a single payment of less than a hundred dollars and get a smart watch or wearable gadget that lets you keep an eye on your own vitals.

Prices depend on the type of device you go for. A few of the high-end products even send alerts to medical professionals if they detect potential health problems.

Elevate your lifestyle with smart home devices

Unlock major savings: Top devices for cutting utility bills

Smart home devices are all the rage these days. And it's easy to see why. They let you remotely control various devices — including lighting, security, and cooling and heating systems — using a smart speaker or a mobile app on your smartphone. What could be more convenient when, say, you're leaving work on a hot summer day? Simply open the app, turn on the air conditioner, and cool your house while driving home.

What's more, smart devices can save you a ton of money. Here's how.

Smart lights. These fixtures and bulbs allow you to control the brightness of your lights and schedule when they should turn on and off. You can also program smart lights to power up or down when you enter or exit a room. What's more, smart bulbs use 75% less energy than incandescents and last 25 times longer.

Smart leak sensors. According to the U.S. Environmental Protection Agency, leaks in the average household account for more than 10,000 gallons of wasted water a year. But you can avoid that if you place smart leak sensors under sinks, around washing machines, and behind toilets. Once the device detects a leak, it will send an alert to your smartphone so that you can address the situation before it gets out of hand.

Smart thermostats. You'll save big on your energy bill with these devices. Many of them can establish a schedule that automatically adjusts to energy-saving temperatures when you're asleep or away from home. Plus they can give you detailed reports on your energy use, allowing you to identify areas where you might be wasting energy.

Smart plugs. Did you know that your appliances — phone charger, television, coffee machine, and hair dryer, for example — leech energy even when they're not in use? This wasted electricity is called "vampire power," and it could account for more than 10% of your total energy use. So you might want to look into smart plugs — you can program them to shut off once you're no longer using the appliance.

Future-proof your smart home investment

Whether you're opting for a smart thermostat or looking to automate a large part of your home, you'll want to consider the following prior to making a purchase.

Determine your goals. It's important to figure out what you want in the long run. Are you looking to have the smartest home in the neighborhood, or do you want just a couple of devices to make your life easier? Either way, it's probably best to start slowly — getting one or two key devices at first will allow you to get accustomed to the technology.

> The smart gadgets in your home could save you money on homeowners insurance if they help prevent water damage, theft, or fire. Discounts are available, for example, on residences with smart water leak sensors, security cameras, and smoke alarms. If you have any of these devices, or plan on buying them, ask your carrier if you're eligible.

Check your internet connection. Smart home devices require a Wi-Fi network and a high-speed internet connection. After all, you don't want any disruptions to your home's smart devices or your remote access. So do some research to determine how much internet speed you'll need and make sure you keep your router up to date.

Look for compatibility. Don't buy a smart device unless it pairs with the central platform you'll use to manage it. Your gadgets must communicate in the same "language" that your home's smart hub speaks, whether that's Amazon's Alexa, Google Assistant, or Apple's Siri. Along with controlling your devices with voice commands when you're at home, you'll be able to remotely manage them with the hub's corresponding app.

Don't forget about privacy. Smart devices collect data on your habits and preferences. Some companies may sell this information to others, including advertisers. So before you buy one of these gadgets, look into the manufacturer's security policies and customer reviews. And make sure your Wi-Fi network is encrypted. Use strong and unique passwords, and enable two-factor authentication on your phone's smart home apps.

Navigate sales days like a pro

Setting up your smart home doesn't have to cost a fortune. Not if you shop at the right times. So mark your calendar with the following sale days.

Black Friday and Cyber Monday. You're bound to get good deals on smart devices, including locks, security cameras, speakers, and lights, on these days. Although Black Friday officially starts the day after Thanksgiving, retailers often launch their sales on the holiday and extend them into the following week on Cyber Monday. You'll find reduced prices on smart appliances online and in stores.

Amazon Prime Day. Look for online discounts on small kitchen items like smart coffee makers, as well as Amazon products like Echo speakers, on this two-day, mid-July sale for Prime members. Don't have a membership? You can sign up for a free 30-day trial before the event to take advantage of savings.

Fortunately, sales on smart home devices aren't limited to twice a year. You'll often find discounts on older models when manufacturers release a new device. And don't forget to look for reduced prices on holidays like the Fourth of July.

5 tips for getting more out of your smart speaker

Home digital assistants like Amazon Alexa and Google Assistant can do so much more than tell you the weather or time. Read on to learn some of the best features these gadgets offer.

It's your own personal encyclopedia. Your know-it-all cousin can be pretty annoying, offering unwanted opinions all the time. But your virtual assistant, on the other hand, really does know everything. And it only talks when you ask it to. Want to know the name of the eighth U.S. president? Or perhaps you can't remember the capital of South Dakota. No need to go to the encyclopedia. Just ask your smart speaker.

Stay on schedule. Your digital assistant can help you keep track of all your scheduled activities. All it needs is a voice command. For example, let's say you have a medical appointment next week.

Just say, "Hey Alexa, remind me at 3 p.m. on Tuesday that I have a doctor's appointment the next day." You can also set an alarm to ensure that you wake up at a certain time.

You can control your home entertainment. You enjoy listening to music while you go about your daily chores. No problem — your digital assistant can play your favorite songs. You can also listen to audiobooks, podcasts, and news reports, all with a simple request. And if you want to hear the same internet radio station in every room in the house? Just add as many devices as you want and they'll sync together — no wires necessary.

Armchair shopping is a breeze. Both Google and Amazon have huge online storefronts, so it's no surprise their digital assistants make shopping easy. That's especially true for items you order on a regular basis. When you run low on Fido's kibble, you can simply say, "Alexa, reorder dog food," and it's done in under 30 seconds.

Home automation is a snap. You can use your smart speaker system to control everything from your thermostat to your lights and even your appliances. Want to set a time for the laundry to start? How about scheduling when the porch lights go on and off? Just tell your digital assistant, and it will get done.

From listing to closing: Tips on selling a technology-savvy home

Thinking of selling your home? If so, you'll want to figure out what to do with your smart devices. So before your house goes on the market, make a list of the gadgets that will stay with the new owner.

You'll probably want to leave behind items — a smart thermostat or light dimmers, for example — if they've been hardwired into the electrical system. It can be difficult and time consuming to remove them. And potential buyers consider video doorbells and smart locks as big draws, so you might want to include them in the sale.

Be sure to strip any personal information from such device-related apps, and do a factory reset on the technology. Finally, give the new owner a list of the brand names and models of the home's smart devices, along with any instruction manuals and related apps.

Don't ask your smart speaker to look up a phone number. It's dangerous because scammers have managed to place fake customer service phone numbers into top search result positions.

Here's how one of these cons work. Let's say you need to cancel a flight. So you ask your speaker to find the number for the airline's customer service department. You make the call, and someone pretending to be a representative answers and says he can help. But the fee is $150. The result if you fall for it? You lose your hard-earned money and your flight is still booked.

The best place to look for a telephone number for customer service, as well as tech support and warranty information, is on your bill, receipt, or on the company's website. If you go online, be sure to check the URL to ensure you're at a legitimate web address.

Be prepared, stay safe with emergency planning

Every smartphone user needs a Medical ID

If you're in an accident, emergency responders need all the information about your health they can get. That's why it's a good idea to set up a Medical ID on your smartphone.

This critical data helps medical professionals make quick, informed, and possibly lifesaving decisions about your health. So you'll want to include your age, blood type, any medical conditions and allergies you might have, your emergency contacts, and the medications you're taking. Health care workers can easily access this information from your phone's lock screen — without requiring a passcode.

Here's how to set up a Medical ID on your iPhone.

1. Open the Health app and tap the *Summary* tab.

2. Tap your profile picture in the upper-right corner.

3. Under your profile picture, tap *Medical ID*.

4. Tap *Edit* in the upper-right corner.

5. To make your Medical ID available from the Lock screen on your iPhone, turn on *Show When Locked*. To share your Medical ID with emergency responders over the phone, turn on *Share During Emergency Call*.

6. Enter your health information, including things like your date of birth, allergies, and blood type.

7. Select *Done*.

Here's how to set up a Medical ID on your Android phone.

1. Open Settings.

2. Tap *Safety and emergency*.

3. Choose *Medical info*.

4. Enter your medical information and select *Save*.

5. Tap the switch button to turn on *Show on Lock screen*.

Here's how to share your Medical ID with emergency responders during a phone call.

1. If the Personal Safety app isn't installed on your device, download it from the Google Play Store.

2. From the app's home page, tap the *Your info* tab.

3. Find and select *Emergency info access*.

4. Turn on *Share during emergency call*.

It's always better to be safe than sorry, especially when it comes to getting help in an emergency. So always keep these seven numbers in your cellphone — your local police and fire departments, your doctor's office, poison control, your local locksmith, roadside assistance, and a trusted neighbor.

Smartphones — your lifeline to first responders

Your iPhone or Android smartphone could save your life, even if it's locked. That's because it has a hidden feature that automatically connects you to — and shares your location with — emergency services. Here's how to get help in case of a medical crisis, fire, car crash, or a crime in progress.

iPhone users. You'll want to do the following to set up your phone for Emergency SOS calls.

- Open the Settings app.

- Tap *Emergency SOS*.

- If you have an iPhone 8 or later version, turn *Call with Hold and Release* to *On*. If you have an iPhone 7 or earlier version, enable *Call with 5 Button Presses*.

Here's how to report an emergency on an iPhone 8 or later version.

- Press and hold the side button and one of the volume buttons until the Emergency SOS slider appears.

- Drag the slider to call for help. If you continue to hold down the side button and volume button, instead of dragging the slider, a countdown will start and an alert will sound. If you release the buttons after the countdown, your iPhone will call emergency services automatically.

Here's how to report an emergency on an iPhone 7 or earlier version:

- Press the side (or top) button five times rapidly. The Emergency Call slider will appear.

- Drag the slider to call emergency services.

After the call has ended, your iPhone will send your emergency contacts a text message with your current location, unless you choose to cancel. If Location Services is turned off, it will turn on temporarily. If your location changes, your contacts will get an update. You'll receive a notification about 10 minutes later.

Here's how to set up emergency contacts on your iPhone.

- Open the Health app and click your profile picture. Tap *Medical ID*.

- Select *Edit*, then scroll to Emergency Contacts.

- Click *Add*, select the person, then add their relationship to you.

- Tap *Done* to save your changes.

You can't set emergency services as an SOS contact.

Android users. The Emergency SOS feature is available on Android 12 and later versions. Here's how to set up the service.

- Open the Settings app. Tap *Safety & emergency* and then *Emergency SOS*. At the bottom right, select *Start setup*.

- To add your emergency services number, click *Start*. If you need to change the local emergency number, tap *Change number*. Once you have the correct number, tap *Next*.

- To share your location information and send updates to your emergency contacts, select *Start setup* and then *Set up*. Tap *Add contact*, and pick a contact to share the information with. Choose what information you want Emergency SOS to share with your contact. Click *Next*.

- To share your location in an emergency, you must give the Personal Safety app permission to access your location. Tap *Next*, and then *While using the app*.

- To have Emergency SOS start an emergency video recording while still using your phone's other features, scroll down and select *Start setup*. If you want to record emergency video, tap *Turn on* and then *While using the app*. You can choose to share your video automatically with your emergency contacts after it's backed up to your device. To do so, click *Share automatically after backup*, and then *Next*.

- To choose the manner in which the above actions will occur, select either *Use touch & hold to start actions* or *Select Start actions immediately after countdown*. If you want an alarm to sound with this option, turn on *Play alarm sound*. Click *Done*.

You can set up Emergency SOS so that the previously mentioned features start automatically, or you can require a confirmation step before they start.

> If you place a call to emergency services by mistake, don't hang up. Tell the operator that the call was accidental and that you don't need assistance. Otherwise, 911 officials may think you need help and send responders to your location.

- Open your phone's Settings app. Tap *Safety & emergency*, and then *Emergency SOS*. Under "How it works," click the *Settings* icon. To add a confirmation step before an emergency action starts, tap *Touch & hold to start actions*. To start emergency actions automatically after a 5-second countdown, select *Start actions automatically*.

Here's how to make an emergency call on these Android devices.

- On your phone, press the power button five times or more.

- Depending on your settings, touch and hold inside the red circle for 3 seconds or wait for the automatic countdown to start the emergency call. After you start the call, emergency actions will begin based on how you set up the service.

You may need to evacuate your home if a flood, storm, or wild-fire is headed your way. Chances are, you won't have time to pack every little thing you need. So it's important to keep a water-proof "go bag" stocked with these essential items.

- Cash. You may not be able to use ATMs and credit cards during a natural disaster, so it's a good idea to include enough money to cover a few days of food and lodging.

- ID. You should have your passport and a copy of your driver's license ready to go. Don't forget to add a list of your account numbers and passwords.

- Emergency contact info. Keep the phone numbers of family and friends inside the bag.

- Important records. Make sure you have copies of your estate planning documents, insurance policies, and the deed to your house.

Turn panic into preparedness with these apps

Apps are fantastic tools that can help you prepare for a natural disaster. Read on to find the most helpful — and free — apps to place in your tool kit. To find and download these apps, search your device's linked app store — either the Apple App Store or the Google Play Store.

The FEMA app. The Federal Emergency Management Agency's app allows you to receive real-time weather alerts, locate emergency shelters, prepare for common hazards, learn if your area is eligible for federal assistance, and gives you answers to your most pressing questions. The app has information on more than 20 emergencies — from avalanches to winter weather.

The American Red Cross First Aid app. This app offers information on handling the most common emergency situations. It also helps you locate nearby hospitals and lets you refresh your first-aid skills with interactive games and quizzes. In addition, the organization's Pet First Aid app provides expert guidance on your pet's health and how to include your furry friend in your emergency plans.

The MyRadar app. This real-time app offers a simple, animated view of the local and national weather. For example, its hurricane layer allows you to track storm patterns as they occur. You can also enable severe weather watches and warnings via push notifications. This way you'll be alerted about any storms, tornados, and hurricanes headed your way. The MyRadar app also provides detailed weather forecasts.

> Your insurance company will require a detailed list of everything destroyed during an emergency. But what if you get writer's cramp just thinking about preparing an inventory before disaster strikes? Use your cellphone to make a video of your valuables instead. Then store the video on a USB flash drive, and stash it in a safe deposit box.

Stay safe with these emergency essentials

Nobody wants to think about getting stuck in a disaster area. Still, it's important that you prepare for just such an occasion.

So keep the following items on hand — they'll help keep you safe and connected.

Power banks. Electricity is often the first thing to fail during sever weather and storms. That's where these portable, rechargeable battery packs come in. They're fantastic for juicing up your laptop, tablet, smartphone, or rechargeable flashlight. Although most quality power banks will hold a charge for an extended period, you should recharge them once every three to four months.

NOAA weather radios. These devices, which are powered by either batteries or a crank, are just what you need to hear emergency weather updates and forecasts from organizations like the National Oceanic and Atmospheric Administration. The radios also broadcast warnings and post-event information on all types of hazards, including earthquakes, avalanches, and chemical spills.

Battery-powered lamps, sconces, or ceiling lights. No need to sit in the dark waiting for the electricity to come back on. Not when you have these gadgets to light up your house. And because battery-powered lighting is cordless, you can place these devices anywhere in a room. Just make sure you have extra batteries — you never know how long the power might be out.

Navigate the world of streaming services with confidence

Cancel your cable and watch your favorite shows for free

The average cable bill costs $83 a month. That's a hefty chunk of change. Fortunately, though, you don't have to spend all that money. Free video streaming services make it easy to access hundreds of TV shows and movies without having to pay for cable. Here are some of the best ones.

- Freevee. This streaming service, which is owned by Amazon, offers a wide variety of shows and movies with ads. If you already have Prime Video, you can watch content from Freevee straight through the Prime Video app. Freevee is also available as a stand-alone app on a variety of devices. To find out how to stream Freevee, go online to *amazon.com/gp/video/splash/freevee_findus* and follow directions for your device.

- The Roku Channel. This channel is available on any Roku smart TV or Roku streaming device. You can also download the Roku Channel app to your smartphone or tablet to start streaming. It also offers several live TV channels, and often includes the first episodes of premium cable shows. Check your smart TV or streaming device to see if it is available, or go to your device's app store.

- Tubi. Want to check out classic movies and TV shows? This service, which is owned by Fox, is a great choice. It offers select content from MGM, Paramount Pictures, and other major studios. Plus it has live TV channels. You can download the Tubi app to your smartphone, tablet, or smart TV. Or you can watch online at *tubi.com*.

- Hoopla and Kanopy. If you have a library card, check to see if you can access these streaming services. They partner with library systems and allow users to digitally check out TV shows and movies. Find out more online at *hoopladigital.com* or *kanopy.com*.

Can't find everything you want to watch on these services? Some mobile phone carriers and internet providers offer their customers free streaming services as a perk. Contact customer support to find out what they offer.

Cutting costs: Access premium packages on a budget

It seems like everything is more expensive these days — including your streaming subscriptions. Most of the major companies, like Hulu, Netflix, and Disney+, have been hiking their prices. In fact, according to one survey, people spend an average of $552 a year for this type of entertainment.

But you don't need to shell out big bucks for these top-tier providers. Here's how to make sure you can still watch your favorite shows while saving money.

Don't pay for several plans. If you keep all of your streaming services active throughout the year, chances are you're spending a lot on shows and movies that you're not even watching. Instead, consider rotating out your services.

For example, get Netflix for a couple of months and catch up on everything you want to watch. Then, cancel or pause your subscription and sign up for Hulu. This way you're not wasting money on a subscription you don't use.

Consider dropping down a tier. Many services offer a premium, ad-free tier so you can watch all your favorite shows without interruptions. And while avoiding those intrusive commercials may sound nice, it can cost a pretty penny. Instead, check to see if your favorite streaming service offers a cheaper plan that has ads.

Check to see if you can still share. While many high-profile streaming services have announced crackdowns on password sharing, several premium options still let you add users from outside your household. Check the terms of service and talk about splitting the streaming costs with a friend or family member.

If you don't want to rotate premium streaming services every few months, you may still be able to save money by bundling them together. Many major media outlets offer package deals that give you access to multiple top-tier platforms for a discounted monthly rate.

Media companies love to push bundled streaming packages because they help reduce cancellation rates. But that doesn't mean these plans are necessarily a wise choice. You'll still spend more than you would on a single streaming service.

But if you already subscribe to multiple platforms and want to keep them, it's worth it to see if you can save by bundling them.

Can't decide on a plan? Try these 3 apps and websites

If you're trying to pick a streaming service to subscribe to, you'll want to make sure that you get your money's worth. That means choosing a service with the types of movies and TV shows that you enjoy. Fortunately, you can use the following free websites and apps to make a watchlist. Doing so will make it easier to decide which streaming service will get you the most bang for your buck.

- ReelGood. You can go online to *reelgood.com* or download the app to your smartphone, tablet, streaming device, or smart TV. This service tracks shows and movies you're interested in, and will even alert you if they move to another streaming platform. It also includes ratings and reviews, so you can get a better idea of whether or not you want to watch something.

- TV Time. Access this service at *tvtime.com* or download the app. You can use TV Time to add shows to your watchlist and find out where they're streaming. It also has an upcoming section, which is a calendar that tracks when the next episodes or seasons of shows you're tracking will be available. TV Time will also recommend new content based on your preferences. And once you mark a show as watched, you can rate it.

- Watchworthy. This smartphone app provides personalized recommendations for TV shows and tells you where you can view them. After you download the app, you'll spend a bit of time swiping through shows and then rating them. Afterwards, Watchworthy will provide recommendations for content you might like. The app even has a feature that helps you decide if a streaming service's library is subscription-worthy. Watchworthy doesn't keep track of movies, but that may change in the future.

Ditch the buffering — say hello to perfectly seamless streaming

Don't you hate it when the movie you're watching gets interrupted by a spinning circle? Or, even worse, when your streaming service quits working altogether. Luckily, you can troubleshoot all your streaming woes with these tips.

Make sure your speed is up to scratch. If you're having problems with the quality of something you're streaming, the first thing to do is make sure that it's not due to slow internet service. So log on to your computer and go to *speedtest.net* or *fast.com*. These websites will test the speed of your internet connection. Then compare that number with what you signed on for with your internet provider.

A slow connection could be the result of too many devices connected to your internet, problems with your router or modem, or an issue with the network itself. If you're using Wi-Fi, move your router to a central location, away from corners and off the floor. Reboot it to reset the connection and test it again. If your service is still slow, reach out to your internet provider.

Check your device's signal strength. Even if you don't have problems with the internet, a weak Wi-Fi signal to your streaming device or smart TV could cause poor video quality. So go to the settings menu on the device you use to stream and search for *Network*. Most devices have an option to test the connection. If you have poor signal strength or a slow connection speed, you may need to move the device closer to your Wi-Fi router or try using a wired internet connection.

Make sure everything is up to date. Go to your device's settings menu and search to see if there are any available software updates. You could experience interruptions with your streaming if the version you have is old.

Try clearing out the cache. Streaming apps store temporary bits of data on your device to help improve video playback. However, sometimes this data gets corrupted. Check to see if this is the problem by accessing your device's settings menu. Then look for an option that says "clear cache," "clear data," or "clear internet data." The exact steps vary depending on the tablet, laptop, streaming device, or smart TV you use. If you're unsure of what to do, search the web for your device with the keywords "clear cache."

You may know that you can get cash-back rewards on your credit card when you go to the gas pump or eat at certain restaurants. But did you know that using your card to pay for streaming subscriptions could get you perks, too?

More and more credit card companies are adding incentives to customers who pay for streaming this way. Some offer statement credits, points, or cash back for anything you spend on these services. Others may offer special discounts from partner retailers, including streaming providers. Just be aware that some of these cards have an annual fee. So it's important to ask yourself if the benefits outweigh the cost.

If you already have a rewards card, reach out to your provider to see if you're making the most of the perks.

Discover the hidden gems Netflix has to offer

Netflix has a secret that makes it easier to find exactly what you want to watch. Every single sub-genre you can think of has a secret code that the company uses to sort its movies. For example, there's a code for Family Movie Night, Faith & Spirituality Movies, TV Mysteries, and more.

Netflix estimates that it has thousands of these codes, and they date all the way back to the days when the company mailed DVDs to customers. Finding some of the most popular ones is a simple feat, though. Simply search the web for "Netflix secret codes" to find websites dedicated to listing the most popular sub-genres.

Once you've found a category that you're interested in, there are a couple of different ways to see what Netflix has to offer in that grouping. If you're using a smart TV or streaming device, all you need to do is type the code into the search bar.

However, if you're browsing on the web, you'll need to search by typing *netflix.com/browse/genre/* followed by the code of your choice. For example, if you wanted to find every 90-minute family movie in Netflix's catalogue, you'd go to *netflix.com/browse/genre/81466229*.

Mark thought he was in luck when he saw a social media posting with a link to stream the local high school's football game. His grandson was starting, but Mark couldn't make the trip to see him play. So he clicked the link without hesitation. Mark then filled in his email address, name, and credit card information, only to discover that the link didn't work.

Even worse, the scammers now had Mark's personal information. The Better Business Bureau says you should watch out for this common scheme. Fraudsters post a message falsely claiming that they're streaming a local game, but in reality they're hoping to steal your identity.

Never click on a link from a random post that says it can stream a game. Instead, reach out to the school or team to see if they have any broadcast options.

Moving? Don't forget to update your streaming services

When changing residences, you know that you need to set up your utilities and get a new driver's license. But did you know that you should also update your streaming service accounts, too? If you don't, you may wind up running into problems. Here's what you need to do with your Netflix account.

1. Open up Netflix on your smart TV. Press left on the remote to open the menu and select *Get Help*.

2. Go to *Manage Netflix Household*.

3. Click *Update Netflix Household* and go to *Send Email* or *Send Text*. You'll receive a verification link that expires in 15 minutes. If you don't get this email or text, click *Resend Email* or *Resend Text*.

4. Once you get that link, select *Yes, This Was Me* in the email, or tap the link in the text message, and then choose *Confirm Update*.

5. You should receive a confirmation email within a few minutes. Your app will refresh, and you should be able to begin watching.

Don't forget to sign into your Netflix account from a computer and update your billing information, too. Otherwise you may be paying the wrong tax rate. To do that, go to *netflix.com*, sign in, and follow these steps.

1. Hover your mouse's cursor over your profile picture in the upper-right corner of the screen.

2. Click *Account* and go to the *Membership & Billing* section.

3. Select *Update Payment Info*, edit your address, and save the changes.

If you have any problems performing these tasks, call Netflix at 844-505-2993 or go to *help.netflix.com/en/contactus*.

Kathy was delighted to discover that she could log in to Netflix on the television in her hotel room. She thought that it would be great to watch her favorite shows after a long day spent sightseeing. Big mistake — her account was hacked only a few days after she returned home.

Kathy didn't realize that public TVs, like those found in hotels and rentals, aren't secure. And if your login information is never cleared, anyone who stays in the room after you will be able to access your account.

If you want to stream your favorite shows and movies while you travel, bring along and plug in a small streaming device, like an Amazon Firestick or Roku stick, that you use at home. Just don't forget it when you leave. Or stream movies and shows on your laptop or tablet. You may also be able to download your shows onto your device before you go on vacation. This way you'll be able to watch them later if you don't have an internet connection.

Don't make these mistakes when bundling services

Many people bundle their phone, internet, and cable plans to score discounts on their bills. And while these plans may seem great on paper, you could wind up paying for services you'll never use. Here's what you should do to make sure you'll save money before signing up for a bundled package.

Keep an eye out for hidden fees and pitfalls. Watch out for bundles that come with unnecessary and expensive features. You'll want to read any contracts carefully to make sure there aren't any early termination fees, internet data caps, or equipment rentals that drive up the cost.

Watch out for rising rates. You may think you're getting an amazing deal if you sign up for a bundle, only to find that the price skyrockets after a certain period of time. That's because it's common for companies to offer a good promotional price that will go up later. So before signing on the dotted line, figure out how much you'll be paying after the discount.

Consider cutting the cord if you're already streaming. It is not necessarily cheaper to bundle your home internet, phone, and cable together. For example, you may find that you're not really watching live TV very often. So why continue paying for it? If you cut the cord and ditch cable, you'll only have to pay for internet. Then you can shop separately for a new cellphone plan to find one that's cheaper.

Live TV streaming: Time to make the switch?

So you want to cancel your expensive cable plan without missing out on live television broadcasts. No problem — you can consider signing up for a live TV streaming service. These plans offer dozens and dozens of TV and cable channels, along with the ability to save content for viewing later on.

Here's how to find out if a live TV streaming subscription is right for you.

Before anything else, you should make sure the programs you're looking to watch aren't already available for free. Some streaming devices and smart TVs come loaded with free apps that give you access to live broadcasts. So you might be able to watch your favorite news show online — without having to pay for it.

Next, consider the price. Some live TV subscriptions are a downright bargain. For example, you can get a Philo subscription for less than $30 a month. However, more premium options could cost you over $100 a month.

Then think about what you'll watch. There's no point in subscribing to a live TV streaming service that doesn't have the local broadcasts or sports that you want to watch. Check out the channels that each service offers before you sign up.

If you do find a plan that you like, hunt around for promo deals and discounts. Just be sure to keep your eyes peeled for price increases. Eventually, you may find that the cost of live TV streaming services isn't cheaper than cable anymore.

Listen to your favorite music without paying top prices

If you want to stream your favorite tunes on demand, you can expect to shell out around $10 a month for streaming services like Apple Music, Spotify, or Amazon Music. But instead of paying these prices, you may be able to listen to all the music you want for a fraction of the price.

Hunt around for discounts. Music streaming services offer a lot of great promotional deals. For example, you may get three months of free music when you sign up with Amazon Music. You can simply cancel your subscription when that deal expires and hop over to Spotify, which could have a deal going for a free month. Unfortunately, most of these perks are only available the first time you sign up for a subscription.

Don't forget about (online) radio stations. You don't need an antenna to tune into your favorite radio stations anymore. Most broadcasters offer a digital stream, so you can use your phone, tablet, or computer to listen to tunes on the go. Simply search the web for online radio stations to see what's available.

Check out your local library. If your local library partners with Hoopla, you can stream all types of music for free. All you need is a library card. Once you're logged into the service, you can "borrow" the songs from the company's website or its mobile app. Most titles can also be downloaded to your phone or tablet. Talk to your local librarian to see if you're eligible for this service.

What smart TVs can do for you

Learn everything you ever wanted to know about your smart TV

Nearly 80 percent of U.S. households have a smart TV. These devices come with built-in apps and features that let you connect to the internet, view your streaming services, and more. But if you're having trouble with a few key features, don't worry. These simple tips will help you get more out of your television.

Make sure your connection is strong enough. Your smart TV needs to have a good internet connection. Otherwise, your streaming may get interrupted just when you're trying to watch your favorite show or movie.

If your connection seems to be lagging, consider moving your television closer to the Wi-Fi router. Or if you don't want to pick a new spot to watch television, look into getting a Wi-Fi extender. These devices may help if your smart TV is far from the router or if the signal is blocked by doors and walls.

Download all your favorite apps. Smart TVs come preloaded with several apps for streaming services, but that doesn't mean you're limited to watching only, say, Netflix and Hulu. Most devices have an app store that you can use to install other channels on your television. Use this to find free streaming services and games.

Use your phone to make sure your never lose your remote again. Hate searching the house for a misplaced remote? If you have a smart TV, you can use your phone instead of having to dig through the couch cushions.

Simply download the television's app to your smartphone. For example, if you own a Samsung TV, you'll need the Samsung SmartThings app. Once you download it and pair it with your TV, you can use the app to do things like turning the TV on or off, changing the volume, and opening streaming services.

Don't waste your time squinting at your phone's screen when you're trying to watch YouTube or home videos. Instead, connect your smartphone to a smart TV. This process, which is known as screen mirroring, lets you sync these devices so that anything on your phone's screen will appear on your TV.

Both devices will need to be connected to the same Wi-Fi network. If you're using an iPhone, open the Control Center by swiping down from the upper-right corner of the screen. Tap the *Screen Mirroring* button and select your TV from the list of devices. You may see a passcode on your TV screen that you'll need to enter on the iPhone.

If you use an Android, open the Google Home app. Tap *Favorites* or *Devices*. Select your TV from the list. Then tap the *Cast* button and select *Cast screen*.

4 fantastic things you never knew your TV could do

Your smart TV is packed with features you probably never realized were there. Here are some of the things you can do with your device.

- Make video calls. Zoom, Google Duo, and other video chat apps are great ways to keep in touch with your loved ones. But communicating through your phone's tiny screen or crowding around a laptop can get annoying. Try using your smart TV instead. Check your television's app store to see if it supports video chat apps. If it does, connect a USB webcam to your smart TV and get talking.

- Use voice commands to control your smart TV. Chances are your television has a built-in microphone near the screen or in the remote. That means you can use voice commands to change the channel, open apps, search for movies and shows, or even adjust the volume. You may even be able to use your voice to search for a misplaced remote.

- Control smart home devices. If you have smart home technology like a video doorbell or smart lights, chances are you can sync them with your TV. That means you can see who's at the door right on your TV screen, dim the lights through your remote, and more.

- Stream your favorite music, audiobooks, radio shows, and podcasts. Smart TVs aren't only good for watching videos. Many of them connect with apps like Spotify, Pandora, and Audible. That means you can use any speakers connected to the TV to listen to your favorite tunes or audio programs.

Protect your smart TV from hackers

Here's some food for thought. Cybercriminals can take control of your smart TV — after all, these devices are connected to the internet. And that means, in a worst-case scenario, these fraudsters could use your television's microphone and camera to listen to your conversations and spy on you. Moreover, hacking into your smart TV could mean gaining access to your router. If that happens, all the smart devices in your home could be compromised. Yikes!

If you want to keep your TV safe, follow these steps.

- Make sure your router is safe. Wi-Fi routers come with a default password, but you should always change it to something more difficult to hack. Keep up with the security updates on your router, too.

- Beef up the security on your smart TV. Check the privacy settings to make sure that your device isn't sharing data. You can also disable your smart TV's microphone and camera if you don't plan on using them. And keep your television's software up to date if you want to have the latest security fixes.

- Watch what you download. Hackers often use fake apps to disguise viruses and malware. Only download apps directly from your smart TV's app store.

Beware of these 3 red flags

Look for these warning signs that your smart TV may have been hacked.

- Watch out if your device starts turning on and off at random or the channels change without you doing anything. While this unusual activity could be just a system glitch, it could also be a caused by malware.

- Strange pop-up messages or ads on your screen are another warning that your smart TV may have a virus. Alerts that demand payment or threaten to prevent you from using your device are surefire signs that your television has been hacked by a cybercriminal.

- If your smart TV starts to operate more slowly, it could also be an indication that your device has malware running in the background.

Stop using your smart TV immediately if you suspect it has been hacked. Don't enter any passwords or other sensitive information, as they could be stolen. Check to see if you can install anti-virus software on your device.

You could also consider performing a complete system reset. You may lose files and apps stored on your television, but you'll also remove any viruses or malicious software that are in it.

You may have heard about a smart television's "refresh rate." This term, which is measured in hertz (Hz), refers to how many times a TV can display an image each second. The higher the number, the more natural on-screen movements appear. You can expect most modern TVs to have a 60 Hz refresh rate.

So if you're out shopping for a new TV, be aware that some manufacturers use misleading terms like "clear motion rate," "clear scan rate," and "effective refresh rate" to advertise how realistic movement appears on their sets. If you see any of that phrasing, divide the hertz measurement in half. That will give you the true refresh rate.

3 ways to make your TV last for years to come

So you just spent $400 on a new smart television. Now you need to make it last. No worries — with the following tips you can keep your TV in top-notch condition.

Keep your TV clean and tidy. Fingerprints and smudges can make it difficult to see the screen clearly. And you definitely don't want dust building up inside the vents at the back of your TV. That could dramatically shorten its life span. Use a microfiber cloth to gently remove smudges and dust at least once a week. Avoid using any chemical cleaners, as they may damage your television.

Cut down on running time. Most televisions last anywhere between 40,000 to 100,000 hours, or about four to 10 years. However, you could dramatically shorten your TV's life span if you keep it on for background noise while you do chores or drift off to sleep. Turn it off when you're not watching it, or consider using a sleep timer so that it will power down after you've nodded off.

Give it plenty of room to breathe. Televisions use a lot of electricity and generate a lot of heat. And getting too hot could cause them to malfunction or break down. To keep your TV cool, use a stand or wall mount that keeps the device at least 4 inches away from the wall. Check to make sure there aren't any vents or openings on your TV that are covered or blocked.

Save when shopping with these hacks

Your movie club is in full swing when you realize it's time for a new TV. But do you really need a pricey OLED model that has individually self-lit pixels?

If not, cut costs by going with a less advanced display. The $480 4K LCD — which uses a backlight to illuminate all the pixels for an overall brighter display — may be a better fit than the $1,100 4K OLED anyway. Especially if your room is brightly lit.

And unless you get a giant screen, you may not notice a difference between 4K and 8K resolution, so that $3,000 splurge might be a waste. Who knew you could spend $2,520 less, and your eyes are none the wiser?

If having the latest and greatest features isn't important to your family, enjoy hefty discounts on refurbished TVs and last year's models. Don't forget to compare prices at traditional, big-box, and online stores. And scour the web — including social media — for coupons and other incentives.

One of the best times to get a deal on a TV is during holiday sales, particularly Black Friday in November. The weeks leading up to the Super Bowl offer super savings as well. Springtime is also perfect for snagging bargains because that's when manufacturers release new models and stores discount their old inventory.

You can save money on your electric bill just by tweaking a few settings on your TV. So take a look at these simple tricks that promise to make your smart television more energy efficient.

First, turn on the energy saving mode on your TV. It will automatically adjust the screen's brightness and contrast to reduce power consumption. Next, consider using a smart plug or power strip so that you can completely shut off electricity to your TV when it's not in use. Finally, you'll want to take advantage of standby mode — a feature that puts the TV in a power-saving mode when it's idle for a period of time.

Transform your old TV into a smart one with a simple device

Why stream video on your computer or tablet when you could be watching it on your nice big TV? After all, you can see just about any movie and TV show available — or listen to any kind of music — from the comfort of your living room.

It's easy to do — one little box or stick will open this world to you. All you have to do is buy a device that provides the streaming service.

Take Roku, for instance. Traditionally, this has been a box that connects to your TV via an HDMI cable. But many people prefer a stick, which plugs into the HDMI slot in the back of your TV. You can purchase these from $29.99 upward, depending on the type of device.

Once you have bought your Roku device, link it to your Wi-Fi router by following the instructions on your TV. After that you can create a Roku account, and then you're all ready to start streaming movies and TV shows.

There is no charge for setting up a Roku account, which allows you to connect to the vast range of content it offers. And a lot of it is free, but you can also use your Roku streaming device to subscribe to services such as Netflix, or to rent or buy movies and TV shows.

Roku is just one of many hardware options you can choose for streaming. Others include the Amazon Fire TV, Apple TV, and Google Chromecast.

Wise ways to eat well for less

10 apps for free food from your favorite restaurants

Love to eat and save? Then you may want to download the apps — and join the rewards programs — of these restaurants. Doing so will make you eligible for freebies and other goodies.

Auntie Anne's. Right off the bat, you'll get a free pretzel after spending $1 at Auntie Anne's establishments. You'll also receive a free pretzel if you purchase at least $10 worth of goods annually at the company's outlets. Plus, Auntie Anne's will give you 10 points for every $1 you spend through the app. Earned 250 points? No surprises here — another free pretzel.

Chili's. If you go to this restaurant at least once every 45 days, you'll be entitled to either free chips and salsa or a non-alcoholic beverage every time you visit a participating location and spend at least $5. You'll also get a free dessert on your birthday.

Chipotle Mexican Grill. Download the app and join Chipotle's rewards program for a free order of guacamole with your first order. You'll also be eligible for a special birthday offer, members-only deals, and free food. And for each dollar you spend, you'll get 10 points. Shell out $8.50 and you'll have enough points for a free tortilla.

DQ. This restaurant — formerly known as Dairy Queen — will give you 10 points each time you spend a dollar. You can redeem your points for treats like fries or ice cream. In addition, you'll receive exclusive benefits like weekly deals, app-only perks, and a special deal on your birthday.

Einstein Bros. Bagels. Sign up for the rewards app, buy something, and you'll be able to snag a free bagel. You'll also get a free egg sandwich on your birthday with a purchase. Not only that — buy something once a month and you'll get unlimited free coffee the next month when you order through the app. You'll also earn two points for every dollar you spend via the app.

Krispy Kreme. Looking for a free doughnut? Just download Krispy Kreme's rewards app. The company will also give you 10 points for every dollar you spend. You can exchange your accrued points for free coffee, hot chocolate, lattes, and doughnuts. Members of Krispy Kreme's rewards program are also entitled to exclusive deals and a birthday gift.

This trick is a favorite among coupon hunters. Open your internet browser, and type a restaurant's name along with the word "coupon" into the search bar to see what pops up. You can also look for special meal-deal perks on sites like *restaurant.com* and *seniordiscounts.com*.

Moe's Southwest Grill. As a thank you for downloading Moe's rewards app, the company will present you with a free cup of queso. Plus you'll receive a special offer on your birthday each year. Moe's will also give you one point for every dollar you spend. Earn 100 points and you'll get $10 in rewards to spend at Moe's.

Popeyes. As a one-time offer, Popeyes will give you free food or a beverage if you spend at least $5. Then you'll earn 10 points for every dollar spent on the Popeyes rewards app, which you can redeem for available menu items. Additionally, benefits like

Happy Hour Tuesday and bonus points on combos and family meals are available.

Quiznos. You'll earn one point for every dollar you spend via the Quiznos rewards app. You can use these points to get discounts off your check. Plus, you'll get a free regular sub if you invite a friend who then signs up for the Quiznos app. You'll also receive $5 off your first app order. And as a birthday present, you're eligible for a buy one, get one free regular sub.

Subway. You'll get 250 points just for signing up for Subway's rewards app. Then you'll earn 10 points for every $1 spent. You can redeem accrued points to get discounts on Subway purchases. The restaurant will also give you extra points when you order food with the app. And every year you'll get birthday deals and reward member freebies.

Planning a night out? If you want to save big, consider shopping for a restaurant gift card before heading out. With a little know-how, you can find surprising discounts. In some cases, you may be able to get cards that offer as much as 20% off the price of a meal. So a $50 entree would cost you only $40.

- Check out websites like *raise.com* and *cardcash.com* to buy discounted cards. Unless you get a digital code online, you'll have to wait several days for the card to be delivered in the mail.

- Big-box stores like Sam's Club and Costco may offer you a deal if you buy in bulk. For example, several restaurant gift cards worth a total of $100 may cost you only $75 at the register.

3 great reasons to order groceries online

Nowadays you can recline in your lounge chair, snack in hand, and load up your grocery cart. Just click submit and in a short amount of time, your groceries will show up at your front door. Curious to know more? Here's why you may want to give online shopping a try.

- Put a stop to impulse purchases by shopping on the web. You might not think twice before grabbing a box of freshly baked cookies at the supermarket, but these indulgences can add up quickly. If you buy your groceries online, it's easier to stick to your shopping list and avoid overspending.

- Buying online makes it easy to get the best deal. That's not true when you're physically pushing a cart. It can be tricky to go back and forth between items and shelves to make sure you're getting the cheapest price per unit. But if you shop electronically, you can effortlessly compare multiple brands of a single item.

- Ever get buyer's remorse when you're in the supermarket's checkout line? You want to put back that apple pie and ice cream, but there's really no place to do so. So you wind up buying both items — and regretting it later.

> Stroll on past those costly, pre-sliced fruits and veggies in the produce aisle. A store might, for example, charge 50 cents for a whole, 8-ounce onion. Buy a similar onion already chopped up and you'll shell out $2.99. That's nearly 500% more. Dice your own onion once a week and save almost $130 a year.

But you can easily empty items from your cart with a single click when shopping virtually. And you're able to keep track of how much you're spending. So no surprises at checkout.

Receipt rewards: Cash in with these powerful apps

So you've just gotten home from the supermarket. Of course, you'll want to unpack your groceries and put them away so that nothing spoils. Next thing to do? Break out your smartphone.

You'll want to do this because cash-back apps like Fetch Rewards and Ibotta let users scan or upload their grocery receipts to earn points. And guess what? Those points can then be converted into Visa gift cards. For example, Fetch gives users a minimum of 25 points for every receipt they upload.

Feel free to download these money savers from your device's app store. You may also want to try similar apps like Dosh and Rakuten.

Having trouble putting food on your table? Your local food bank can help. To find assistance near you, go to *feedingamerica.org/ need-help-find-food*. And The Emergency Food Assistance Program helps supplement the diets of people with low incomes. For more information, go to *fns.usda.gov/tefap/emergency-food-assistance-program*.

A frugal shopper's guide to grocery delivery services

Jamie got a $5 coupon in the mail for an online grocery delivery service, so he decided to give it a shot. After all, shopping over the internet is super convenient. And you can even schedule a delivery time. What could be easier?

So Jamie placed his order and applied the discount at checkout. That's when he learned he would have to pay a fee for same-day delivery, along with a service charge. Add on the tip to the driver, and even with the coupon Jamie wound up spending more than if he had gone to the store himself.

Don't fall for similar gimmicks. If you want your groceries delivered for less, try the following hacks.

- Stagger free trials with different grocery stores and delivery services. For example, Kroger has a 30-day trial offer for it's free delivery service on orders totaling $35 and up. You can cancel any time during that period. Walmart has a similar program. And you can sign up for a two-week trial on Instacart's free delivery service on orders of at least $35.

- Consider memberships that you already have. For example, Amazon Prime members in select regions can shop products across multiple grocery categories on *amazon.com* and get same-day delivery. Prime members also get 2-hour grocery delivery from Amazon Fresh, Whole Foods Market, and other local stores on Amazon. Not only that — members also get free restaurant deliveries from Grubhub.

Grocery lists have never been easier to create. Apps like Out of Milk and Listonic let you speak yours into existence on your smartphone or computer. Set up your free account and create your first list before you head to the grocery store.

Here's another tip. You can quickly compare prices across stores with apps like Basket, Grocery Buddy, and Flipp. In under one minute, you can find the price of your favorite cereal at two competing grocers. This technology even predicts your needs and tailors suggestions to help you save time.

Enjoy restaurant-quality meals for a fraction of the cost

You don't want to cook dinner tonight, but you don't feel like getting dressed up to go out to a restaurant. So instead, you go online and order your favorite meal from an app. Tonight it's spaghetti and meatballs and a Caesar salad.

It seems like a great idea, until you see just how much it costs. In fact, all the fees for the convenience could have you paying between 25% and 90% more than if you'd gone out and eaten at the restaurant.

Fortunately, though, it's possible to still eat an easy, nutritious meal in the comfort of your own home without worrying about all that prep work and cleanup. All you need to do is sign up for a meal delivery service.

Feeling particularly tired and hungry after a long day? Some companies offer completely prepped meals that are ready to cook right out of the box.

All you need to do is pop them in the oven or microwave, and you'll have dinner ready faster than you can say Jack Robinson. Expect to pay between $11 and $15 a serving, depending on the service and meal plan you choose. But you may be able to get a better price if you're a new customer.

If you're up for cooking but don't want to deal with cutting and chopping every night, you can opt for meal kits that offer pre-portioned ingredients and recipes.

Like to eat out in restaurants? Consider ordering a less expensive appetizer as your main course. Or set aside half of your entree for lunch the next day. That way you'll get two meals for the price of one. And don't waste your money on pricey drinks and desserts.

They typically cost between $8 and $12 a serving. Before placing an order, look for promo codes to reduce the cost of delivery.

Of course, you'll want to make sure that any perishable food deliveries don't go bad. So when you're looking for a meal kit company, ask a representative how the food packages are kept cold after being shipped out.

And don't let your meal kits sit at your front door unattended. Try to schedule their arrival to coincide with a time when somebody is home to put them away. If you can't be there to bring your food inside, talk to a friend or a neighbor to see if they can accept the package for you.

Finally, before you put things up, examine the packaging to check if anything is damaged. If you have a food thermometer, test your perishable items — like meat, precooked foods, and leafy greens — to ensure none are warmer than 40 degrees. Store them in your fridge as soon as possible.

Drive into the future with these high-tech tools

Ready to buy a new car? Shop virtually to save time and money

You can save a fortune on a new car if you shop online. Here's how to find the best deal.

Determine your options. Decide on the type of car that best fits your needs. You'll want to consider things like your budget, fuel economy, and safety features. Then search for your new ride from the comfort of your own home. Try *truecar.com* and *cars.usnews.com* to get started.

These web resources will ask you to enter information about the model you want. They'll also need your email address, phone number, and ZIP code. Then, hang on. Offers by the dozens will start rolling in from internet salesmen at local dealerships.

Have a loan offer in hand.
Your search doesn't stop here. You'll want to go online to look for the best loan terms and interest rates. Doing so will give you a baseline for negotiations with the dealership later on. By having your financing lined up, you won't have to settle for the high interest rates that some showrooms offer.

Each year, the Department of Energy releases an annual report on fuel economy for new cars in the U.S. market. This report can help you make a better decision about the best car for your budget. Check it out at *fueleconomy.gov*.

Test drive your email. Communicating with salespeople via email allows you to shop around and compare prices with ease. When you start getting quotes, tell those who want to charge you more that you have lower offers, and ask them if they can do better. They'll either reduce their prices or drop out.

The best part of this? You'll never have to talk to a salesperson directly. That means you won't be pressured into making a hasty decision.

Work out the details. Once the last two or three dealerships have gotten down to their lowest quotes, ask them what else can they do to win your business. Maybe free oil changes? Or perhaps a car care kit at no cost. After you've snagged a great deal, you'll want to agree to that quote. Then print out your paperwork before going to buy your car.

And remember — your chance of getting the best price is at the end of the month when salespeople need to reach their quotas.

Between websites and social media, you have all the tools you need to find the best and least expensive car. You can start with free professional reviews to narrow your car choices. Edmunds, NADA Guides, and Kelley Blue Book are all trusted sources for straight talk on prices, safety features, and more.

When you're ready to look for the right dealer or seller, you'll find helpful feedback at *autotrader.com* and *dealerrater.com*.

Finally, check out the opinions of influencers on social media who share their experiences with the cars you're considering. Search for your car in videos and posts on Facebook, Twitter, Instagram, and YouTube.

Get the best deal with an online auto loan

Shopping on your computer for auto loans certainly has its advantages. For starters, it's convenient. You no longer have to schedule an in-person meeting at a bank or credit union. Nor do you have to fill out mountains of paperwork. And you can get quotes from multiple lenders at the same time so you can easily compare interest rates and loan terms.

Still, you should do a couple of things before you start to shop. You'll want to use an online auto loan calculator to help you budget a monthly payment that you can afford. In addition, you should check your credit score. If it's low, consider raising it before applying for a loan. Keeping your balances to a minimum, making timely payments, and not taking out any new lines of credit will help increase your score. That means more favorable loan terms.

> What if your navigation app could plot the best way to get somewhere and route you around bad traffic? Waze can do that. People who use it can report traffic jams, accidents, and road closures, and the app includes that information when it plots your route.

With that in mind, you can shop and compare loans online at websites like *bankrate.com/loans/auto-loans/rates*. But before you sign on the bottom line, be sure to do the following.

- Read and understand all the terms of your contract, including the fine print.

- Have a down payment of at least 20% of the car's cost. This will decrease the amount of interest you'll have to pay.

- If you're financially able, opt for a shorter term loan so that you'll pay less overall for your vehicle.

4 tools that make your car safer and easier to drive

Let's face it — getting older can affect your driving skills. For example, if you have arthritis, turning your head to see what's behind you might be difficult. But there's no need to despair. You can update your car with do-it-yourself, tech-savvy equipment that puts you right back in the driver's seat. You can find the following items online.

- Back-up camera. This device helps you see the area behind your car when driving in reverse. It's a great tool for parallel parking and backing out of your driveway. You can buy one of these gadgets and install it yourself for less than $50.

- Wide-angle rearview mirror. This item provides a panoramic view of the cars traveling behind you. That makes it perfect for minimizing blind spots when you're changing lanes on the highway. You can easily purchase one of these mirrors for less than $20.

- Pedal extender. Nerve issues and knee pain can make it difficult to reach the pedals of your car. But moving your seat forward would place you dangerously close to the steering wheel if you're in an accident. The answer? An extender that reduces the distance your foot has to travel before touching the pedals. Expect to pay around $50 for this device.

- Dash cam. This type of camera is often used to capture video during a fender bender. But some come with advanced features like front and rear collision alerts. They can also notify you if you're veering out of your lane, if a pedestrian is in front of you, and if the car ahead of you at a traffic light starts moving. You can get these more elaborate dash cams for less than $200.

You'll want to avoid this new scam at all costs. Fraudsters are targeting drivers with text messages seeking payment for overdue toll charges.

The texts, which appear to come from toll collection agencies, advise you to click a link to settle up and avoid late fees. But don't do it. Clicking the link can lead to a phishing attack, where the scammer tries to get your personal information and even steal your identity. And if you pay, the cybercriminal will have both your money and credit card number.

Your best bet? Don't react to the text. Instead, contact your state's tolling agency. Use a phone number or website that you know is legitimate instead of the info contained in the text.

Stay independent and mobile with ride-share services

Need to go somewhere but don't drive? No worries — you can use your smartphone to get picked up safely, at your own home, day or night.

In fact, you'll never have to worry about getting a lift again with ride-share companies like Uber and Lyft. With Uber, for example, all you have to do is log in to the Uber app on your smartphone. Then do the following.

- Type your destination into the *Where to?* section.

- Tap to confirm your pickup location and tap *Confirm* again to be matched to a driver nearby.

You can check the driver's location on the in-app map. It's a good way to know when you should be waiting for him at your pickup location. Of course, you'll want to make sure that you get into the right car. So match the license plate, car make and model, and driver's photo with what's in your app. You can pay for your ride with cash, with a credit card linked to your Uber account, or with an Uber Cash balance.

You can still hitch a ride even if you don't have a smartphone. Here's how.

- Both Uber and Lyft have apps that let family and friends reserve, track, and pay for rides for their loved ones.

- For a monthly subscription fee, senior-friendly companies such as GoGoGrandparent and GreatCall connect you with ride-sharing services like Uber and Lyft. To use the service, seniors call a member number to reserve a ride.

- Lively is a wireless service provider for seniors. Using a Jitterbug phone, seniors can request a Lyft ride by pressing zero on their phone. A Lively Care Advisor will set up the ride, provide an estimated cost, and arrival time. This plan requires a monthly subscription fee.

Unplug and enjoy hobbies in the digital world

From fitness to fun: The 15 most useful apps for seniors

The hands-down best thing about apps is how much they can enrich your life. Take, for example the SilverSneakers GO app. It makes it easy for you to get fit, stay active, and develop healthy exercise habits.

Download the free app and you'll find dozens of guided workouts that you can customize to your fitness level. You can attend classes virtually, or the app will help you find locations where you can exercise with others.

Here are more great apps for your smartphone. All of them are free to download, many cost nothing to use, while others have free trial periods.

Audible. You can listen to books anytime, anywhere with this app. Whatever genre you're in the mood for — whether it's mysteries, memoirs, fiction, or thrillers — this app has them all. Audible is also great for people with visual difficulties.

Duolingo. Want to brush up on your Spanish? Or perhaps you've always wanted to learn Korean. Either way, this app — which teaches nearly 40 languages — will help get you there. Choose how long you want to study each day, take a quiz to learn your level of fluency, and start lessons in your chosen language.

Empower Personal Dashboard. This app will help you track your IRA and 401(k), along with your budget, mortgage, cash, and other assets. You can view all your financial accounts in one place, see your net worth, plan your retirement, and track your investment portfolio.

Envision. Have poor eyesight? Envision has your back. It uses your smartphone's camera to turn text into speech. Envision will read out any words — from food labels and menus to subway signs and electricity bills. The app can also describe your surroundings.

Facebook. This social media app makes it easy to stay up to date with family and friends. You can also find and catch up with old schoolmates by sending and receive messages, posts, videos, and photos.

GasBuddy. This app lets you find the cheapest gas near you. Just select the type of fuel you're looking for and enter your ZIP code. The app will tell you exactly how much each gas station in charging in your area.

GoodRx. Find the lowest local prices for your prescriptions at more than 70,000 pharmacies with this app. GoodRx also tracks prices, provides coupons, and notifies you with saving alerts for your prescriptions.

Krazy Coupon Lady. You can learn about lots of sales with Krazy Coupon Lady. And once you set your alerts, the app will notify you as soon as it finds a coupon or price drop. It also has tips and tricks to coupon like a pro.

Luminosity. The app's cognitive training program is a fun, interactive way to train your brain and improve your memory, attention, and processing speed. You'll begin with a 10-minute test to set your baseline scores and show your improvement over time.

MyFitnessPal. This app is right up your alley if you're looking to shed some pounds. Just enter your height, weight, sex, workout frequency, and goal weight, and MyFitnessPal will tell you exactly how many calories you should eat each day. It also helps you track calories consumed and burned.

Recipe Keeper. Collect all your favorite recipes in one place and organize them just the way you want with this app. You can add your own recipes, import them from websites, or snap a photo of a recipe from a book. Recipe Keeper also helps you plan meals and create shopping lists.

> Learning about your ancestors has never been so simple — especially now that other folks have done much of the legwork. You can find the branches of your family tree that have already been drawn and more by going to websites like *familysearch.org* and *usgenweb.org*.

Snapseed. Quickly tidy up photographs with this easy-to-use photo editor. With this app you can fine-tune exposure, contrast, and color and make localized adjustments to specific areas of images. Want to experiment with your edits? No problem. This app saves your original image.

Step Tracker. It can be hard to know how many steps you've taken each day. The Step Tracker app can help monitor your progress. It counts your daily steps, burned calories, and walking distance with its built-in sensor, whether your phone is in your hand, your pocket, or your bag.

Words with Friends. This solo and multiplayer app lets you expand your vocabulary and show off your spelling skills as you search for the highest scoring word in a virtual game of Scrabble. Returning after a break? Words With Friends saves all of your past games, friends, and progress.

Gardening is great fun and even greater exercise. Connect with others while enjoying this healthy hobby through online gardening groups. Search social media platforms — like Meetup and Facebook — as well as organizations like The Garden Club of America at *gcamerica.org* for local clubs offering plant and seed swaps, free expertise and advice, and inspiration.

Not interested in gardening? You can still use the internet to find info on a ton of hobbies without spending a dime. Let these websites lend a hand.

- Visit *eventbrite.com/b/online/hobbies* for a long list of possibilities, from photography to story writing or singing. Explore the free how-to videos to get started with minimal investment.

- Whatever hobby you come up with, *youtube.com* is a terrific resource for honing your skills and learning from others.

Get back in touch with help from these websites

Thanks to the internet, it's easier than ever to find old friends and long-lost relatives. In fact, you'll wonder why you didn't do this sooner.

First, you'll want to jot down any information you remember about this person. Their name, age, birth date, last known job or location, and where they went to school are good starting points. Then check out one or more of the following tools.

Search engines. Go to *google.com* and type in their name and any additional details you have. For more common names — like John Smith — using quotation marks around the search term helps to filter results. You can also try other search engines like Bing, DuckDuckGo, and Yahoo.

People finder sites. Websites like *whitepages.com*, and *thatsthem.com* offer basic information for free. They can also provide valuable leads for tracking down someone. Other sites, including *peoplefinders.com*, *intelius.com*, and *truthfinder.com* require a fee for detailed reports.

No reason to feel guilty about playing video games. They're great for boosting your memory. Plus they reduce stress, connect you with others, and are fun. Maybe that's why nearly half of seniors play video games at least once a month.

Social media. Platforms like LinkedIn, Facebook, and Instagram often contain details about an individual's whereabouts. Simply type in the person's name in the search bar. If you find them, send a friend request and then a brief private message.

Niche search sites. Looking for an old classmate? You can register at *classmates.com* and search for that person. Or you could check to see if your school has an alumni website. You can also look for former elementary, high school, and college friends at *alumniclass.com*. And if you're looking to catch up with a fellow military veteran, you'll want to check out *vetfriends.com* or *togetherweserved.com*.

3 fun ways to boost your brainpower

Want to keep your mind agile? Try these games when you're tired of the crossword — they're especially designed to help your memory and cognition.

- Happy Neuron. The website *happy-neuron.com* divides its games into several brain areas, including attention span, language, and memory. It also personalizes your training and tracks your progress. There's a subscription fee for the service, but Happy Neuron offers a free seven-day trial period.

- Tricky Test 2 Genius Brain. Like brain teasers? If so, this is the app you've been waiting for. It's full of clever trick questions that will keep you challenged, entertained, and amused. And new questions are added regularly. This free app also features memory, logic, and trivia games.

- Braingle. Give your brain a workout by checking out *braingle.com*. You'll find loads of fun activities, including puzzles, games, optical illusions, quizzes, vocabulary builders, and codes and ciphers. You can create a free account, but subscribers get added benefits.

Look no further than your smart speaker for fun games that can keep your mind sharp. You can use one of these devices to play games such as Jeopardy, Who Wants to Be a Millionaire, Trivia Battle, and Name That Song. You can play by yourself or invite some friends over for an exciting night of entertainment.

Here's what else a smart speaker can do.

- It can make hands-free phone calls and send text messages.

- It allows you to talk to family members in other rooms if you have more than one smart speaker in your home.

- It can help you learn a foreign language. For example, if you have an Amazon Alexa, simply say "Alexa, open Rosetta Stone," for vocabulary and grammar lessons.

Tech transforms your access to books

Choose the right store with this e-book buyers's guide

Are you a big Amazon fan? Have a place in your heart for Barnes and Noble? Those things may play into your decision on what e-book provider to choose. Here's a quick rundown of the major sellers to help you decide.

Amazon (*amazon.com/ebooks*). The largest online retailer in the world, Amazon started life as an online bookseller. Books are still central to Amazon. They helped pioneer the e-reader, but you don't need a Kindle to buy e-books from Amazon. That's because Kindle books can be read on most mobile devices and desktop computers, using the Kindle app from Amazon.

Kobo Books (*kobo.com*). Kobo sells its own e-readers and tablets and features a large online store. Kobo books are in a proprietary format, so they can't be read in other apps or other e-readers. However, the Kobo app is available for all major platforms, so Kobo books can be read on most tablets and smartphones.

Apple Books (*apple.com/apple-books*). Apple doesn't sell a dedicated e-reader. Instead, you can read ebooks on your Apple phone or tablet using the Apple Books app. The app's store features a broad selection, including audiobooks. Apple Books has no website. You must purchase books through the Books app.

Barnes and Noble (*barnesandnoble.com*). This company has a strong online presence for e-books. Barnes and Noble sells its own line of Nook e-readers and tablets. Like many other e-book sellers, Barnes and Noble's Nook app lets you read Nook books on any mobile device. But the company no longer supports reading Nook content on desktop computers.

Google Play (*play.google.com/books*). You can read Google's books through the Google Play Books app on your phone or tablet. Because of Google's efforts to digitize most books that have been published, many of them are available for free through Google's bookstore. You can search for the company's full set of free books at *books.google.com/googlebooks/about/free_books.html*.

Looking for a free read? These sites have you covered

E-books can cost a pretty penny. But if you don't want to spend big bucks to stock your e-library, check out these four tips.

Take advantage of your public library. If you have a library card, chances are you also have access to free e-books and digital magazines. You'll need to log in to your library's online card catalog and search for books available in e-book format. Many libraries deliver e-books through third-party sites, so you may need to register with that site as well to gain access to the content. Typically, books are active on your device or computer for a set amount of time, after which they become unreadable.

Check out Project Gutenberg. Looking for more free e-books? You can't do any better than Project Gutenberg, which is found at *gutenberg.org*. That's right — you can gain access to over 75,000 free titles when you visit this site. You'll find numerous classics, such as *The Adventures of Tom Sawyer* by Mark Twain and *Oliver Twist* by Charles Dickens. You can download and read these books on any e-reader. Or you can read them on the Project Gutenberg website. And you don't even need to register or have a library card to use this service.

Don't miss the Open Library. You can go to the Open Library's lending library at *openlibrary.org* to pick among millions of titles. That's because contributors add their legally owned physical copy of a book to a library, which is then converted to e-book format for others to borrow. You won't be able to download a PDF of the publications. Instead, you'll flip through images of the book on your computer screen. All you have to do to gain access is register with an email address. No library card necessary.

Scan digital stores for free titles. Amazon's Kindle store and Barnes and Noble's Nook are two of the biggest online retailers for e-books. But if you're a savvy shopper, you may be able to find your next new read for free. All you have to do is go online to *amazon.com/kindle-dbs/storefront* and type "free ebooks" into the search bar at the top of the page. Or head to *barnesandnoble.com*, hover your cursor over the eBooks tab, and select *Free eBooks*.

Discover the best ways to read your e-books

You can have hundreds of books that take up only inches of space. How? By downloading and reading e-books on a portable electronic device. You have a couple of types to choose from.

General-purpose tablets and phones. Most e-book sellers offer apps you can use to read their books on Android and iOS tablets and smartphones. If you already use one of these devices, this is the quickest and easiest way for you to start reading e-books. Simply download the Kindle app and you're ready to find some books.

E-ink readers. Sometimes called "digital paper," these are simple e-readers that most closely imitate the experience of reading black ink on white paper. Barnes and Noble's version is called the Nook GlowLight. Amazon's Kindle E-reader and Kindle Paperwhite series both use versions of the technology. Another company, Kobo, offers similar devices.

Unlike some other types of tablets, they're easy to read even in direct sunlight. They're also lightweight and can be held in one hand. E-ink readers are designed almost exclusively for reading books and have limited other functions.

Opt for audiobooks and bring your favorite stories to life

Missing out on the fun of reading because it strains your eyes? No worries — you can give your peepers a rest while still enjoying the books you love with digital audiobooks.

Book lovers can listen to stories in the car, on walks, at the beach, and while doing household chores. And where only one or two digital audiobook providers once existed, readers now have more options than ever. Here are three of the biggest.

Audible (*audible.com*). You can listen to Audible books on virtually any device — Apple and Android phones and tablets, desktop computers, and Amazon Echo digital assistant speakers. Audible, which is owned by Amazon, remains the largest seller of audiobooks. If you subscribe to this service, you get a monthly credit that can be redeemed for one audiobook, regardless of its price. Plans start at $14.95 a month. You can also purchase titles individually, even if you're not a subscriber.

Google Audiobooks (*play.google.com/store/books/category/audiobooks*). Unlike Audible, Google offers no subscription for audiobooks. Instead, Google only sells audiobooks individually. A single title tends to cost less than a monthly Audible subscription. So if you don't listen to many books, this may be a cheaper option. You can listen to Google audiobooks on any Google OS device, such as Android and Chromecast products. There is also a Google Audiobook app for Apple products.

Kobo Audiobooks (*kobo.com/audiobooks*). In addition to the company's e-book business, Kobo also offers an audiobook service. The selection at Kobo is not as large as Audible's, but you can also purchase stand-alone titles through the Kobo store. Their subscription price — good for one book per month — is $9.99 per month. But you can try the service out for free for 30 days.

To listen to audiobooks, you'll need to use the Kobo Books app for iOS or Android, or a compatible Kobo eReader.

Don't miss these 5 free audiobook resources

Audiobooks are great. But free audiobooks are even better. Luckily, you have a number of ways to get them, and not by asking Uncle Fred for his Audible password.

Participate in crowdsourcing with LibriVox. Volunteers from around the world record public domain books and a few more recent titles. The selection is not as large as other sites, and the recording qualities can vary a lot. But it's free, and it has a lot of the classics. Check it out at *librivox.org*.

Enjoy the resources of Open Culture. This site catalogs free audiobooks from a number of sources and brings them together.

You'll discover mostly classics, but there are some new titles from independent authors. You can sometimes find some real gems. Look for them at *openculture.com.*

Check out audiobooks with Chirp. You can discover all sorts of free audiobooks at *chirpbooks.com/discover-free-audiobooks.* You can stream the books using the company's web player or listen anywhere by downloading the free Chirp mobile app.

Take advantage of the original free bookstore. Project Gutenberg at *gutenberg.org* has free audiobooks, mostly classics. As with other sites, quality can be good or not so good. Some text-to-speech computer-generated audio can be difficult to listen to.

If you have an Amazon account, you can stream hundreds of free audiobooks — from classics, novels, and romance to mysteries, thrillers, and nonfiction — at *audible.com/ep/FreeListens.* Amazon members can also access free podcasts at this site.

Don't forget your public library. Your library card gives you access to free audiobooks. You'll need to log in to your library's online card catalog and search for books available in audio format. Of course, you can also check them out from your local brick-and-mortar location.

Streamline your travels with these hacks

Top apps for your next international adventure

You'll want to take a look at the following apps before going abroad. They're guaranteed to make your foreign travels a breeze.

Language. No need to worry about the dreaded language barrier anymore. With the Google Translate app, all you have to do is type in a word or sentence and then indicate the language you want to read it in. This software also lets you take a picture of a word to translate it into English and other languages. With this app, you can even have a real-time conversation with locals through its speech recognition feature. Similar apps include Triplingo and Waygo.

Currency. You no longer have to do the math in your head when it comes to figuring out the value of the euro, yen, and peso. The XE Currency app will automatically give you the latest exchange rates on more than 100 currencies and convert them into U.S. dollars within seconds. Other options include the Currency app. Speaking of money, you might also want to download the Trail Wallet app to track your expenses. When you buy something, simply enter the price to see how much money is left in your travel budget.

Food. Check out the World of Mouth app, where hundreds of chefs, food critics, and street food aficionados provide recommendations on thousands of restaurants around the world. And if you don't eat meat, you'll love the HappyCow app. Simply type in the name of the city in which you want to eat, and a map will pop up featuring all the vegetarian and vegan restaurants in the area. The software even provides information on the eatery's pricing, ratings, and hours of operation.

It's every traveler's nightmare. You're at the airport's baggage carousel and your suitcase is nowhere in sight. You wait and wait but it never arrives. What in the world are you going to wear while you're on vacation?

Unfortunately, situations like these occur all too often. But you can prevent them from happening to you if you keep a digital leash, called a luggage tracker, on your belongings. This product is a small electronic gadget that you place in your bag. The device can then connect to your smartphone and allow you to pinpoint your suitcase's location.

If you're considering buying a luggage tracker — you can get one for under $20 — be aware that most trackers are compatible with either iPhones or Android smartphones. However, there are a few products that can connect with both. Be sure to look at the tracker's specifications before making a purchase.

Stop hackers from ruining your trip

You may be on vacation, but it's a sure bet that cybercriminals are still hard at work. That means you've got to keep your guard up each time you go online — wherever you are. Here are some tips to prevent a security breach.

Take these steps before you go. Keep your software and apps updated to help your device defend itself from malware. You'll also want to set up the "Find My" feature on your smartphone, laptop, or tablet. This will help you remotely locate the device if it gets lost and, if necessary, wipe any data on it. Make sure you have strong usernames and passwords, and use the Lock screen feature on your smartphone. And if you haven't already done so, set up multifactor authentication.

Protect your data while you're on vacation. Using your mobile network connection is generally more secure than using a public wireless network. That's why you'll want to disable any features on your electronic devices that automatically connect them to public Wi-Fi. If you have to use a public network in an airport, restaurant, or hotel, ask someone on staff for the name of the network and the login procedures. Otherwise you might connect to a scammer's fake Wi-Fi hotspot. Never shop or bank online when using public Wi-Fi.

And avoid using public computers. If you absolutely must use one, don't save any passwords on it, clear your browsing history and cache, and log out when you're finished.

Save on travel with these 8 super sites

Travel can be expensive. But it doesn't have to be. In fact, you can find hotel rooms with discounts of up to 60% on websites like *priceline.com*. Not only that — you can also find the best deals on flights, car rentals, and travel insurance on the internet. So next time you're planning a trip, be sure to visit these other websites, too.

- *hoteltonight.com*
- *kayak.com*
- *expedia.com*
- *squaremouth.com*

- *hotwire.com*
- *google.com/travel/flights*
- *autoslash.com*

Golden years, great savings: Score the best travel discounts

So you've finally decided to take that long-awaited vacation. Whether you're traveling internationally or exploring closer to home, you'll want to take advantage of the very lowest rates for seniors. Just remember that you'll probably have to show proof of your age to get them.

- Airlines. Carriers change their discount policies often, so always call the airline to see if perks are available for seniors. Here are some concessions you may be eligible for. United Airlines and American Airlines offer reduced fares to select destinations for people 65 and older. And for around $50, folks in that same age group can purchase Air France's Senior Pass to get rewards and discounts of up to 30% on air fare.

- Auto rentals. Many car rental companies offer discounts to AAA or AARP members. For example, AARP members can enjoy savings of up to 35% on Avis and Budget Rent-A-Car base rates when renting a vehicle from a participating location in the contiguous United States and Canada. And travelers 50 and over can save up to 20% off base rates at Hertz.

- Hotels. Are you 55 or older? Then consider a stay at a Best Western hotel for a discount of up to 15% on your room rate. In addition, AARP members and guests who are 60 or older are eligible for a discount of up to 10% at Choice Hotels. Red Roof, Marriott, and Aqua-Aston Hospitality offer similar deals.

- Activities. If you're a nature lover age 62 or older, you'll love the America the Beautiful senior passes that provide admittance to more than 2,000 national parks and federal recreational sites. Get an annual pass for $20 or a lifetime pass for $80. Discounted senior admissions to world class museums are also available, including The Metropolitan Museum of Art in New York City, the Prado in Madrid, and The Art Institute of Chicago.

Can you guess what you never should do in a hotel room? It's really pretty simple — don't leave your valuables unattended. Otherwise, they could be stolen.

So here's what you should do before heading out for some sightseeing. Place any expensive or important items that you're leaving at the hotel — extra credit and debit cards, your jewelry and laptop, for example — in the safe in your room. If there isn't one, ask the staff if you can use the hotel safe.

You may also want to place a single shoe in the room safe. It may sound crazy, but you'll notice the missing shoe when you're packing and remember to check the safe for your valuables.

Maximize travel awards with a tracking app

Travel rewards credit cards are a great way to save on vacations. You receive points or miles each time you make a purchase. And once you accumulate enough rewards, you could be eligible for a free — or discounted — flight or hotel stay.

If you have more that one of these cards, you're not alone. Frequent travelers often end up having several accounts with airlines, hotels, and credit card companies. In the past, juggling these programs was time consuming. That's because cardholders had to log into each account to check how many points or miles they accrued. But not anymore.

Tracking apps let you check all your balances with a single login. They'll give you an accurate picture of all the rewards you have, allowing you to know which card's points or miles you should use when reserving a hotel room or flight. These apps will also warn you if any of your rewards are about to expire.

What's more, checking several balances at once means that you'll probably view them more often. That's a good thing because you'll be more likely to catch any missing miles or points that could indicate you're a victim of fraud.

Ready to download a rewards tracker? AwardWallet does all of the above, and sends email alerts about flight delays, tracks travel plans, and analyzes your spending to make sure you get the most points. Other apps you'll want to check out include Cardpointers, MaxRewards, Travel Freely, Uthrive, and The Points Guy.

Never get lost again with these handy apps

No need to lug paper maps with you on your next trip. Not when you can download navigation apps onto your smartphone.

Take, for example, the Google Maps app. With this technology you can get directions for driving, walking, and biking, along with information on public transit. If there are multiple ways to get somewhere, the best route to your destination will be marked blue. Alternate routes appear in gray. Google Maps also lets you compare ride services and their prices with other ways of getting to your destination. And if you're driving for long distances, you can find gas stations, restaurants, and rest areas along your route.

Google Maps isn't the only navigation app for you to choose from. Other ones include Apple Maps, Waze, Mapquest, HERE WeGo, and Roadtrippers.

Never swipe your debit card when booking travel reservations online — it's dangerous. That's because hotels, like many other businesses, have been victims of data breaches. And you don't want your debit card info, which is directly linked to the money in your checking account, to be vulnerable to hackers.

Same goes for when you check in. If you use a debit card, the hotel will deduct money from your account for a deposit on any incidentals — mini-bar, laundry, and room service, for example — that you may incur during your stay. Of course, the hotel will put all that money back in your bank account if you haven't, say, ordered delivery from the hotel restaurant. But it could take several days.

Instead, use a credit card. The deposits on incidentals is considered a temporary hold on your credit card that will be removed at checkout. And credit cards offer more protection to the consumer than debit cards.

Need a passport? Learn to spot this common scam

Before you go abroad, you may need to apply for or renew your passport. So be on the lookout for fraudulent websites that say they can help you — for a fee. These sites, which may have official looking flags and seals, aren't actually affiliated with the federal government.

For $60 to a few hundred dollars (on top of the regular passport fee), these sites claim they can help you get your passport. But if you take them up on their offer, you'll lose your money. And the con artists running these sites will have your personal information.

Here are a few other things you need to know to avoid these scams.

- The U.S. Department of State is the government agency that handles passport services. Go directly to *travel.state.gov* to avoid clicking on a fake website.

- There's a charge to get a passport, but the forms to renew or apply for one are free. Anyone who asks you to pay for forms is a scammer.

- It's free to set up an appointment if you need a passport to travel right away. The U.S. Department of State's passport agencies and centers don't charge for appointments, and paying someone to set it up for you won't help you get your passport any faster.

$

Lots of folks go online and book their vacations at sea directly with a cruise line. That's a smart move if you know the type of trip — whether it's a classic, elegant cruise or one that caters to families and children — you want to take. But you may miss out on some good deals.

If saving money is important to you, you might want to check out *cruisedirect.com* to review several cruise prices at once. You can search by destination, cruise line, or port of departure. To top things off, *cruisedirect.com* offers bonuses, including discounts on shore excursions, for booking through the website. Another similar option is *cruisecritic.com*.

Want to get reward miles when you book your cruise? Check out airline-affiliated websites like *cruises.united.com*, *cruises.delta.com*, and *bookaacruises.com*.

Index